WORLD® AIR POWER

JOURNAL

Aerospace Publishing Ltd

Airtime Publishing Inc.

Published quarterly by
Aerospace Publishing Ltd
179 Dalling Road
London W6 0ES
UK

Copyright © 1993 Aerospace
Publishing Ltd

Cutaway drawings
copyright © 1993 Greenborough
Associates Ltd

ISSN 0959-7050

Aerospace ISBN 1 874023 32 8
                (softback)
                1 874023 33 6
                (hardback)
Airtime ISBN   1-880588-07-2
                (hardback)

Published under licence in USA and
Canada by Airtime Publishing Inc.,
10 Bay Street, Westport,
CT 06880, USA

Editorial Offices:
WORLD AIR POWER JOURNAL
Aerospace Publishing Ltd
179 Dalling Road
London W6 0ES
UK

Publisher: Stan Morse
Managing Editor: David Donald
Editor: Jon Lake
Production Editors:
  Karen Leverington
  Trisha Palmer
Design: Barry Savage
      Robert Hewson
Typesetting: SX Composing Ltd
Origination and printing by
  Imago Publishing Ltd
Printed in Singapore

Europe Correspondent:
  Paul Jackson
Washington Correspondent:
  Robert F. Dorr
USA West Coast Correspondent:
  René J. Francillon
Asia Correspondent:
  Pushpindar Singh

The editors of WORLD AIR
POWER JOURNAL welcome
photographs for possible
publication, but cannot accept any
responsibility for loss or damage to
unsolicited material.

The publishers gratefully acknowledge
the assistance given by the following
people:
Tenientes Franco and Magallanes for
their help with the Fuerza Aérea
Venezolana article.
Gabor Szekeres for his help with the
Hungary article.

World Air Power Journal is a
registered trademark in the
United States of America of
Airtime Publishing Inc.

World Air Power Journal
is published quarterly
and is available by
subscription

SUBSCRIPTION AND BACK
NUMBERS:

UK and World (except USA and
Canada) write to:
Aerospace Publishing Ltd
FREEPOST
PO Box 2822
London
W6 0BR
UK

(No stamp required if posted
within the UK)

USA and Canada, write to:
Airtime Publishing Inc.
Subscription Dept
10 Bay Street
Westport, CT 06880
USA

Prevailing subscription rates are
available on request.
For single and back issues of the
soft-cover edition (subject to
availability):
$17.95 each for delivery within
mainland USA, Alaska and
Hawaii. $22 (Can) each for
delivery to Canada. $22 (US)
each for delivery overseas.
Please enclose payment with
your order. Visa, MasterCard
and American Express accepted.
Include your card number,
expiration date and signature.
Hard-cover subscription rates
available on request.

Publisher, North America:
  Melvyn Williams
Subscription Director:
  Linda DeAngelis
Charter Member Services
Manager:
  Jill Brooks

WORLD AIR POWER ®

JOURNAL

CONTENTS

International

GEC Ferranti are flight-testing the ECR-90 radar for the Eurofighter in a BAC One-Eleven from Prestwick. Luftwaffe EFAs will likely have the American APG-65.

Eurofighter programme salvaged

A dramatic reversal of fortunes at a defence ministers' meeting on 10 December 1992 put the troubled European Fighter Aircraft (EFA) back on track for service with the air forces of Germany, Italy, Spain and the UK, albeit later than at first hoped. At the heart of EFA's problems had been demands by German Defence Minister Volker Rühe for a substantial cut in costs and a radical re-design of the airframe. These were over-come by a cosmetic change of the aircraft's name to Eurofighter 2000 and resort to some off-the-shelf equipment for the Ger-man version, thereby allowing Rühe to save political face and claim a 'victory' with up to 30 per cent cut from the unit price.

While of undoubted importance, the defence ministers' decision left many vital questions unanswered. Still to be decided are important issues such as the technology content, work-share and production aspects of the programme, although it seemed certain that the concept of four assembly centres has been abandoned. Equally vague are terms for the start-up of production. Germany agreed that its partners should have the aircraft entering service in 2000 (up to three years later than planned), while Berlin will make a decision on the production phase in 1996 (after the next general election) and take first de-liveries six years later. However, the pro-duction decision *must* be taken in 1995 to allow the UK, Italian and Spanish pro-grammes to proceed as agreed.

Pleasure at Germany's decision to con-tinue with the Eurofighter 2000 lasted only a month, until fresh clouds appeared on the horizon. Addressing the funding of its renewed commitment, Germany dis-covered in January that after rectifying in-adequate payments assigned to EFA in 1992 (when Rühe was attempting to kill the pro-gramme) it has only half the cash needed to pay its share of 1993 work. According to some sources, 1993 German Eurofighter funds would run out in April. An even longer stretch-out of development was then being mooted as one means of keep-ing the project running.

The German Eurofighter 2000 will, in all probability, have AN/APG-65 radar (as being retrofitted to F-4F Phantoms) in-stead of the purpose-designed ECR-90 being developed by a GEC Ferranti-led consortium. Reductions will be made in the self-protection systems and possibly in the weapons to be carried, although the de-cision to arm interceptor Eurofighters with Hughes AIM-120 AMRAAMs has re-cently been reconfirmed. The RAF Euro-fighter is expected to be the most compre-hensively equipped, including the full defensive aids sub-system.

Eurofighter's second EFA prototype, built by BAe at Warton, appeared to have leapfrogged Development Aircraft 1 (DA1) in Germany and was expected to take to the air first. In readiness for its maiden sortie, DA2 was wheeled into the paint shop at Warton on 8 January and emerged on 12 January in overall air defence grey and bearing the serial ZH588 on the fin. Also taking shape in the UK is

DA4 (ZH590), which will be the first two-seat Eurofighter, and probably the third to fly. DA3, the Italian-built test aircraft for the Eurojet EJ200 powerplant, has been held back in assembly. Because it is scheduled to undertake some trials in the UK, DA1 has been assigned the 'shadow' RAF serial number ZH586.

F-16 MLU trimmed

Planned cuts in the strengths of the Belgian and Netherlands air forces have been re-sponsible for a reduction in the size of the projected mid-life update (MLU) of NATO's F-16 fleets. Compared with an original target of 130, Belgium is now only committed to modernising 48 F-16s, although an option is held on 24 more. The Netherlands' programme has been cut from 172 to 136. Totals for Denmark (61), Norway (56) and the USAF (220) re-mained unaltered when the MLU Steering Committee agreed the changes on 28 January.

NATO considers J-STARS force

During December, NATO was studying the practicability of obtaining its own fleet of battlefield surveillance aircraft, which would be operated in a common pool like the E-3A force at Geilenkirchen. One obvious contender for an order would be the Grumman E-8C J-STARS which will enter US service in 1997, despite having had its operational debut (as E-8A) in the 1991 Gulf War. However, a more attractive European option would be to install the J-STARS avionics on one of the Airbus family. Presently, there are several com-parable national programmes in Europe: the UK is pursuing its own long-running ASTOR programme, possibly to be mounted in an executive jet; France has the Horizon system to be carried by Cougar helicopters; and Italy is developing Creso. The German LAPAS system was cancelled in February.

Right: As part of the Belgian reshuffle, the SF.260s of 5 Sm/Esc are to move from Goetsenhoven to Beauvechain.

Western Europe

BELGIUM:

Force reductions

Strong reaction to the drastic cuts planned for the Belgian air force resulted in a 12-month reprieve for No. 42 Squadron's Mirage 5s. Due to disband at the end of 1992, the unit is now to disappear on 31 December 1993. Perversely, upgrading is to proceed on its 20 Mirage 5BRs and 5BDs. Having established that to cancel the planned MIRSIP (Mirage Safety Im-provement Programme) would cost as much as completing it, the FAB/BLu decided to let it continue. The last aircraft will be redelivered a month before the squadron disbands.

The air base at Beauvechain/Bevekom lost its two F-16 squadrons (349 and 350) on 31 December as planned, but will re-main in being as a training base, housing the Alpha Jets of Nos 7, 9 and 11 Squad-rons, Magisters of No. 33 Squadron, and SF.260s of 5 Squadron. These will move from Brustem and (SF.260s) Gossoncourt/ Goetsenhoven, both of which are being closed. Support bases to be vacated are the air traffic control centre at Semmerzake (duties assumed by Glons/Tongeren) and air force ammunition dump – 25 Logistics Wing – at Meerdal (to Bertrix).

The famous Nos 349 and 350 Squad-rons, which flew with the RAF in World War II, have been saved from extinction following the disbandment of 1 Wing. One

squadron will join 2 Wing at Florennes (1 and 2 Squadrons) and the other is to reform in 10 Wing at Kleine Brogel (23 and 31 Squadrons). Net strength of the dimi-nished F-16 force will be unchanged, as unit establishments are being reduced from 18 to 12. Hungary has emerged as a possible customer for 15 of the 45 F-16A/Bs which Belgium is to sell.

FRANCE:

Squadron re-equipments

Early in the new year, Escadron de Chasse 2/12 'Picardie' became the second squadron within 12 Wing at Cambrai to replace its Mirage F1Cs with Mirage 2000Cs. The positions of the squadron's two flight badges have been reversed on the 2000C so that they now conform to usual practice: right side, first escadrille (SPA173) a blue-bird; left side, second escadrille (SPA172) a parakeet. It is believed that the curtailment of Mirage 2000C orders will result in EC 3/12 'Cornouaille' being disbanded.

Conversion also started early in 1993 at Colmar/Meyenheim of the second Mirage F1CT squadron, EC 3/13 'Auvergne'. EC 1/13 'Artois' is already equipped, but contrary to original plans EC 2/13 'Alpes' is to disband with Mirage 5Fs in 1994 and not receive F1CTs. The strength of 13 Wing will then be two squadrons, each of 20 F1CTs and about 30 pilots. The remain-ing 15 conversions will be held as reserve.

Right: Latest Mirage 2000 unit is EC 2/12 'Picardie', which has the latest S5 standard of 2000C.

Below: A French rarity is this Eurocopter Fennec, based at Cayenne, French Guyana, with Escadron d'Hélicoptère d'Outre Mêr 68 'Guyane'. The badge is that of SPA 152, and the squadron falls under Groupe Aérien Antilles-Guyane 375.

Modernised Crusaders introduced

French navy squadron 12F at Landivisiau received its first two remanufactured F-8E(FN) Crusader interceptors in January. The modification programme, devised by Dassault and undertaken at the naval workshops at Cuers, will involve 17 aircraft to be redelivered at the rate of one every six weeks. France received 42 Crusaders from 1964 onwards, and the installation of radar warning receivers, new navigation equipment, uprated ejection seats and new wiring will keep them operational until the Rafale is received in the late 1990s.

Also currently at Cuers, the ferry squadron (ERC) is to move to Hyères this year and combine with experimental unit, 10S from St Raphaël, to become the Escadrille de Reception, de Convoyage et d'Essai.

Tankers on lease

A surprise arrival at Avord on 20 December was a flight of three USAF KC-135R Stratotankers delivered from Tinker AFB for use by ERV 93, the French air force tanker wing. They have been hired to augment the fleet of 11 C-135FRs as the result of it being over-stretched by the demands of deployments to Cambodia, Somalia, Turkey and Saudi Arabia, plus the need to stand down C-135FRs during their conversion to three-point status with the addition of two FRL Mk 32 wing pods.

Squadron renamed

The air force's 59 Squadron was renamed late in 1992 as Escadron de Transporte 1/59 'Bigorre', taking the title name from a Noratlas transport unit (ET 3/64 'Bigorre') disbanded on 1 July 1981. Formed at Evreux on 1 September 1987, Escadron Electronique 1/59 received four Transall C.160Hs equipped with Rockwell-Collins VLF communications equipment (like the US Navy's E-6A Mercurys) for liaison with nuclear missile-armed submarines on patrol. Though part of Transport Command, the unit has been assigned to oper-

ational control of the Strategic Air Forces since 9 September 1992 and appears to be designated as a transport squadron for security reasons. No official pictures of its aircraft have been published.

Mirage 2000 plans change

Following an earlier reduction in Mirage 2000 orders from 372 to 318, it was revealed that 11 aircraft ordered as 2000C interceptors will be built as 2000B two-seat trainers. Therefore, at the beginning of 1993, the order book for the Armée de l'Air stood at 135 Mirage 2000Cs, 33 Mirage 2000Bs, 75 Mirage 2000Ns and 75 Mirage 2000Ds.

Late production interceptors are being built to S5 standard, at last meeting the specification originally laid down for the aircraft. Individual versions (refer to *World Air Power Journal*, Volume 10) are:
S3 Interim standard with RDM radar and M53-5 engine, only Super 530F missiles. All surviving S1 and S2 aircraft upgraded. Mirage 2000C Nos 1-37 and 2000B Nos 501-514 (plus 516 and 517 downgraded). All to be modified to Mirage 2000-5 with RDY radar and MICA missile capability.
S4 RDI J1-1 radar, introducing Super 530D missile capability. Mirage 2000C Nos 38-48 with M53-P2 engine and 2000B Nos 515, 518-520 with M53-5. All upgraded to S4-1.
S4-1 Retrofit of S4, plus new-built Mirage 2000C Nos 49-63. All with RDI J1-2 radar and M53-P2 engines. All upgraded to S4-2A.
S4-2 RDI J2-4 radar. Mirage 2000C Nos 64-74 and 2000B No. 522 with M53-P2 engine and 2000B No. 521 with M53-5. All upgraded to S4-2A.
S4-2A Retrofit standard for Nos 38-74, 515 and 518-522. HOTAS-type throttle and RDI J2-5 radar.
S5 RDI J3-13 radar and M53-P2 engine. Mirage 2000C Nos 75-135 and 2000B Nos 522-533.

A first flight was imminent at the start of 1993 by the initial production Mirage

Small numbers of Piaggio PD.808s remain in Italian service. This example flies with the Reparto Sperimentale di Volo (311° Gruppo).

2000D, No. 601. This conventional attack version will initially go to complete 3 Wing at Nancy. EC 2/3 reformed (ex-Mirage IIIE) with Mirage 2000Ns on 1 September 1991 and the wing will establish its initial 2000D squadron (EC 1/3) on 1 January 1994. Finally, EC 2/3 will pass its 2000Ns to EB 91 as Mirage IVP replacements in 1995 and receive 2000Ds. The two prototype Mirage 2000Ds were D01 (ex-N01) flown 19 February 1991 and D02 (ex-N02) flown 24 February 1992.

1993 defence budget

France's 1993 defence budget includes a mere two combat aircraft (Rafales) to be funded during the year. Receipts of previously-ordered machines by the air force during 1993 are planned to include the last three of 75 Mirage 2000Ns, first 12 of 75 Mirage 2000Ds, six Mirage 2000C/Ds and 18 Mirage F1CT conversions. Arrival of four more Airtech CN.235s during 1993 will boost the fleet to six, while the first Airbus is to arrive before December, followed by another in 1994. Helicopter deliveries in 1993 will comprise the last two Eurocopter AS 555 Fennecs.

GERMANY:
Double defence cuts

No less than two series of cuts in German defence spending were announced around the turn of the year as the government wrestled with the seemingly impossible tasks of balancing the books, funding the immense cost of modernising former East Germany and not appearing to renege on international collaborative weapon development agreements.

The major item in a wide-ranging package of reductions and changes of plan announced on 15 December was the acceptance of the Eurofighter 2000 for Luftwaffe service. However, procurement will be cut from an envisaged 250 to only 140 (including 20 two-seat trainers) and delayed three years, first production funds to be allocated in 1996 instead of 1993. Overall,

defence equipment budgets were being trimmed by 21 per cent, resulting in cancellations and stretch-outs in other programmes.

Westland in the UK will benefit from a follow-on order for up to 12 more Lynxes (augmenting 19 Mk 88s delivered) as a result of the Marineflieger abandoning plans to obtain the anti-submarine version of NH-90. All 38 NH-90s to be delivered to the navy from 2003 onwards will be in transport/SAR configuration. Lessening of Russian submarine activity has also resulted in postponement of plans to replace the Dassault-Breguet Atlantic. The existing aircraft of MFG 3 will receive a further upgrade and remain in service at least until 2005.

The Heeresflieger is affected by disappearance of the Warsaw Pact tank threat. As a result, the Eurocopter Tiger will be recast as a multi-role helicopter instead of specifically anti-tank, and its procurement target cut from 212 to 138. The new version is to be known as the Unterstutzungshubschrauber (UHU – Support Helicopter) and, although armed with HOT 2 and, later, TriGAT anti-tank missiles, will not have the previously planned air-to-air missiles. The last-mentioned will be replaced for escort duties by a podded 27-mm Mauser cannon. Plans to convert 54 PAH-1s (BO 105Ps) to armed escort/anti-helicopter BSH-1s have been dropped and upgrading of remaining PAH-1s has been halted at the 70th aircraft.

As previously reported, conversion will proceed of the Luftwaffe's four Boeing 707s to tankers from 1995. Upgrading of the Tornado IDS force will include FLIR, GPS and provision for the APACHE stand-off munitions dispenser. The upgrade, as well as purchase of 30 reconnaissance pods for about 40 naval Tornados being transferred to the Luftwaffe, will be funded in 1994.

German armed forces are to be orientated more towards intervention outside the NATO area on UN-authorised policing operations. Political approval for such missions may be difficult to obtain and will, in any case, require an amendment to the German constitution. Despite this re-

striction, Germany announced plans to send 1,500 troops to join the UN force in Somalia. The new outlook was soon to undergo political testing when Germany threatened to withdraw its personnel from the NATO AWACS force because E-3As from Geilenkirchen might be used to enforce the 'No-Fly Zone' in former Yugoslavia, a non-NATO area.

The new NATO Rapid Reaction Force is assigned Phantoms of JG 71 and JG 74 as well as one Roland, three Patriot and two Hawk SAM squadrons. Phantoms are being modified to carry the AIM-120, of which 328 – cut from 440 – will be ordered in 1994. By late 1992, six trial launches of the missile had been conducted by German F-4s in the USA.

A second round of programme reductions, the third in 12 months, was announced on 3 February. Plans to transfer some Luftwaffe F-4E/ICE Phantoms to former East Germany have been postponed, perhaps indefinitely. The units concerned were JG 72 from Hopsten to Laage as JG 75, and JG 35 from Pferdsfeld to Falkenberg as JG 73 (additionally with one squadron of MiG-29s). LTG 62's move to the east has been switched from Neubrandenburg to Holzdorf: UH-1Ds in 1995 and the C.160Ds by 2000. Also abandoned on 3 February was the LAPAS high-altitude reconnaissance programme involving Grob D-500 aircraft. This had recently been given the green light after protracted delays, but then stalled (just before the planned contract signature date of 16 January) following allegations of financial impropriety against two officials. Days after the government announced that the bribery charges had no bearing on its commitment to LAPAS, the entire project was axed.

Antonovs sold off

Offered for sale in January were seven more Antonov An-26s (5201, 5202, 5203, 5206, 5207, 5211 and 5212). Only two of the type now remain, An-26SM calibration aircraft 5209 and the Elint machine, An-26M 5210.

ITALY:
Self-defence for G222s

Following the loss of an Alenia G222 to a shoulder-launched SAM in Bosnia during September, the AMI was urgently looking at ways of installing self-defence aids in its transport fleet. A radar warning receiver and chaff/flare dispensers are being tested on a Hercules and are likely to be installed in both types of tactical transport. The 12 remaining Italian Hercules are currently undergoing a wing replacement programme and may be joined by four new aircraft if funding permits. Modernisation of the G222 with new radar and navigation equipment is under consideration.

The Maltese Air Squadron has received two Nardi-Hughes 500s (above) from Italy. Two of the three ex-Libyan Alouette IIIs have been put back in the air (right) following overhaul by Eurocopter.

Below: This SIAI-Marchetti S.208 serves with the 636ª Squadriglia Collegamenti (training/liaison flight), 36° Stormo.

Based at Villanubla-Valladolid, Ala 37 has recently completed replacement of the DHC-4 Caribou with the CASA C.212 (T.12B).

Starfighter modifications planned

In the final stages of converting 147 F-104S Starfighters to F-104S-ASA standard, the Italian air force was drawing up plans late in 1992 for a further life extension as the result of delays with the Eurofighter 2000. Of 143 aircraft remaining, 44 will be retired from fighter-bomber roles and the remainder given new wings, a new inertial navigation system and partial re-wiring.

NETHERLANDS:
F-16 cuts

Cuts in the Netherlands' F-16 force will be greater than expected, it was revealed in January, with 36 being sold, instead of 14. The number of aircraft committed to NATO will accordingly fall from 162, through the planned target of 144 to a new low of 108, resulting in the disappearance in 1996 of Nos 313 and 314 Squadrons at Gilze-Rijen and Twenthe respectively. One squadron from each Fighting Falcon base – No. 306 at Volkel, No. 315 at Twenthe and No. 322 at Leeuwarden – will be assigned to UN peacekeeping operations. The KLu will sell 20 F-16s by 1996 and the other 16 before 2000.

Helicopter plans

Plans have been cancelled to lease armed helicopters before buying a more capable type. Instead, purchase of a definitive attack helicopter will be brought forward to 1994 for delivery in 1996-2001 to Nos 298 and 302 Squadrons at Gilze-Rijen. In addition, No. 300 Squadron will move from Deelen to Eindhoven in 1994 and re-equip from Alouette IIIs to transport helicopters: Chinooks in 1994-95, followed by either Black Hawks or Cougars in 1996.

SWEDEN:
Viggen squadron swap

Planned disbandment of Sweden's No. 6 Wing (F6) at Karlsborg has been postponed from 30 June 1992 to 31 December 1993, when half a squadron's worth of AJ

37 Viggens will go to F10 and half to F15, those aircraft of the remaining squadron being condemned to scrap. F15 at Söderhamn currently has one AJ 37 squadron and one which is half OCU, but the new aircraft will give it two full AJ 37 components on 1 January 1994, the Sk 37-equipped Typingflygingskola becoming a separate training unit.

F13 at Norrköping disbands on 30 June 1993, but its two component squadrons are to be reassigned, the beneficiaries being F10 and F17. F10 at Angelhölm will augment its two J 35J Draken squadrons with No. 3 Recce Squadron (amalgamating the old 1/F13 and 2/F17) on 1 July, this equipped with SF 37s and SH 37s. On 1 January 1994 the same squadron will gain several AJ 37s from F6, as mentioned above, prior to all its aircraft being reworked to AJS 37 standard. At Ronneby, F17's loss of its recce squadron (2/F17) will be compensated for on 1 July by arrival of the old 2/F13 with AJ 37s.

Swedish combat units in January 1994 will therefore be:

F4 – Östersund	1 & 2 Sqn, JA 37	
F7 – Sätenäs	1 & 2 Sqn, AJ 37; Tspt Sqn, C-130H	
F10 – Angelhölm	1 & 2 Sqn, J 35J; 3 Sqn SF/SH/AJ 37; OCU, Sk 35C	
F15 – Söderhamn	1 & 2 Sqn, AJ 37; OCU, Sk 37	
F16 – Uppsala	2 & 3 Sqn, JA 37; 5 Sqn, Sk 60	
F17 – Ronneby	1 & 2 Sqn, AJ 37	
F21 – Luleå	1 Sqn, SF/SH 37; 2 & 3 Sqn, JA 37	

AEW contract

Confirming earlier plans, the Defence Material Administration (FMV) awarded a contract to Saab and Ericsson radar on 8 January for production of a prototype Saab 340 fitted with PS890 EriEye radar and including options on five further systems. The system is a follow-on to the trials undertaken with PS890 radar on the spine of a Swearingen Metro III. Delivery of the prototype Saab 340 conversion is scheduled for early 1995.

Radar trials by Sabre

Rockwell Sabre Series 40 86001 of F 13M at Malmslätt has begun a series of flight trials with the Coherent All Radio Band Sensing (Carabas) system which is able to detect forces hidden beneath trees and even locate objects under 15-30 ft (4.5-9.1 m) of earth. The antennas for Carabas are in two 18-ft (5.9-m) long flexible tubes trailing from

the base of the fin. The tubes are inflated with air from a compressor before landing and take-off but remain rigid due to the ram air effect when in flight.

TURKEY:
More Black Hawks

An additional 20 Sikorsky UH-60L Black Hawks were added to a previously-planned Turkish order when it was signed in December. Discussions held in September were for 75 of the utility helicopters, but in consideration for Sikorsky promising to accelerate deliveries, 95 were ordered. Of these, 45 are being delivered from the USA between January and September of this year. The remaining 50 are to be assembled locally by TUSAS at Mürted, with indigenous content increasing from 18 to 50 per cent during the production run. A dozen similar S-70A-17s serve with the Turkish gendarmerie and national police.

Extended Comfort

Turkey's parliament voted late in December to extend for a further six months the permission for USAF, French and UK aircraft to fly from Incirlik (Operation Provide Comfort) in protection of the Kurdish safe haven in northern Iraq.

UNITED KINGDOM:
CIS bids for RAF contracts

Media interest was generated during December by speculation that CIS-built aircraft might be bought to satisfy RAF re-equipment requirements: Beriev Be-42 flying-boats as a Nimrod follow-on and Antonov An-70T transports to replace the Hercules. The MoD acknowledged that it was examining the two aircraft. However, most observers agree that any CIS aircraft bought for a NATO country would need

Above: Farewell, Lightning – three of BAe's Lightnings on the last sortie demonstrate the three main colour schemes which graced the type through its career.

Right: No. 230 Sqn's Pumas have adopted this two-tone camouflage.

Western avionics and, probably, engines, thereby reducing its competitive edge. Unhindered supplies of spare parts is another worry for potential operators.

Lynx replacement launched

Despite earlier hopes, Russian attack helicopter manufacturers were not contacted when the long-expected invitation to tender for the British Army's Lynx replacement programme (AST 428) was issued in February to five consortia: Westland/McDonnell Douglas AH-64 Apache, BAe/Eurocopter Tiger, GEC-Marconi/Bell AH-1 Cobra Venom, Agusta A 129 Mangusta and Boeing Sikorsky RAH-66 Comanche. Approximately 100 helicopters are required for anti-armour operations, but with secondary air-to-air and ground-suppression capability. Bids have to be in by October and finalised by August 1994, so that the winner can be announced in May 1995 and production begun for 1998 service entry. A scout version of the chosen helicopter may be procured later.

First Chinook Mk 2

RAF Chinook ZA718 – the only one of its type to escape sinking of the MV *Atlantic Conveyor* during the Falklands War in 1982 – was rolled out at Boeing's Ridley plant on 19 January after conversion from HC.Mk 1B to HC.Mk 2 standard. Approximating to the CH-47D, the helicopter is the first of 33 to receive new

dynamic components, engines, instrumentation, flight control system and APU. The comprehensive array of self-defence systems (chaff/flare dispensers, IR jammers, missile-approach warners and door machine-gun mountings) applied to some Chinooks will be standardised and a new colour scheme applied in IR-absorbent paint. After ZA718 is delivered to A&AEE at Boscombe Down for trials, remaining conversions will be received between August 1993 and July 1995.

Sea Harrier 2 in view

The Fleet Air Arm announced its intention of forming a Sea Harrier FRS.Mk 2 Operational Evaluation Unit at Boscombe Down in June, preparing the way for the new variant to enter service with 899 Squadron at Yeovilton in 1994. In the interim, diversion of FRS.Mk 1s to BAe for modification will result in the two operational squadrons, 800 and 801, falling below their normal establishment of eight aircraft each.

Harriers practise night operations

RAF Harrier GR.Mk 7 squadrons were working up on their night vision systems early in 1993 in advance of the aircraft replacing Jaguars based at Incirlik, Turkey, from 1 April onwards, to support Operation Provide Comfort. The two Ger-

many-based units had just completed a move from Gütersloh to Laarbruch: No. 3 Squadron on 16 November, and No. IV on 27 November (while the Pumas and Chinooks of No. 18 Squadron followed on 9 December). One of the Germany-based squadrons was expected to begin the Turkish detachment, rotating after two months.

Most advanced in night operations is No. 1 Squadron at Wittering, UK. Last to convert to the Mk 7 – having only flown its first sortie (with Squadron Leader Mark Green in ZD434) on 2 June 1992 – the squadron was undergoing intensive training during the winter months, each of its 18 pilots receiving some 50 hours of night conversion training. On six of the squadron's aircraft, the GEC-Ferranti FIN1075 inertial navigation system has been upgraded to 1075G with the incorporation of a global positioning system receiver. Betrayed by a small, circular antenna on the aircraft's spine, the GPS was first flown by ZD437 (Flight Lieutenant Lance Nicol) on 19 November 1992. Early in 1993, No. 1 Squadron began augmenting its low-level armament of Improved BL755 cluster bombs, 1,000-lb retarded bombs and MATRA 155 68-mm rocket pods with medium-level weapons first used by RAF Jaguars in the 1991 Gulf War: CRV-7 rockets and CBU-87 cluster bombs. For reconnaissance, the GR.Mk 7 can carry the Harrier GR.Mk 3's sensor pod, or one of two others undergoing trials late in 1992: the Vinten VICON 18 long-range optical and VICON 57 multi-sensor.

SAR in 1992

Data announced in January showed that UK SAR helicopters attended 2,017 incidents during 1992, for a total of 2,098 call-outs: 1,445 RAF, 539 Fleet Air Arm, 85 Coastguard and 29 others (not counting operations entirely by Coastguard S-61s with no military assistance). Additionally, 54 Nimrods were launched and RAF Mountain Rescue Teams attended on 125 occasions. In all, 1,353 people were assisted.

Last Lightnings

Disposal of the last four airworthy Lightnings followed the final sortie in the Tornado F.Mk 3 radar development programme, which was flown from Warton on 16 December by XP693, XR773 and XS904. BAe has used five Lightning F.Mk 6s to provide airborne targets for Foxhunter radar. XR724, XR773, XS904 and XS928 previously saw RAF service, while XP693 (first flown as an F.Mk 3 on 16 June 1962) was the manufacturer's trials installation aircraft. XR724 was withdrawn from Warton in July 1990. On 31 December G-FSIX (XP693) and G-OPIB (XR773) were registered as civil aircraft to B. J. Pover.

Nuclear depth charges withdrawn

Disbandment on 1 December of a US Marine Corps guard detachment at RAF St Mawgan appears to have signalled the end of the UK's capability to drop nuclear depth charges. Between 6 and 13 April 1992, seven C-141B StarLifters collected weapons from St Mawgan, followed by 13 more sorties between 17 and 30 June, allowing the UK government to announce that month that tactical nuclear weapons were no longer carried by Royal Navy ships, and Fleet Air Arm and RAF maritime patrol aircraft. The weapons concerned are believed to have been the 700-lb B57 bomb, which has a yield variable between 1 and 20 kT (the upper limit of Hiroshima proportions). Applications would have been to FAA Sea Kings and RAF Nimrods under 'dual key' agreements with the US, but apparently only since 1974, when the first Marines arrived at St Mawgan.

The lack of a comparable USMC unit at Kinloss, the largest (and now only) Nimrod base, raises the question of a UK depth bomb and its fate. An official error in December 1986 revealed WE177 to be the designation of a British nuclear bomb for which new fuses had been bought by the Navy's contracts department at Bath, implying a depth charge application. The weapon originated from Red Beard, the low-level bomb developed for the Buccaneer naval strike aircraft. When the V-Bomber force resorted to low-level operations in the early 1960s, Air Staff Requirement 1177 was issued for a larger version of Red Beard for lay-down delivery, replacing Yellow Sun Mk 2 with most Vulcan and Victor squadrons. WE177 entered service in September 1966 and a version designated WE177B is believed to be current with some RAF Tornado GR.Mk 1 units. According to unofficial estimates in the 1980s, 245 WE177-type weapons were shared by Tornados and Buccaneers, while 140 more were configured as depth charges.

Staff Requirement (Air) 1244 has been issued for a WE177 replacement having stand-off capability, and £5.5 million has been spent since 1989 on associated studies. In 1993, £1.5 million will be spent and a decision reached on the replacement weapon, for which the Martin TASM, Aérospatiale ASLP and Boeing SRAM 2 are in contention. In order to beat a forthcoming US

The 'Tigers' of No. 74 Sqn are now a 'shadow' squadron for 4 FTS, flying Hawks at Valley.

embargo on underground testing, work has already begun on an SR(A) 1244 warhead, which it is hoped can be detonated beneath Nevada in 1996. Even if it meets this deadline, it is now certain that the new stand-off weapon will not meet its original in-service date of the late 1990s. Meanwhile, in February, the MoD selected Hunting-BRAE to manage the four Atomic Weapons Establishment sites at Aldermaston, Burghfield, Cardiff and Foulness from 1 April.

Eastern Europe

CIS:
Smaller states' nuclear weapons

Apparent reluctance by Ukraine to join Russia and the US in signing nuclear arms control accords was causing some concern in the West early in 1993. This coincided with the publication of a report estimating the number of nuclear delivery systems outside Russian control to be 431 and the total of associated warheads as 3,147. Ukraine is reckoned to have 14 Tu-142

As part of the 50th anniversary celebrations for the 'Normandie-Niémen' squadron, Mirage F1s from EC 2/30 visited Kubinka (left). Among host aircraft were Su-25s of the 'Sky Hussars' (below).

'Bear-H' (224 warheads) and 16 Tu-160 'Blackjack' (192) bombers, as well as 46 SS-24 (460) and 130 SS-19 (780) intercontinental missiles. Only slightly less potent is Kazakhstan's inventory of 40 'Bear-Hs' (370) and 104 SS-18s (1040), while Belorussia possesses 81 single-warhead SS-21 missiles.

CZECH REPUBLIC:
Air force split

Two new air forces came into being on 1 January when Czechoslovakia was dismembered to become the Czech Republic and Slovakia, with a 3:2 share-out of the armed forces. The Czech air force has been assigned 80 interceptors (MiG-21, MiG-23 and MiG-29), 72 fighter-bombers (MiG-21, MiG-23 and Su-22), 25 attack aircraft (Su-25), 24 reconnaissance machines (MiG-21 and Su-22), 26 advanced trainers (MiG-21), 32 transports (Tu-134, Tu-154, An-12, An-24 and An-26), 30 liaison aircraft (L-410), 76 trainers (L-29 and L-39) and 122 helicopters (Mi-2, Mi-8, Mi-17 and Mi-24).

Agreement has been reached on cross-supply of spares from factories in the 'other' halves of former Czechoslovakia, but there have been further disruptions, such as the Czech requirement to establish a new air academy at Brno.

ROMANIA:
Air force plans

Avionics modernisation for MiG-21s and MiG-23s will be one of the first priorities for the reorganised Romanian air force, according to plans revealed early in 1993.

With a sizeable force of 430 aeroplanes and 120 helicopters, the air force is intending to reorganise on Western lines, reverting to its pre-World War II lines of command, but is being hampered by spares supply and overhaul problems. The MiG-23MF force of some 45 interceptors has encountered difficulties with support from Bulgaria, while Mi-8 helicopters are no longer being overhauled by Hungary. The 13 MiG-29s delivered in 1990 have flown only 200 hours each since then, but the prospect of their 700-hour overhaul is already looming and it may be that they are replaced by Western fighters. In hand is an avionics upgrade for the IAR-93B attack aircraft, while IAI of Israel is beginning a MiG-21 update programme.

RUSSIA:

Faster withdrawals

Although returns of Russian units from eastern Germany slowed during the winter months, they are to be slightly accelerated in future. As the result of an agreement with Germany announced on 16 December, departure of Russian military units is being brought forward by four months, the last now to be withdrawn by 31 August 1994.

New combat aircraft designations

Russia assigned the designation Su-30 to the 'Flanker' variant previously known as Su-27PU and now in production at Irkutsk. Although able to function as a conventional long-range interceptor, the two-seat, refuelling probe-equipped Su-30 is primarily a command post. Operational tactics are for it to fly in company with four Su-27Ps, using its radar to locate targets for its associates. The latter are assigned by datalink to intercept and so do not have to use their own radar until late in the attack, thereby gaining the advantage of surprise.

Information only recently made public included Mikoyan design bureau numbers for several variants of 'Foxbat'. Interceptor versions of the aircraft are collectively known as the Type 84, their air force designations being MiG-25P, D, PD, PDS and SD-SL. Type 02 covers basic reconnaissance versions MiG-25R, RB, RBV and RBT, while Type 02K is the MiG-25RBK, Type 02S covers MiG-25RBS and RBSH and Type 02F is the MiG-25RBF. The anti-radar 'Foxbat-F' is Type 02M/MiG-25BN. Trainers are Type 22/MiG-25RU and Type 39/MiG-25PU. Two special record-breaking aircraft were both Type 99s: Ye-155M and Ye-266M.

UKRAINE:

Arms bazaar

Surplus military equipment was offered in unprecedented quantities by Ukraine on 26 January, generating interest from African and other nations. The Universal Ukrainian-Siberian Commodities Exchange at Kharkov advertised the availability of 27 MiG-27Ks (at $16 million each), 30 Su-17Ms ($7 million), 14 Yak-28s ($13

million), 10 Mi-2s ($0.7 million), three Mi-8Ts ($2 million) and unspecified numbers of Su-25Ks ($11 million), Su-27SK/UBs ($31 million), Il-76TDs ($32 million) and Mi-24s ($7 million). Of particular interest was the fact that the Yak-28s were recorded as having been built in 1985-88, long after the type was presumed to have ended its production run.

(Former) YUGOSLAVIA:

UN shies from aerial interventions

In spite of political pressure from some quarters eager that something should be seen to be done to punish Serbian aggression, UN members involved with the civil war in Bosnia-Herzegovina failed to agree to implement by force the 'No-Fly Zone' declared on 8 October and disregarded by all sides. It was feared that the projected use of USAF aircraft based in Italy and USN fighters afloat to enforce the ban would lead to to further Serbian attacks on Western ground forces, despite their UN status. As 1992 turned into 1993, therefore, NATO armed forces remained in their established roles of escorting food convoys, providing the air lift to Sarajevo and enforcing the sea blockade.

Serb fixed-wing aircraft had not flown a combat mission since 13 October, but helicopters were active, their sorties monitored by NATO, USAF, RAF and French E-3 Sentries. Locally-built Eurocopter SA 341/342 Gazelles predominate, several armed with anti-tank and air-to-air missiles, while some Mil Mi-8s were alleged to have been painted white to resemble UN helicopters. However, new intelligence was beginning to show that Serbia was no longer the main violator of the zone. Since December, increasing numbers of supply flights were noted between Croatia and the Croat- and Muslim-held parts of Bosnia in contrast to the marked decline in flights by Serb helicopters based near Banja Luka.

In appreciation of Hungarian permission for E-3 Sentry overflights to monitor former Yugoslavia, a NATO E-3A and RAF E-3D made a courtesy visit to Budapest on 19 January. E-3s began using Hungarian skies on 31 October.

At sea, US Navy P-3C Orions had flown 1,075 sorties from Sigonella, Sicily, by early December. Co-located have been

Portuguese Orions (50+ sorties), RAF Nimrods (12 sorties), Netherlands Orions and Italian Atlantics. Additionally, German Atlantics were operating out of Decimomannu, Sardinia and French Atlantics from their home base at Nîmes/Garons.

Naval vessels were investigating possible gun-runners, landing some boarding parties by helicopter. Those involved included the Italian navy's destroyer *Audace* with Agusta Bell 212ASWs aboard. Main power at sea has been provided by the USS *Kennedy* with CVW-3 embarked: VF-14 and VF-32 with F-14As; VFA-37 and VFA-105, F/A-18Cs; VA-75, A-6Es and KA-6Ds; VAW-126, E-2Cs; HS-7, SH-3Hs; VAQ-130, EA-6Bs; and VS-22, S-3Bs. Replacement was due in March by USS *Roosevelt* and CVW-8: VF-41 and VF-84, F-14As; VFA-15, VFA-87 and VMFA-312, F/A-18Cs; VA-36, A-6Es; VAW-124, E-2C; HS-9, SH-3H; VAQ-141, EA-6B; and VS-24, S-3B.

HMS *Ark Royal* left Britain for the Adriatic on 17 January, carrying eight Sea Harrier FRS.Mk 1s of 801 Squadron, six Sea King HAS.Mk 6s of 820 Squadron and three Sea King AEW.Mk 2As of 849 Squadron 'B' Flight. RFA *Argus* had arrived earlier with four Sea King HC.Mk

The first two of 48 Aero L-59E advanced trainers were handed over to the Egyptian air force at Aero's plant on 29 January.

4s of 845 Squadron, while also committed were frigates HMS *Brilliant* and *Coventry* with two Lynx HAS.Mk 3s each, all from 829 Squadron. *Ark Royal* took up station on 27 January and was joined, two days later, by the USMC carrier *Guam* with 20 helicopters aboard. The French carrier *Clemenceau* left Toulon for the Adriatic on 24 January, carrying two squadrons of Super Etendards and 15 army Puma and Gazelle helicopters and supported by seven smaller ships. The role of the UK and French aircraft-carriers is to support ground troops if they come under attack or are ordered to withdraw from relief supply escort and policing duties.

On 22 January, Croat forces attacked the Serb enclave of Krajina, a UN-protected area within Croatia, capturing the airport at Zemunic on 25 January.

In preparation for possible intervention in Bosnia, RAF Jaguars based at Coltishall were put on alert in late January.

The air bridge to Sarajevo, suspended on 1 December, was resumed on 21 December, the first aircraft to arrive being an RAF Hercules. Deliveries slowed significantly during mid-February when the citizens of Sarajevo refused to accept more supplies unless the UN redoubled its efforts to send aid to their compatriots in less accessible parts of Bosnia. At the turn of the year, the USAF element of Operation Provide Promise included four Hercules of the 37th Airlift Squadron based at Pleso Airport, near Zagreb, assisted by other Hercules from the West Virginia ANG, 96th ALS/AFRes and the Bravo rotationary detachment (then 314th AW from Little Rock) at Mildenhall.

Middle East

ISRAEL:

Albatross extension

On 2 February, the IDF/AF took delivery of the first Sikorsky Stallion upgraded to CH-53-2000 standard by IAI's Mata helicopter plant in Jerusalem. Known locally as the Yas'ur (Albatross), the Israeli CH-53s are being modified for a further 20 years of service. The service operates the survivors of 33 CH-53Ds, two ex-Austrian S-65s and 10 US-surplus CH-53As delivered in 1990-91. Six more CH-53As were promised in August 1992.

LEBANON:

RAF mercy mission

Three Wessex HC.Mk 5Cs of Cyprus-based No. 84 Squadron, RAF, deployed to southern Lebanon on 23 January to airlift 17 Palestinians from the Marj-as-Zahour deportee camp. The lift, under UN auspices, returned the 17 to Israel, from where 13 had been mistakenly deported and four required medical treatment.

SAUDI ARABIA:

Tornado purchase

Announcement by Saudi Arabia on 28 January that it was to proceed with long-awaited purchase of 48 Panavia Tornado IDS attack aircraft signalled the formal launch of the Al Yamamah II arms contract agreed in 1988, but repeatedly delayed. Welcome though the order was to British industry, it fell far short of the original 'AY II' intent, which was also to embrace 60 BAe Hawk 100/200s, 88 Westland-built

WS-70 Black Hawk helicopters, four BAe Jetstream 31 Tornado systems trainers and 12 BAe 125 and four BAe 146 executive aircraft.

To be delivered from 1996, the Tornados are believed to be all of the interdictor variant (IDS). The initial Saudi purchase under 'AY I' was 24 ADV interceptors and 48 interdictors, with a view to increasing quantities to 72 of each. However, the Tornado ADV's indifferent performance during the Gulf War and the US willingness to supply F-15 Eagles is understood to have moved the Saudi preference towards an all-IDS follow-up.

The Tornado contract came as BAe's Warton plant had only the last two RAF aircraft on the production line. These were from the eight ADVs ordered for Oman, then cancelled and added to the RAF Tornado F.Mk 3 contract as ZH552-ZH559. All have been completed with dual controls. ZH559 is the 197th Tornado ADV and 929th production Tornado (not counting 15 prototypes and pre-series), the new order therefore taking the number built up to a mere eight short of 1,000.

Far East

INDONESIA:

Hawk order agreed

UK sources were unable to confirm Indonesian reports claiming that an order had been placed in January for up to 24 BAe Hawk 100/200 advanced trainer/light attack aircraft. The TNI-AU plans to buy 144 Hawk 100s and single-seat 200s to augment the 20 Series 50 aircraft obtained for training during the 1980s.

JAPAN:

Defence budget for 1993

Announced in January, the defence budget for Fiscal Year 5 (beginning 1 April 1993) incorporated some last-minute changes to accommodate the substantial cost of two Boeing 'E-767' AWACS aircraft, in addition to the cuts already announced in the 1991-95 defence plan. In 1993, the Air Self-Defence Force is to buy four more Mitsubishi/McDonnell Douglas F-15Js (making

Below: Seen in Hong Kong, this is one of India's two Boeing 707s which fly from Palam.

New for the JASDF is the BAe U-125 (125-800), equipped for navaid calibration duties.

156, plus 37 F-15DJ trainers), nine Kawasaki T-4 trainers (= 144), one Mitsubishi/Sikorsky UH-60J (= 14), one SAR-configured BAe 125 (= four, plus one for calibration), three Beech 400 crew trainers (= six) and the two 'E-767' aircraft. The Maritime SDF gains a single Kawasaki/Lockheed P-3C patroller (= 100), one EP-3E (= six EP/NP-3 variants), two SH-60J (= 51) and four UH-60J (= 12) helicopters, one US-1 SAR amphibian (= 15) and the first four T-4 jet trainers. Finally, Ground SDF procurement in 1993 comprises two Fuji/Bell AH-1S Cobra helicopter gunships (= 85), 13 Kawasaki/Hughes OH-6Ds (= 283 OH-6J/D) and two Kawasaki/Boeing CH-47J Chinooks (= 36).

Japan launches 'E-767'

In the absence of a US military designation, the combination of a Boeing 767 airliner and detection systems installed in the E-3 Sentry has adopted the working title of E-767. Japan had not acted on its requirement for four large jet AWACS aircraft before the E-3 line closed, so the 767-200ER airframe was studied in 1991 as a platform for the APY-2 radar system and Block 20/25 avionics package. Plans are for the two 767s to be built at Seattle and structurally modified at Wichita, beginning in January 1995, before returning to Seattle

for installation of basic equipment and seven months of flight testing. Final fitting-out is due to begin (on the No. 2 aircraft first) in October 1996 and both will be ready for handing over in January 1998.

First BAe U-125

On 18 December, British Aerospace handed over to the ASDF at Utsunomiya the first of three U-125 variants of the BAe 125 Series 800 business jet equipped for flight inspection duties. Ordered in 1990, and fitted with equipment produced by LTV/Sierra research, the aircraft will be used to calibrate radar and radio aids at airfields throughout Japan. The ASDF also plans to obtain 27 U-125As equipped for SAR between 1995 and 2003.

MALAYSIA:

Fighter competition intensifies

Competition to supply the RMAF with 18 air superiority/attack aircraft intensified early in 1993 when representatives of McDonnell (F/A-18 Hornet) and Dassault (Mirage 2000), among others, stepped up their lobbying. An interesting development was the signature of a military training and logistics support agreement by India and Malaysia, viewed by some observers as a means of overcoming RMAF objections to the Mikoyan MiG-29 'Fulcrum'. As a major operator of MiG-29s, India would be able to guarantee support, although that would still have no effect upon the aircraft's high maintenance demands.

SINGAPORE:

Enforcer Mk 2 flies

Destined for delivery to Singapore, the prototype Fokker Maritime Enforcer Mk 2, based on the Fokker 50, made its first flight at Schiphol, Netherlands, on 27 January. As the first of four on order by Singapore, it will be delivered in 1994. The Fokker 50 is equipped with two Pratt & Whitney PW125B turboprops in place of the Rolls-Royce Darts which powered the F27 Friendship for three decades. In its maritime guise, the aircraft is equipped with 360° radar (Litton APS-140 or Texas

Primary rotary-wing training for the Chilean army is provided by 15 Enstrom 280FXs. This is a refined version of the basic design, with a covered tail rotor shaft and fully-faired landing skids.

Instruments APS-134), a GEC FLIR, CAE ASQ-504(V) internal MAD and the CDC UYS-503 sonobuoy data processing suite.

SRI LANKA:
Pucará delivery

Latest equipment for SLAF operations against Tamil separatist guerrillas arrived in December in the form of the first of four FMA IA-58A Pucará COIN turboprop twins supplied by Argentina. For several years, Argentina has been attempting to dispose of late-production Pucarás held in storage, but has succeeded only in selling small numbers to Colombia and Uruguay. The SLAF is also beginning to operate the four Chengdu F-7M Airguards (MiG-21s) and two Shenyang FT-5s (MiG-17Us) obtained from China in 1992. Hitherto, the main fixed-wing combat equipment has comprised a half-squadron of SIAI-Marchetti SF.260TP Warriors. It expects to receive two Mil Mi-8 helicopters from an eastern European supplier and may buy more.

TAIWAN:
F-5 upgrade planned

Despite recent purchases of 150 General Dynamics F-16 Fighting Falcons and 60 Dassault Mirage 2000s, Taiwan was considering during January an upgrade to its force of 270 Northrop F-5E/F Chung Cheng (Tiger II) light fighters. The pro-

Above: Canada has also adopted all-over mid-grey for its transports. This is a No. 435 Sqn CC-130.

Right: In Canadian Forces service, the A310 is known as the CC-150 Polaris. The three aircraft serve with No. 437 Squadron at Trenton.

posed F-5E-SX would virtually reinvent the F-5G Tigershark by replacing the two General Electric J85 turbojets with a single powerplant: either the GE J101 (a development of the F404 used in the Hornet and other aircraft) or the Allied Signal F125X (developed from the TFE1042 used by the indigenous Ching Kuo fighter). With a new radar – possibly the indigenous Sky Dragon, based on the General Electric Aerospace AN/APG-67 – the F-5E-SX would be equipped with Hughes AIM-120 AMRAAM missiles for beyond visual range, fire-and-forget interception.

Australasia

AUSTRALIA:
Third 'bare base'

A go-ahead was given in December for the RAAF to construct its third and last 'bare base' in the northern regions of Australia. Intended to host operational units in the event of an emergency, RAAFB Sherger (named for a former Chief of Air Staff) will be begun in March 1993. By 1999 it is intended to have a 9,800-ft (2990-m) runway and 20 hardened aircraft shelters. Sherger, which is near the town of Weipa, is on the Cape York peninsula in the north-west. The remainder of the northern air base chain comprises Curtin near Derby, Learmonth (WA) and the fully operational station at Tindal, which is home to No. 75 Squadron's F/A-18 Hornets.

Africa

SOUTH AFRICA:
More SAAF contractions

Additional cuts in the SAAF announced

during December included 2,552 of its 10,000 personnel, with a further 1,000 to go before 1995. Aircraft strength will continue to fall during the next few years to reach 390 by 1995, compared with a peak of 775 in 1988. Accordingly, the number of squadrons is in the process of being cut from 36 to 17.

As planned, the SAAF's nine Transall

C.160Zs were withdrawn from 28 Squadron at Waterkloof on 8 January, having flown a total of 61,000 hours since 1969. They will be maintained in an airworthy state until a buyer can be found.

PC-7 choice

Erroneous reports that it had chosen the EMBRAER Tucano as its next basic trainer were disproved in December when the SAAF announced a contract for 60 Pilatus PC-7 Mk IIs to be delivered from July 1994 onwards as replacements for veteran North American T-6 Harvards. The Mk II has a four-bladed propeller and other, unspecified, improvements. Following the first one or two aircraft built at Stans, Switzerland, the remaining PC-7s will be assembled in South Africa, allowing 55 per cent of their value to comprise indigenous work and materials. When instructor training is complete, the PC-7 will enter service early in 1996 at the Central Flying School, Langebaanweg.

New aircraft required

In spite of cuts, the SAAF is planning to modernise its remaining equipment. The Atlas Impala (Aermacchi M.B.326) jet trainer is to be replaced or upgraded from 1996 in order to provide a suitable aircraft on which to train student pilots after their PC-7 courses. The Alouette III light transport helicopter, which proved to be such a valuable workhorse in the Namibian bush war, is also due for replacement from 1996.

South America

CHILE:
Israel upgrades Tiger IIs

Having at one time considered selling its Northrop F-5E/F Tiger IIs, the FACh is currently preparing to reaccept the first of approximately 15 aircraft after a modernisation programme. By early 1993, the first of each variant was undergoing flight trials in Israel, where the Bedek Division of IAI had installed a new avionics package including HOTAS controls, multi-function displays, a HUD, air data computer, inertial navigation system and a new radar (originally developed for the stillborn IAI

Procured to replace ancient Bell 47s, 10 Enstrom F28Fs are operated by the Peruvian army for basic training. This example is seen at the manufacturer's plant at Menominee, Michigan, which has produced over 900 helicopters.

Lavi programme) installed in an Israeli-built radome. The F-5s also gain an integrated self-defence system comprising a passive warner, jammer and chaff/flare dispenser. Remaining aircraft will be upgraded in Chile under Israeli supervision.

COLOMBIA:
EMBRAER trainers and transports

Delivery was effected on 10 December of seven EMBRAER EMB-312 Tucano turboprop trainers (from 14 on order) and two EMB-110P1A Bandeirante VIP transports ordered earlier in 1992. The Tucanos, finished in training colours, have entered service at Apiay with Grupo Aéreo de Combate II, alongside Cessna T-37s, FMA Pucarás and Lockheed T-33s. Both Bandeirantes are for the Grupo Aéreo de Transporte Militar at Bogotá.

The Naval Research Laboratory at NAS Patuxent River, Maryland, operates this NP-3B Orion, seen with various unidentified pods.

North America

CANADA:

Arcturus into service

Following completion of equipment installation by IMP Group at Halifax, Nova Scotia, the first of three Lockheed CP-140A Arcturus patrol aircraft was delivered to the Canadian Forces at Greenwood in December. The aircraft are a version of the CP-140 Aurora lacking anti-submarine equipment, but instead outfitted for fisheries patrol, maritime surveillance and SAR. They will also be used as flight deck crew trainers for the CP-140 fleet. The third machine, delivered to IMP on 30 May 1991, was the last of the Orion family built at Palmdale, but production has resumed at Marietta, with first roll-out due for May 1994.

Air forces withdrawn from Europe

Canada's permanent air commitment to NATO ended on 31 December when 439 Squadron stood down at Söllingen prior to returning home on 19 January. The unit was the last of three (409, 421 and 439) operating CF-18 Hornets as the major element in No. 1 Canadian Air Division in south-eastern Germany. Withdrawal of the Hornet ended a European presence unbroken since Canadair CL-13 Sabres were deployed (initially to North Luffenham, England) in 1952.

UNITED STATES:

F-111 activities in Europe

The 48th Fighter Wing at RAF Lakenheath withdrew the last examples of the F-111F from United States Air Forces in Europe during December 1992 after 15 years of operations. The final squadron to fly the type was the 493rd Fighter Squadron, which was deactivated on the afternoon of 14 December 1992 in a ceremony held in one of the hangars at the base. The disbandment of the squadron effectively ended the operational career of the F-111F with the 48th FW. Present for the formal deactivation were members of the squadron flanked by the 493rd FS Commander's aircraft, 71-0889, and the 48th FW Commander's F-111F, 74-0178.

Both aircraft were painted with additional markings on the nose and tail for their respective squadron and wing commanders. 71-0889 had a yellow '493 FS' on the tail, while elaborate artwork on the port side of the nose featured an F-111 overflying the flags of the USA and the United Kingdom, surrounded by a circle containing the national emblems of countries to which the squadron had deployed or paid goodwill visits during its 15 years operating the type. These included Saudi Arabia, Turkey, France, Belgium, Germany, Spain, Kuwait, Greece and Italy. In addition, two gold sections contained the inscriptions 'Farewell F-111F' and '1977 – 1992'. 74-0178 was inscribed '48 FW' across the fin with all three squadron colours on the fin with all three squadron colours on the fin cap. The port side of the nose was marked with an eagle holding a red spear and a scroll inscribed 'Provide Comfort'. Adjacent was a green map of England, with a smaller eagle overflying holding a second scroll inscribed 'Desert Shield/ Desert Storm' and 'El Dorado Canyon'. The two aircraft were participants in both operations, the latter performing 56 Gulf combat missions to become the wings' sortie leader during Desert Storm.

The final four F-111s were scheduled to depart Lakenheath early on the morning of 15 December for reassignment to the 27th Fighter Wing at Cannon AFB, New Mexico. As the four aircraft were conducting their pre-flight checks, a serious leak from 74-0178 resulted in fuel spilling on to the flight line. F-111F 71-0889, which was parked alongside, was hurriedly repositioned to a safer area as the fire department quickly responded to place foam on the spilt fuel. 74-0178 was towed away as the other three, serials 71-0888, 71-0889 and 71-0890, took off shortly after 0930 local time for Wright-Patterson AFB, Ohio, on the first leg of their journey to Cannon AFB. Following repairs and a test flight, 74-0178 completed its journey to the USA on 18 December.

The first three F-111s were delivered to Lakenheath on 1 March 1977, replacing the F-4D in an operation named Ready Switch. The majority were previously operated by the 366th TFW at Mountain Home AFB, Idaho, and were flown to Lakenheath directly from the former facility. Close to 100 aircraft were stationed at Lakenheath throughout the 15 years of operations.

Attrition and reassignment to test duties resulted in approximately 72 F-111Fs joining the 27th FW, being distributed between the 522nd, 523rd and 524th Fighter Squadrons. The wing also has the 430th ECS with the EF-111A and is shortly to receive the F-111E to be assigned to the 428th FS. The latter squadron will receive its equipment from the 20th FW at RAF Upper Heyford, which is scheduled to return its aircraft to the USA commencing April 1993. The 79th FS will be first to wind down between April and June, followed by the 77th FS from July to September and finally the 55th FS between October and December. Once the aircraft have left, each squadron will deactivate before the wing inactivates early in 1994.

December was an active month with aircraft and crews on assignment in the Gulf completing their period of temporary duty and being replaced by fresh personnel and aircraft. Lakenheath hosted some of the swap-overs, including EF-111As of the 366th Wing stationed at Dhahran AB, Saudi Arabia. 67-0044 and 67-0048 arrived from the USA on 4 December and departed for Dhahran four days later, although they were forced to divert to Ramstein. These replaced 66-0055 and 67-0052, which arrived at Lakenheath on 15 December and departed for the USA on 18 December in company with the final 48th FW F-111F (mentioned earlier). Another pair (67-0035 and 67-0037) landed on 13 December and stayed for two days on their flight from Dhahran to Mountain Home AFB. The replacements for these had presumably accomplished their flight to the Middle East through a different route.

Lakenheath also supported the return to the USA of 131st FW Eagles which had completed their period of temporary assignment at Dhahran. Twelve F-15Cs of the 71st FS, along with one displaying special markings for the 94th FS C.O., arrived from Saudi Arabia on 14 December and departed for Langley AFB two days later, having been replaced by 12 F-15Cs of 58th FS/33rd FW which deployed from Eglin AFB to the Middle East via Bitburg during mid-December. The 1st Fighter Wing lost 83-0021 of the 71st FS, which crashed in Saudi Arabia on 30 November.

Air Force test unit designation changes

Air Force Materiel Command (AFMC) has implemented a number of changes, including the redesignation of some of its flying units to eliminate those with four-digit identities. At Edwards AFB, California, the flying component of the Air Force Flight Test Center (AFFTC), the 6510th Test Wing, became the 412th Test Wing on 2 October 1992. The nine flying units assigned to the wing, within the range 6510th to 6520th Test Squadrons, were redesignated, although not all were reassigned in numerical sequence. At Hill AFB, Utah, the 6545th Test Group and its associated flying unit, the 6514th Test Squadron, had their designations changed with the simple elimination of the prefix number 6 in both cases. The 545th TG is a subordinate organisation of the AFFTC, whose primary role is the development and evaluation of air-launched drone technology. The 'ED' tailcode allocated to the 412th TW is displayed by most, but not all, of the aircraft at Edwards AFB. None of the aircraft or helicopters of the 545th TG at Hill AFB carry a tailcode, apart from the HH-1Hs which display 'HL', which is the identifier for the resident 388th FW.

At Eglin AFB, Florida, the 3246th Test Wing and its single flying unit, the 3247th Test Squadron, were abbreviated to 46th TW and 40th TS respectively on 3 October. The wing is the flying component of the Air Force Development Test Center (AFDTC) and has tailcode 'ET'. The unit is responsible for the evaluation of new or upgraded tactical weapons prior to their introduction into service, with the majority of tests taking place over the vast Eglin ranges which encompass almost half a million acres. Whereas the AFFTC and the contractors at Edwards AFB are assigned close to 100 aircraft, the AFDTC has approximately two dozen.

The bulk of transport-orientated test aircraft are assigned to the 4950th Test Wing at Wright-Patterson AFB, Ohio, which has two squadrons consisting of the 4952nd TS flying the C-18A, EC-18B/D, NKC-135A and EC-135E, and the 4953rd TS with the NC-141A, CT-39A, NT-39A and T-39B. The wing is the flying unit of the Aeronautical Systems Center, whose

An F-15E of the 40th Test Squadron during tests with the AGM-130 2,000-lb rocket-boosted EO-guided bomb. In addition to LANTIRN and Sparrows, it carries an AXQ-14 datalink pod.

Left: *On 10 February 1993, McDD's St Louis plant delivered its 10,000th jet, an F/A-18 for VFA-137. The occasion was marked with this display of current types.*

Above: *The New Orleans-based 706th Fighter Squadron is now an F-16C operator. These replace the A-10s in which the squadron saw much action in Desert Storm.*

primary duties are to evaluate avionics suites, reconnaissance sensors, radars and a host of other other new or modified aircraft systems prior to operational service. The Center has conducted evaluation of advanced aviation-related technology, including the High Energy Laser Laboratory which was housed in a highly modified NKC-135A as part of the 'Star Wars' programme.

The unit designation is to remain unchanged as the aircraft are in the process of moving to Edwards AFB to join the 412th TW as part of a consolidation programme. The 4953rd TS will be the first to relocate, commencing April 1993, followed by the 4952nd TS which will complete the move by February 1994. Once the move is complete the two squadrons will be redesignated in line with the other units at Edwards AFB, with the 4950th TW being deactivated. Resident flying units at Wright-Patterson AFB will then be restricted to the Air Force Reserve and Air National Guard.

The five Air Logistics Centers have a single flying squadron directly assigned whose duties are primarily to perform flight testing of aircraft following major overhaul. These squadrons have also been redesignated from four to those with two- or three-digit identities. Three of the five squadrons have a small number of aircraft allocated to conduct a limited amount of test work. The five centers are the Warner Robins ALC at Robins AFB, Georgia (C-130, C-141, F-15), Sacramento ALC at McClellan AFB, California (A-10, F-111, F-117 and a small number of KC-135s on behalf of the Oklahoma City ALC), San Antonio ALC at Kelly AFB, Texas (B-52H, C-5), Ogden ALC at Hill AFB, Utah (F-16, FMS F-4 plus limited C-130 overhauls on behalf of Warner Robins ALC), and the Oklahoma City ALC at Tinker AFB, Oklahoma (B-1, B-52G, C-135/KC-135, E-3).

Most major aircraft types receive major overhaul 'in house' at one of the Air Logistics Centers as detailed in the preceding paragraph, although not all, as it would be impracticable and uneconomic to undertake this work completely. Some types are maintained by the manufacturer, such as the C-21A Learjets which return to the Learjet Corporation facility at Tucson, Arizona, and the U-2Rs which are overhauled by Lockheed at Palmdale, California. Other maintenance contracts are issued by AFMC to airlines such as Pan Am at Miami International Airport, which

overhauled SAC KC-10As during the late 1980s. Specialist corporations such as Chrysler Technologies at Waco's TSTI Airport, Texas, and E Systems Inc. at Majors Field, Greenville, Texas, both perform conversions on behalf of AFMC. These include various electronic and reconnaissance versions of the C-130 and C-135 which were originally converted by these companies and return periodically for maintenance of both the airframe and the onboard sensors.

Air Combat Command has implemented unit redesignation to its small test organisation. The 4485th Test Squadron at Eglin AFB, which was formerly accountable directly to the Air Warfare Center, has been shortened to the 85th Test and Evaluation Squadron and is now responsible to the newly-created 79th TEG. The squadron operates approximately a dozen fighter aircraft including the F-15A/C and F-16A/C/D, plus an RF-4C. The prime function of the 85th TES is to develop procedures for weapons delivery after test programmes have been completed by AFMC and before issue to operational fighter units. The 89th Tactical Aerial Targets Squadron at Tyndall AFB, Florida, changed to the 84th TS with assignment to the 79th TEG. The squadron has no aircraft assigned but borrows from the parent unit at Eglin AFB as required. Details of the former and current unit identities are as follows:

Air Force Materiel Command Units

Old Unit	New Unit	Aircraft Types
Air Force Development Test Center		
3246th TW	46th TW	
3247th TS	40th TS	F-15A/B/C, F-15E, F-16A/B/C, F-111E/F, UH-1N, T-38A 'ET'
Air Force Flight Test Center		
6510th TW	412th TW	
6510th TS	410th TS	B-1B 'ED'
6511th TS	411th TS	YF-22A
6512th TS	445th TS	OA-37B, NOA-37B, C-23A, UH-1N, T-38A 'ED'
6515th TS	15th TS	F-15A/B/D, F-15E 'ED'
6516th TS	416th TS	F-16A/B/C 'ED'
6517th TS	417th TS	C-17A 'ED'
6518th TS	418th TS	MC-130H, AC-130U 'ED'
6519th TS	419th TS	B-52G/H 'ED'
6520th TS	420th TS	B-2A
6545th TG	545th TG	
6514th TS	514th TS	DC-130A, C-130B, NC-130B, DC-130H, HC-130H, HH-1H, NCH-53A, HH-53C

Operational Support

2871st TS	10th TS Oklahoma City ALC	nil
2872nd TS	15th TS Ogden ALC	RF-4C, F-16A/B
2873rd TS	313th TS San Antonio ALC	nil
2874th TS	337th TS Sacramento ALC	A-10A, F-111A/D, FB-111A, YF-117A, T-38A
2875th TS	339th TS Warner Robins ALC	F-15A 'RG'

Air Force training update

The Air Force has released additional information concerning the proposed formation of Air Force Training and Education Command (AFTEC). The amalgamation of existing Air Training Command (ATC) resources with the combat crew training units (CCTU) at Davis-Monthan AFB (OA/A-10A), Luke AFB (F-16C), and Tyndall AFB (F-15A/C) currently under Air Combat Command control has already been announced. The new Command will assume control of both Luke AFB and Tyndall AFB on 1 July 1993 and gain Altus AFB, Oklahoma, at a later date. The latter facility has the 97th AMW in residence which conducts aircrew training with the C-5B and C-141B. The wing also has two KC-135R air refuelling squadrons assigned which are not dedicated to the training role. AFTEC will gain the 398th ARG at Castle AFB, California, which trains KC-135 tanker aircrew. Special forces training is performed by the 542nd Crew Training Wing at Kirtland AFB, New Mexico, with a mixed fleet including the MC-130H, HC-130P,

One of the recent 'players' in Red Flag at Nellis AFB was this B-52H from the 5th Bomb Wing at Minot.

UH-1N, HH-3E, TH-53A, MH-53J and HH-60G which will also join AFTEC. At the Air Force Academy the T-41s of the 557th FTS will transfer to the new Command, although all other aircraft activities will remain under the control of the Academy. Finally, the 4315th CCTS which performs missile training at Vandenberg AFB, California, will also become part of AFTEC.

B-52 training is currently performed by the 93rd BW at Castle AFB and is scheduled to switch to the 92nd BW at Fairchild AFB by the middle of the decade. This activity, together with the CCTUs for the B-1B, RC-135, U-2 and the F-15E, are fairly small organisations and will remain under Air Combat Command. The retention of the F-15E by ACC instead of transfer to AFTEC is surprising, as two squadrons are dedicated to 'Strike Eagle' training at Luke AFB and will therefore be transferred from the 58th FW to another unit.

Three Air National Guard groups may also be transferred to the new organisation, although this is likely to be as a gaining command in the event of mobilisation. The units concerned are the 162nd FG at Tucson IAP, Arizona, 184th FG at McConnell AFB, Kansas, and 142nd FG at Kingsley Field, Oregon. These three units conduct F-16 aircrew training for Air National Guard and Air Force Reserve personnel, although consideration is being given to all Fighting Falcon training being consolidated at Luke AFB within AFTEC. The ANG units would either switch to operational duties or be inactivated.

Small detachments of four Air Training Command T-37Bs or T-38As have been assigned at SAC bomber and tanker bases for several years to perform Accelerated

The first and the last – Boeing's recently restored 'Dash Eighty' prototype meets a Navy E-6 Mercury, the 1,010th and last Model 707 airframe to be produced by the company. 'Dash Eighty' also acted as prototype for 820 C-135s.

Co-pilot Enrichment (ACE). The detachments provide additional flight hours for co-pilots at a fraction of the cost of actually operating bombers and tankers. On 1 January 1993 the ACE dets were transferred to the host wings, joining either ACC or AMC. Details are still being released, but it is believed the Tweets and Talons will be repainted with the colour scheme of the aircraft of the host wing. The ACE trainers at ACC B-1 and B-52 bases will change from white to bomber grey, while the T-38s of the 9th RW at Beale AFB, California, will be painted black overall with red markings. The trainers at tanker bases will be repainted in the new mid-grey scheme. Those trainers joining ACC will have tailcodes applied, while the AMC aircraft will display the command's tail stripe. The dets at Carswell and Wurtsmith should have been withdrawn by the end of 1992 as the bomber and tanker units are inactivating prior to the facilities closing in 1993.

Active 'Wild Weasel' capability retained

The Air Force has undertaken a review of its F-4G 'Wild Weasel' requirement and has decided to retain a single squadron within the active inventory rather than transfer the remaining aircraft to the Air National Guard. The 190th Fighter Squadron at Boise Air Terminal, Idaho, has already re-equipped with the type, although the 192nd Reconnaissance Squadron at Reno, Nevada, was due to exchange their RF-4Cs for the F-4G during 1992. The latter plan was placed on hold pending the review and, instead, the F-4G will be stationed at Nellis AFB, Nevada, with the 561st Fighter Squadron being activated on 1 February 1993 under the 57th Fighter Wing. The squadron will receive the majority of its aircraft from the 81st FS, 52nd FW, at Spangdahlem AB, Germany, which has commenced returning aircraft to the USA. The 81st FS should have relinquished the F-4G by April 1993.

At the end of 1992 the squadron had 28 aircraft assigned, including 12 at Dhahran AB, Saudi Arabia, for Southern Watch and an unspecified number (probably four) at Incirlik AB, Turkey, for Provide Comfort. It would seem likely these will be reassigned to the 57th FW *in situ* in the same manner as responsibility for the EF-111As in the Gulf was transferred from the 20th FW (USAFE) to the 366th Wing (ACC) without disruption to operations. The 81st FS will re-equip with the F-16C receiving Block 50 versions at the same time as its sister squadrons, the 23rd and 480th FSs.

Air rescue squadron update

Details of the transfer of Air Rescue Service units from Air Mobility Command to Air Combat Command and Pacific Air Forces were presented in *World Air Power Journal*, Volume 13. The proposed transfer date of 1 October 1992 has been revised to 1 January 1993. Seven of the eight 'Twin Huey' detachments provide direct support to the former SAC missile units spread across the central United States. As stated in Volume 13, Detachment 8/37th RQS at Vandenberg AFB, California, has become the 76th RQS under the 310th Training and Test Wing.

Apart from Det 24 at Fairchild AFB, Washington, the remaining detachments have been reassigned to the missile wings as follows: Det 2 at Ellsworth AFB, South Dakota, with the 44th MW; Det 3 at Grand Forks AFB, North Dakota, with the 321st MW; Det 5 at Malmstrom AFB, Montana, with the 341st MW; Det 7 at Minot AFB, North Dakota, with the 91st MW; Det 9 at Whiteman AFB, Missouri, with the 351st MW; and the Det 10 at Francis E. Warren AFB, Wyoming, with the 90th MW. Det 24 at Fairchild AFB which supports the USAF Survival School has joined the 92nd BW.

The 48th RQS at Holloman AFB, New Mexico, has been assigned to the 49th FW while the 66th RQS at Nellis AFB, Nevada, has joined the 57th FW. The HH-60Gs of these two squadrons have applied tailcodes 'HO' and 'WA' respectively. Patrick AFB, Florida, is the home of the 41st RQS operating the HH-60G and the 71st RQS flying the HC-130N/P. The two squadrons have been assigned to the 1st Operations Group, which is the flying organisation of the 1st FW at Langley AFB, Virginia, and will probably assign the tailcode 'FF'.

Air Rescue Service Detachments

Air Combat Command

37th RQS	Francis E Warren AFB, WY	
det 2 'EL'	Ellsworth AFB, SD	HH-1H
det 3 'GF'	Grand Forks AFB, ND	HH-1H
det 5 'MM'	Malmstrom AFB, MT	UH-1N
det 7 'MT'	Minot AFB, ND	HH-1H
det 9 'WM'	Whiteman AFB, MO	HH-1H
det 10 'FE'	Francis E. Warren AFB, WY	UH-1N
det 24 'FC'?	Fairchild AFB, WA	UH-1N
41st RQS 'FF'?	Patrick AFB, FL	HH-60G
48th RQS 'HO'	Holloman AFB, NM	HH-60G
56th RQS	NS Keflavik, Iceland	HH-60G
66th RQS 'WA'	Nellis AFB, NV	HH-60G
71st RQS 'FF'?	Patrick AFB, FL	HC-130N/P
76th RQS 'HV'	Vandenberg AFB, CA	UH-1N

USAF unit news

Air Force Special Operations Command (AFSOC) has redesignated and changed

The 57th FWW at Nellis maintains a few 'aggressor' F-16Cs for cadre training and for 'red force' work during Red Flag exercises.

the status of their two overseas-based units. At Kadena AB, Okinawa, the 33rd SOW changed to the 353rd SOG, while the 39th SOW at RAF Alconbury, UK, has become the 352nd SOG. The latter redesignation occurred on 1 December 1992. The 1st SOW at Hurlburt Field, Florida, has remained unchanged. The reduction from wing to group status has been brought about as a result of the 'one base/one wing' concept (below). The major unit at Kadena AB is the 18th Wing, which controls the base on behalf of PACAF. RAF Alconbury should have been administered by the 10th Support Wing, although the 10th Tactical Fighter Wing was still extant in July 1992. The latter facility was due to have been operated by the 628th SW towards the end of 1992.

The 21st SOS and 67th SOS moved from Woodbridge to Alconbury on 20 May 1992, followed by the 7th SOS from Rhein Main AB, Germany, during the late summer. The first MC-130H for the 7th SOS was delivered to Alconbury on 10 September, with a further two examples received by the end of December 1992. The MC-130Es stationed at Rhein Main AB began to depart for the USA during the autumn, with the final pair leaving on 16 December.

The 1st SOW added the MC-130H 'Combat Talon II'-equipped 15th SOS during October 1992, as the 8th SOS will retain the MC-130E 'Combat Talon I' version for the time being. The 1st SOS at Kadena AB was expected to receive their complement of MC-130Hs during the first half of 1993, enabling the MC-130Es to relocate to Hurlburt Field.

During 1992 AFSOC MH-53Js began to be repainted in a mid-grey colour scheme instead of the low-visibility 'European One' green and slate camouflage, with the MC-130s expected to receive a similar paint scheme in due course. The command became responsible for Hurlburt Field during October 1992, when the facility was transferred from Air Mobility Command.

Air Combat Command took one major step on 1 January towards the Northrop B-2A 'Stealth Bomber' becoming operational when the 509th BW was reactivated at Whiteman AFB, Missouri. The 509th Operations Group was activated on the same day, along with the 393rd and 715th Bombardment Squadrons. The two squadrons were the same units that had been assigned to the wing when it was stationed at Pease AFB, New Hampshire, with the FB-111A. The activation of the flying units at Whiteman will enable operational plans to be laid and the infrastructure of the base to be prepared for the first aircraft to be delivered at the end of 1993.

The trend towards relocating as many units as possible to the host command at each facility is being extended to include Operational Support Activity (OSA) airlift squadrons and detachments. Three squadrons and 11 detachments operating the C-12F and C-21A were assigned to the 375th Airlift Wing at the end of 1992, with headquarters at Scott AFB, Illinois, under Air Mobility Command. The latter wing will retain the 11th AAS operating the C-9A for stateside aeromedical evacuation duties, as well as the 375th FTS to train USAF Huron and Learjet aircrew. In addition, the wing will probably retain the 458th ALS. The remainder will join their

host wings, including the 89th Wg at Andrews AFB, Maryland, and 63rd AW at Norton AFB, California (to relocate to nearby March AFB, joining the 22nd ARW), which will assume control of OSA aircraft under AMC.

ACC units destined to receive OSA units will include the 1st FW at Langley AFB, Virginia, 2nd BW at Barksdale AFB, Louisiana, and 55th RW at Offutt AFB, Nebraska. A detachment of C-12Fs at Nellis AFB, Nevada, was established during the late 1980s with four aircraft obtained from Langley AFB. The aircraft concerned were allocated civil registrations and re-painted with a corporate cheat line, lacking the star and bar. These C-12s were frequently noted at air shows which had an F-117A on display, giving rise to speculation that these were in support of the 'Stealth Fighter'. It was by no means a co-incidence that C-12F operations at Nellis AFB ceased around the same time as the F-117s were moved to Holloman AFB, and the Hurons emerged back at Langley AFB in military guise. An 'FF'-coded C-12F from the 1st FW at Langley was seen visiting Hickam AFB, Hawaii, during February 1993.

Air Force Materiel Command will likely become responsible for those C-12F units at Eglin AFB, Florida, McClellan AFB, California, and Wright-Patterson AFB, Ohio. Air Training Command may assume the unit at Randolph AFB, Texas, while the Air University will probably gain the detachment at Maxwell AFB, Alabama. The remaining unit is located at Peterson AFB, Colorado, which is administered by Air Force Space Command which has no aircraft directly assigned at present.

The Air Force is gradually implementing its policy of 'one wing/one base' whereby a single operational wing will manage and administer all operations at each major facility. The concept is being introduced to streamline the chain of command as it will reduce the hierarchy and enable responsibility to be transferred to the lowest level available. Some restructuring has already taken place, including the amalgamation of squadrons from various units into a single wing, while other smaller wings have been reduced to group status. At Altus AFB, Oklahoma, for example, the 340th ARW and 443rd AW were inactivated and replaced by the 97th AMW encompassing both the air refuelling and airlift roles. Amalgamation of re-

sources in the latter example is only possible where the units involved are assigned to the same command. Where units are assigned to wings from several commands, the host wing will administer the base and its own squadrons, while the remaining units will either be transferred or be responsible to a group. A good example is the Air Force Special Operations Command units at Kadena and Alconbury mentioned at the beginning of this feature.

There are still a number of facilities which have more than one operational wing in residence, including Dyess AFB, Texas, with the 96th Wg of ACC as the major unit and 463rd AW of AMC as tenant; Eglin AFB, Florida, whose 46th TW of AMC is the host wing with the 33rd FW of ACC as tenant; and Pope AFB, North Carolina, with the 23rd Wing of ACC and the 317th AW as tenant. The two C-130 squadrons of the 317th AW are to relocate to Little Rock AFB, Arkansas, in due course, although the other future of the unit assignments at Dyess and Eglin have yet to be determined. Several former SAC facilities have both a flying wing and a missile wing assigned, including Ellsworth AFB (ACC), Grand Forks AFB (ACC), Malmstrom AFB (AMC), Minot AFB (ACC) and Whiteman AFB (ACC). This situation also remains unresolved at present. Air National Guard and Air Force Reserve units at front-line facilities are not affected by the rationalisation.

Lockheed L-100-20 Hercules HTTB crash

A crash destroyed Lockheed's L-100-20 Hercules HTTB (High Technology Test Bed) at the Marietta, Georgia, factory on 3 February 1992, killing seven including engineering test pilot George D. Mitchell. The solid-black L-100-20 was serving as a 'flying laboratory' for STOL technologies, improved flight controls and cockpit displays, and precision navigation. Originally built for the Kuwaiti air force, it had been in the hands of a civil operator before returning to Lockheed for extensive modifications, which were completed in June 1984 and included extensions forward from its horizontal and vertical stabilisers.

The loss of Lockheed's L-100-20 HTTB dealt the company a blow in its programme to develop a second-generation Hercules.

The L-100-20 had been upgraded in April 1989 with 5,250-shp (3916-kW) Allison T56-A-501-M71K series IV engines, a one-of-a-kind powerplant. The HTTB was capable of carrying a Mobile Data Center Van, equipped with data processing equipment. When the HTTB landed at a new test site, the van could be driven off and quickly set up to analyse data relayed by telemetry from the test aircraft. On 18-19 May 1989, the HTTB set four US and world time-to-climb and payload/climb records.

The crash occurred after the L-100-20 became airborne during what were to have been high-speed taxi tests evaluating rudder control with a simulated failure of the left outboard engine. "The mystery is how it got airborne," says Lockheed's Julius Alexander. It was the fourth fatal crash of an American Hercules in less than a year. Loss of the HTTB is certain to be a blow to Lockheed, which has kept the Hercules in continuous production since 1954, longer than any other aircraft.

F-22 development stretched

Pentagon officials on 25 January 1992 approved a US Air Force plan to extend development of the F-22 fighter by nearly two years and delay full-scale production

by 18 months. The changes, caused by a $750 million funding shortfall in 1993, will result in nine, instead of 11, F-22 engineering and development airframes and in production being increased from eight to 10 years. First flight of the fighter will be delayed from July 1995 to June 1996. The new 'mix' will include seven F-22A single-seat and two F-22B two-seat aircraft.

NATO AWACS upgrades

NATO's 18 Boeing E-3A Sentry AWACS aircraft are to be upgraded in a $294.6 million programme which will add colour displays, Have Quick UHF radio, and the Link 16 version of the JTIDS. The NATO 'Mod Block 1' aircraft will be retrofitted through 1997 by Deutsche Aerospace.

JPATS first flights

The first Beech-manufactured production prototype Beech/Pilatus PC-9 Mk 2 trainer made its maiden flight at Wichita on 23 December 1992. The first Rockwell/Deutsche Aerospace Fan Ranger trainer made its first flight at the German builder's Manching facility on 15 January 1993. Both are among the seven primary trainers being put forward in the US Air Force/Navy Joint Primary Aircraft Trainer System programme.

Back to Iraq

After months of increasing provocation from Iraq, the coalition finally lost patience with Baghdad.

In December 1992 and January 1993, coinciding with the last days of the Bush administration in Washington, Iraq mounted a series of challenges to United Nations sanctions regarding 'No-Fly Zones' above the 36th Parallel and below the 32nd. The challenges included moving SA-2, SA-3, and SA-6 SAM sites into, or close to, the 'No-Fly Zones' patrolled by coalition warplanes. In addition, Iraqi fighters penetrated the banned zones.

On 27 December 1992, Iraqi fighters challenged F-15E Eagles of the 335th Fighter Squadron, 4th Fighter Wing in the southern part of the country. Soon afterward, two MiG-25 'Foxbat-E' fighters crossed the 32nd Parallel into the southern 'No-Fly Zones' and were engaged, under direction from Boeing E-3C Sentry AWACS, by F-16C/D Block 42 Fighting Falcons of the 33rd Fighter Squadron 'Falcons', part of the 363rd Fighter Wing deployed to the region as part of the 4440th Composite Wing. US officials said that the MiG-25s "turned to confront" the F-16s 20 miles (32 km) inside the zone and that the rules of engagement authorised the F-16C pilots to react. After the MiGs fired at least one missile at the American aircraft, Lieutenant

Colonel Gary North, 33rd FS commander, flying an F-16D (90-0778), callsign BANSHEE 41, with an empty back seat, used an AIM-120A AMRAAM to shoot down one MiG-25, apparently beyond visual range. North's was a relatively new F-16, which had just 456 flying hours on its airframe as of the previous month. This was the first aerial victory for an American F-16 and the first for the AMRAAM. US forces allowed an Iraqi SAR helicopter to operate in the area after the shootdown. That day, USS *Kitty Hawk* (CV-63) was diverted from Operation Restore Hope and sent to the Persian Gulf region.

On 2 January, a MiG-25 'Foxbat-E' attempted to intercept a US Air Force U-2 and was chased off by F-15Cs. On 13 January, beginning at 9:15 p.m. Baghdad time, 100 coalition warplanes from four bases and from *Kitty Hawk* (which provided 35 of the aircraft) attacked targets in south-east Iraq. Primary targets were four air defence command and control centres and two concentrations of SA-3 SAMs, all located between the southern cities of Kut and Basra. The strike had been decided upon on 11 January, but was scrubbed by Joint Chiefs Chairman General Colin Powell on 12 January because of inclement weather. The strike force included six F-117As (49th FW), four F-16Cs (33rd FS/363rd FW), 10 F-15Es (335th FS/4th FW), eight A-6E Intruders (VA-52), six F/A-18 Hornets (VFA-27/97), and four British Tornado GR.Mk 1s. Cover was provided by 10 F-15C Eagles (1st FW), eight F-14A Tomcats (VF-51/114), two F/A-18A Hornets (VFA-27/97), and six French Mirage 2000s. Elec-

Seen immediately prior to deployment to Dhahran, this is the F-16D which shot down the MiG-25 on 27 December 1992. The kill was the first for a US F-16 and the first for AMRAAM.

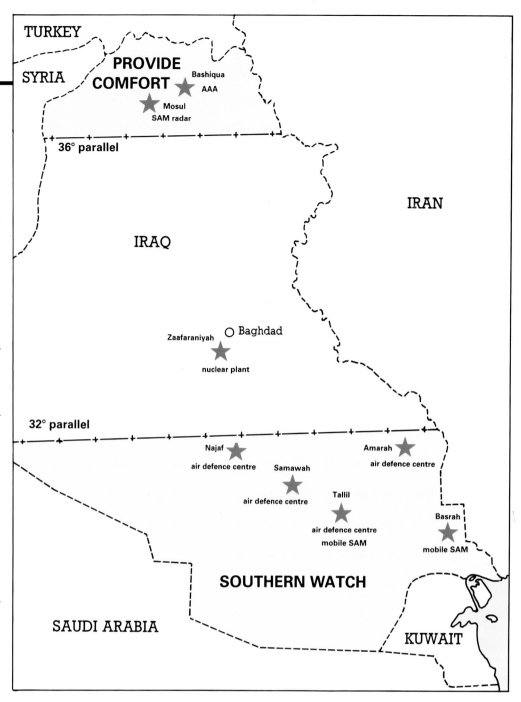

Left: A HARM-equipped F/A-18C from VFA-97 launches from Kitty Hawk on a Southern Watch mission. Shown inset is a Hornet being prepared for the raid with Mk 82s.

Right: Map of Iraq, showing the 'No-Fly Zones' and targets attacked.

tronic warfare, AWACS, reconnaissance, and SAR aircraft took part.

The six targets reportedly involved 17 separate aim points, some of which were bombed more than once with cluster bomb units, 1,000-lb (454-kg) and 2,000-lb (907-kg) LGBs, and gravity bombs. F-117As were first into the area, followed by F-15Es, both encountering continued bad weather. Cloud cover reportedly caused the F-117As to hit only two of six aim points. Two lost laser lock-on, one pilot declined to drop because he could not see his target, and one F-117A hit the wrong target. F-15Es hit eight of 10 aim points. US Navy A-6Es and F/A-18s followed in better weather and hit seven of 14 aim points. Most bombs were dropped from above 10,000 ft (3096 m) to evade AAA. Footage released the following day showed a number of bombs falling wide of their targets.

Ignoring all evidence of who was shooting down whom, on 16 January Iraq threatened to down coalition aircraft if tensions continued. The following day, an F-16C Block 30 Fighting Falcon (86-0262) from the 23rd Fighter Squadron 'Hawks', 52nd Fighter Wing, deployed with the 7440th Composite Wing, Incirlik, Turkey, downed a MiG-29 (not a MiG-23 as widely reported) over the northern 'No-Fly Zone', and American and British aircraft struck missile sites. Four US warships fired 45 BGM-109 Tomahawk cruise missiles at the Zaafaraniyah nuclear fabrication facility 8 miles (13 km) south-west of Baghdad. The Pentagon claimed that one failed upon launch and 37 struck their targets. Initial bomb damage assessments showed seven buildings in the complex that were targeted were all hit. One Tomahawk, apparently hit by anti-aircraft fire, crashed into the Al Rashid Hotel in Baghdad, killing two.

The following day, 18 January, in the first daylight raids on Iraq, US and British strike aircraft, covered by French fighters, bombed Iraqi command and control facilities and SAM sites in the southern zone which had survived earlier strikes. Originally scheduled to involve 75 aircraft, the number was reduced to 69 when it was discovered that some SAMs which were to be attacked had been moved. One of the first targets was the Tallil air defence centre, hit during the nocturnal hours. Lieutenant Colonel North led four 33rd FS F-16Cs which participated in the strikes with AGM-65 Maverick missiles, cluster bombs and conventional bombs. F-15E Eagles of the 335th FS made day strikes against Tallil, Samawah and Najaf. Other US strikes were mounted in the northern zone and Iraq reported 21 killed.

Also on 18 January, an F-15C Eagle encountered a MiG-25 which, the US said, "took an attack posture." The F-15C launched an AMRAAM from 27 miles (43 km) away, then launched an AIM-9M Sidewinder from closer range. Though the MiG was initially reported as

F-15C Eagles from the 33rd Fighter Wing deployed to Dhahran in late 1992, just in time to cover the raids. 85-0101 still wears a star for a MiG-25 kill from Desert Storm.

a kill, it was later determined that the 'Foxbat-E' had landed safely.

On 19 January, an F-4G 'Advanced Wild Weasel' fired an AGM-88A HARM missile at a SAM radar installation after the radar locked on to the aircraft 14 miles (23 km) east of Mosul. An hour later, an F-16C on a reconnaissance mission was fired on by AAA but not hit. Two hours later, two F-16Cs were fired on by AAA about 12 miles (19 km) north of Mosul and dropped cluster bombs on the site.

On 21 January, 29 hours after Iraq declared a ceasefire as a goodwill gesture to President Clinton's inauguration, an F-4G and an F-16C attacked an Iraqi radar 10 miles (16 km) south of Mosul with a HARM and cluster bombs. Two more HARMS were fired at Iraqi radars by F-4Gs on 22 January. On 23 January, an A-6E In-

truder apparently from VA-52 'Knight Riders' aboard *Kitty Hawk*, escorted by two F/A-18 Hornets, responded to flashes in the sky by dropping a laser-guided 1,000-lb (454-kg) bomb on the apparent source of gunfire; US sources later acknowledged that Iraqi radar was not tracking the A-6E and that the flashes may not have been gunfire.

On board USS *Kitty Hawk* (CV-63), CVW-15

VF-51	'Screaming Eagles'	F-14A
VF-111	'Sundowners'	F-14A
VFA-27	'Chargers'	F/A-18A
VFA-97	'Warhawks'	F/A-18A
VA-52	'Knight Riders'	A-6E
VAQ-134	'Garudas'	EA-6B
VS-37	'Sawbucks'	S-3B
VAW-114	'Hormel Hawgs'	E-2C
VRC-50	'Foo Dogs'	C-2A
HS-4	'Black Knights'	SH-60F

SOMALIA: Relief and Hope

Ravaged by famine and attendant disease, and left without law by a civil war and feuding gangs, Somalia was in a desperate situation. A multi-national air effort met with only limited success until military intervention restored order.

Luftwaffe Transall C.160Ds have been flying relief aid into Somalia since August 1992, this aircraft being loaded with food at the main airlift centre at Mombasa, Kenya.

Vital to the Restore Hope landing operation were the KC-130Rs of VMGR-352, which not only ferried in equipment and personnel, but provided refuelling for other aircraft.

Operation Restore Hope, the humanitarian 'invasion' of Somalia by US Marines in December 1992, was but the middle chapter in a longer story of famine, its defeat and the United Nations' continuing effort to restore stability to a lawless African country in which, until recently, the only guaranteed meal-ticket was a gun. Aid agencies had launched their food supply air lift in Somalia the previous August, helped in no small measure by the Americans' Operation Provide Relief but, with 80 per cent of aid looted by bandits, prospects for the defeat of famine in southern Somalia continued to be bleak. Now, however, strong policing action by the UN has, if not defeated then at least driven to earth, the warlords who terrorised Somalia, fought each other and even extorted money from the organisations attempting to feed their countrymen.

What has now become a multi-nation security and air lift operation began with the approval by America's then-President George Bush of Operation Provide Relief. Intended as passive assistance to the relief agencies already working in Somalia, Provide Relief gathered momentum when a command team arrived by StarLifter at Moi International Airport, Mombasa, Kenya, on 19 August to establish a base inside a US Navy warehouse at the airport. This would be the hub from which food shipped into Mombasa harbour could be carried to refugee camps just inside the Kenyan border and to airheads within Somalia itself.

Into Somalia

Four StarLifters from the 437th and 438th AW and eight C-130E Hercules of the 314th AW were stationed at Mombasa, initially for flights to Wajir, a refugee camp in Kenya, the first on 21 August. After a week of operations, on 28 August they began operating into Somalia, initially to Belet Uen. At the same time, 437th AW StarLifters began direct flights into Mombasa, bringing food from the USA.

Operations by Mombasa-based StarLifters ended on 1 September and the aircraft were withdrawn from theatre two days later, on replacement by more Hercules from the Reserve and National Guard. Hercules were by then operating into other air bases and strips, although the

Belet Uen leg was temporarily suspended on 18 September when a 314th crew was threatened during cargo unloading and their aircraft (63-7888) struck by a bullet.

By October, the Hercules force at Mombasa had stabilised at 14 C-130Es. On 25 October, 63-7832 of the 327th was also hit in a wing fuel tank by small-arms fire at Iscia Baidoa. Provide Relief had delivered 78,000 tonnes of food in 792 sorties by all aircraft types up to 1 November.

Because of the uncertain security situation in Somalia, Hercules were unloaded with all engines running and flew only during the day. Unbroken contact was maintained with Joint Task Force (JTF) HQ at Mombasa through a Hercules assigned to radio relay, orbiting for eight hours. A scheduled rotation of crews and aircraft at Mombasa took place on 6 December when the 772nd ALS/463rd AW arrived with C-130H models, the 314th bowing out after having contributed 17,000 tonnes and 1,600 sorties to the airlift.

The Mogadishu operation became two-pronged, greatly enlarged and more complex when military forces entered Somalia early in

Above: Some idea of the scale of the Somali problem can be gained from the size of Mandera refugee camp, just inside Kenya.

Right: View from the observation 'bubble' as an RAF Hercules approaches the strip at Mandera.

Left: The vital foodstuffs and medicines get through to the refugees, courtesy of a multi-national transport effort.

December as Operation Restore Hope. Provide Relief continued, but aircraft were also tasked for support of Restore Hope in the way of taking fuel and supplies to US Army and Marine Corps detachments 'up country'. As the major element of US forces in-theatre, the Marines assumed control of the JTF at Mombasa Airport and extra aircraft were drafted in, including two RAF Hercules. The USAF C-130Hs, RAF aircraft and three German Transall C.160Ds already at Mombasa operate a joint tasking plan, all except the Germans taking part in both Restore Hope and Provide Relief. For reasons of propriety, each sortie is dedicated to one or other operation.

The 772nd ALS deployed eight C-130Es, augmented by four shark-mouthed C-130Es of the 2nd ALS, and single C-130Hs from 144th AS/ Alaska ANG and Ohio ANG. The Alaska aircraft was replaced in January by a brand-new C-130H2 from 165th ALS/Kentucky ANG. As delivery of aid to its intended recipients became more certain, the 772nd was able to withdraw

four Hercules on 28 January. A squadron change-over effective from 12 February brought the 773rd ALS to Mogadishu, although the four remaining aircraft from parent 463rd AW were retained.

More Hercules had been crammed into Mombasa airport when KC-130Rs of the USMC arrived to support Restore Hope. VMGR-352 began operations from Aden, Yemen, on 15 December with three aircraft, at which time a further four were at Rota. One of the Aden-based machines transferred to Mombasa in the early hours of 19 December, to be joined by the four from Rota the following day. After a re-adjustment and transfer of an eighth Hercules from the squadron's pool of 14 at El Toro, a detachment of five was retained at Aden until the end of the year, when an attempted terrorist attack on the Americans' hotel (the perpetrator blew himself up) underlined the advantages of operating from Mombasa.

In the initial phase of the USMC move into Somalia, Hercules had undertaken aerial tanking of A-6 Intruders and CH-53E helicopters, interspersed with leaflet dropping and acting as airborne radio relay stations between units ashore and the command ship, USS *Tripoli*. With helicopters ashore in considerable numbers, VMGR-352 began rapid ground refuelling operations, involving landing at a pre-deter-

mined place and time to dispense fuel. Helicopters kept engines running, while the Hercules had one T56 operating to provide power and expedite departure, if necessary. For crews used to taking off heavy and landing light after an aerial off-load, ferrying of fuel was a new experience as Hercules lumbered in to strange and unkempt airfields at weights up to 168,000 lb (76205 kg).

Once the situation in Somalia settled down, VMGR-352 was able to dispatch two aircraft back to El Toro on 2 January and another a fortnight later. By mid-February it was preparing to leave, its job virtually complete as road convoys were then able to deliver bulk fuel into the Somali hinterland. Operations from Mombasa by UK, US and German aircraft are co-ordinated by the American air commander and his staff. With a scaling down of operations, the task of managing the JTF reverted to the USAF's Air Mobility Command on 15 February.

RAF and Luftwaffe

Southern Air Transport – the well-known 'secret' US government airline – provided five civilian Hercules for the Mombasa-Somalia airlift, its aircraft carrying the logo UN WFP to identify their work for the World Food Programme. It was on WFP business that the German Luftwaffe arrived at Mombasa on 22 August with three Transall C.160Ds of Lufttransportgeschwader 61. After two months, LTG 63 took over, then LTG 62, the cycle repeating itself during early 1993.

Transalls operate outside the close RAF-USAF tasking, despite being co-located and, from 23 December, officially dedicated to Pro-

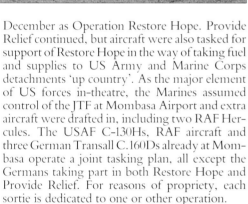

Covering the Marine landings on 9 December, and subsequent security operations, were AH-1W Cobras and UH-1Ns. They were provided by HMLA-369 'Gunfighters', shore-based at Camp Pendleton as part of the 3rd MAW.

Marine Corps Sikorsky CH-53s provide useful heavylift capability, and have supported the move by troops deep into the country to secure villages and landing strips.

vide Relief. They fly to the same refugee camps, but also undertake some low-level air-dropping, in the course of which one C.160D suffered slight damage in an argument with a tree early in February. This had little effect on the detachment's duties, which require it to fly seven missions per four days. With justifiable pride, the Germans note that the Somalian operation is the 118th humanitarian venture in which LTG 61 has been involved since 1970. Belgium, another nation with a record of recent good works in Africa, has a pair of C-130H Hercules of 20 Escadrille/Smaldeel operating from Mombasa, using (like Southern Air Transport) the civil terminal.

The UK's contribution to Restore Hope was a pair of Hercules C.Mk 1s detached from the Lyneham Transport Wing as Operation Vigour. Personnel were drawn from Nos 24, 30, 47 and 70 Squadrons, the UK Mobile Air Movements Squadron, Joint Air Transport Establishment, Tactical Communications Wing (from Brize Norton) and the RAF Police, one member of the last-mentioned flying on each sortie. Following the announcement on 4 December of UK support for the American initiative, the two aircraft and 90 personnel left Lyneham at 0600 on 9 December and arrived at Mombasa two days later.

The four deployed RAF crews are regularly changed every four weeks on a staggered basis, so that the new personnel have opportunity to learn the ropes from their companions. The USAF, by contrast, changes all its squadron personnel at the same time, giving the newcomers a steep learning curve during their first few days. Similarly thrown in at the deep end were the Kenyan air traffic controllers. The vast influx of international aircraft in mid-December came as a severe shock to the normal leisurely pace of issuing flight clearances, so any aircraft which could not make its slot was forced to abandon the mission. Gradually, however, flexibility was introduced to the system.

Operations began on 12 December when XV195 lifted 22,500 lb (10205 kg) of food to Bardera and XV300 took off soon afterwards to deliver a 30,000-lb (13605-kg) load to Waajid. The following day, XV300 became the first RAF aircraft into newly-secured Mogadishu airport, where it collected vehicles and grain for transport to Baledogle. Because some trips involve intermediate landings, the mission tally is measured in legs, rather than sorties. Therefore, by 1 January,

the RAF detachment had flown 92 legs in 150 hours for Provide Relief and 59 legs in 104.25 hours for Restore Hope. Thereafter, the balance tipped heavily in favour of famine relief. In total, the Mombasa-based JTF aircraft have been delivering 480,000 meals per day.

Food is normally carried in 100-lb (45-kg) bags on three or four pallets, four representing the maximum load of 30,000-32,000 lb (13605-14515 kg). Starting at dawn, the two duty crews for each day usually fly two missions each, then hand the aircraft over to engineers for maintenance which carries on into the night, if necessary.

Restore Hope logistics resupply is a military matter, but Provide Relief needs are defined by DART (Disaster Aid Relief Team), the US government-funded civilian agency. DART processes food requirements issued by the many aid agencies operating Somali refugee camps, including the UN, Red Cross, HRO, IMC, CARE, Save the Children, Concern and others. At their daily meeting, detachment commanders from the US, UK, Germany, Canada, Belgium and Southern Air Transport 'bid' for the next day's tasks. The USAF plan then has to be sent by satellite to Scott AFB (AMC HQ) for daily approval, a somewhat unwieldy procedure.

Somali airfields

The landing strips used by aid flights vary greatly. Mogadishu, constructed in the early 1970s by the Soviet Union during a period of good relations with Somalia, offers an international-size runway, but others are short, gravel strips which normally regard Cessna and Piper twins as big movements. Principal locations in southern and central Somalia are: Baledogle, 6,000 ft; Bardera, 3,500 ft; Belet Uen, 5,700 ft; Gialalassi, 5,000 ft; Iscia Baidoa, 10,007 ft (of which 5,000 ft is usable); Kisimayu, 11,000 ft; Mogadishu, 10,335 ft; Oddur strip, 4,000 ft; Waajid strip, 3,500 ft.

In the north, where food is more readily available, aircraft operating from Aden and the French protectorate of Djibouti are able to use Berbera, Bosaso, Dusa-Marreb, Galcao, Garoe and Obbia. Refugee camps inside Kenya are Garissa, Mandera strip (3,200 ft/975 m) and Wajir (9,193 ft/2802 m). Mogadishu is able to accept aircraft up to C-5 size and Baledogle can accommodate a C-141. The abbreviated strip at Iscia Baidoa was tried by a C-141, but proved to be a little short.

Aircraft management is necessary on the smallest strips in view of the dust cloud thrown up by each movement. On still days, this can last for 30 minutes, so spacing of arrivals and departures is

practised. Should a strip suddenly become unusable, an inbound aircraft will be rerouted to another camp so as not to waste the load. Cargoes could be larger, were it not for the fact that absence of fuel at the destination makes it necessary for the Hercules to carry enough for the return to Mombasa, plus normal peacetime reserves.

Restore Hope: the military option

Few, indeed, are the operations which begin with farce and go on to apparent success. One such has been Restore Hope. When the US Marine Corps made their night beach landing at Mogadishu in the glare of TV lights and to the blinking of camera flash-guns, detractors revelled in the incongruity of the situation. Were some of the world's toughest fighting men *really* necessary to liberate a stretch of sand over-populated by the media, and wasn't Uncle Sam, yet again, going over the top?

What was not made clear at the time was that the media representatives were only there to film the landing because they had paid hefty bribes to local gangsters who otherwise threatened to take their equipment, and even their lives. Like the aid agencies before them, they had been forced into the compromising position of having to pay protection money which, because it could not be put on the expense account as such, was disguised as 'local technical assistance'. Thus did the warlords' heavily-gunned trucks come to be known as 'technicals'. One American TV team was charged a $17,000 moving fee to rent a house to cover the landings, and even a month afterwards a BBC team was forced to flee Somalia after refusing to pay thugs' demands for over $30,000.

Following the conception of Restore Hope, a USMC amphibious task unit of 1,800 men arrived off the Somalian coast on 3 December as the vanguard of a force planned to number 28,150 from the 1st Marine Expeditionary Force at Camp Pendleton, CA, and the army's 10th Mountain Division (Light Infantry) from Fort

With support vessels lying offshore, US Navy helicopters have played a part in the relief effort, and are regular visitors to Mogadishu. Shown is a Kaman SH-2F of HSL-33.

USAF C-130s are prominent on the aid distribution network. This shark-mouthed C-130E is from the 2nd Airlift Squadron, 23rd Wing, operating from Mombasa.

Drum, NY. The same day, the UN Security Council passed a resolution (No. 794) authorising members to "establish a secure environment for humanitarian relief operations in Somalia." However, US troops were not the first ashore, as a contingent of 500 Pakistanis had taken control of the airport at Mogadishu three months earlier, but was insufficiently strong to venture beyond its confines.

Leading the Marine force was the carrier USS *Tripoli*, assisted by the dock landing ship USS *Rushmore* and amphibious assault ship USS *Juneau*. *Tripoli* carried the same aircraft complement as the assault ship it had just replaced: USS *Tarawa* had been on station since mid-September, carrying five AV-8Bs of VMA-211, four AH-1Ws and three UH-1Ns of HMLA-367, four CH-53Es of HMH-466 and 11 CH-46Es of parenting unit HMM-161. Aboard *Tripoli*, HMM-164 was the controlling unit, it being USMC practice to title the group after its CH-46 squadron. UH/AH-1s on *Tripoli* came from HMLA-369. Slightly farther back, available if required, was the USS *Ranger* with Carrier Air Wing 2 (CVW-2) embarked. Making its final voyage before going into reserve, *Ranger* had an atypical mixture of aircraft, notable for the omission of any Hornet squadrons. Instead, it carried VF-1 and VF-2 with F-14A Tomcats equipped to carry TARPS reconnaissance pods; VA-145 and VA-155 operating A-6E Intruders; VAW-116 with E-2C Hawkeyes; VAQ-131, the electronic warfare unit of EA-6B Prowlers; HS-14 with SH-3H Sea Kings; and VS-38 flying S-3B Vikings.

Opening the airheads

First Marine landings took place before dawn on 9 December, although aircraft from *Ranger* had made low-level flights over Mogadishu, Iscia Baidoa and other towns the previous day in a show of strength. With Mogadishu and (a few days later) Baledogle airfields secure, airlifting began of 16,000 Marines and 10,000 infantrymen direct from the US. Baledogle, with 6,000 ft (1830 m) available, was chosen for C-141s after the intended secondary at Kisimayu was considered insecure until more troops were available. Units involved included the 60th AW (C-5 Galaxy and C-141 StarLifter), 62nd AW (C-141), 63rd AW (C-141), 433rd AW/AFRes (C-5), 436th AW (C-5), 437th AW (C-141), 438th AW (C-141), 439th AW/AFRes (C-5) and 907th AG/AFRes (C-141B). En-route refuelling was necessary to support the flights, and so detachments of tankers were established at Lajes, Moron (Spain), Souda (Crete), and Cairo, provided by the 22nd ARW (KC-10), 100th ARW (KC-135R), 108th ARG/New Jersey ANG (KC-135E), 141st ARW/Washington ANG (KC-135E), 151st ARW/Utah ANG (KC-135E), 157th ARG/New Hampshire ANG (KC-135E), 172nd ARG/Kansas ANG (KC-135E), 434th AW/AFRes (KC-135E), 452nd ARW/AFRes (KC-135E and KC-10A) and 940th ARG/AFRes (KC-135E).

With no fuel available in Somalia, and Mogadishu only able to accommodate two C-5s or one C-5 and two C-141s on the ground at any one time, AMC adopted a rigid inbound and outbound route plan. West Coast-based C-141s refuelled over the north-east USA and again over Spain before landing at a staging post (usually Cairo) for a crew change and the shorter flight to

Italian forces support the Marine Corps on armed patrols in Somalia, and several helicopters are in-country for this task. Two Agusta A 129 Mangusta attack helicopters (above) are deployed from the army, and two armed Agusta-Sikorsky HH-3Fs (right), from the air force.

Mogadishu (about 11 aircraft per day; no night flights) or Mombasa. At both these centres, palletised freight – now in smaller quantities – is transferred to Hercules for distribution. On leaving Mogadishu with minimal fuel, jet transports fly to Addis Ababa (Ethiopia) or Djibouti to replenish tanks, a third location at Aden having closed down in late December after Muslim fundamentalist demonstrations. Saudi Arabia is also used as a staging post; Jeddah was used until early January when Taif took over. By the end of December, AMC had flown 395 strategic missions, comprising 198 by C-141, 98 by C-5 and 76 by KC-10, carrying 13,000 passengers and 12,600 tonnes of cargo, during which 536 aerial refuellings were made. With most of the US troops installed, AMC began ferrying contingents from some of the 42 nations which would take over policing of Somalia after the American departure. (The Botswana Defence Force contingent, for example, was collected from Ascension Island, the RAF staging post in mid-Atlantic.)

While this influx of aircraft severely strained Kenyan air traffic controllers, their Somalian compatriots had no such problems; there was no Somalian air traffic control. A team of American controllers landed at Mogadishu on 7 December to organise local airspace, but over most of Somalia pilots resorted to a common frequency (126.9 mHz; after 28 December, 127.45 mHz) to advise others of their position and intentions. Some measure of airspace administration was afforded by the duty E-2C Hawkeye, providing an advisory service for aircraft visiting Mogadishu. At 60 nm (69 miles; 110 km) from destination, aircraft were transferred to approach control, which used an air-transportable radar to obtain positive identification. Within a week a portable ILS had been installed.

Elsewhere, the main routes of transport aircraft coming from the USA, Europe, Kenya (Mombasa and Nairobi) and Djibouti were crossed by light civil aircraft operating for the aid agencies. Mercifully, not one collision occurred. As normality returned, the airfields at Baledogle, Bardera, Iscia Baidoa, Kisimayu, Gialalassi and Oddur had all gained VHF/UHF control by late December, four of them also with TACAN. Efforts are now being made to rebuild the air traffic control infrastructure with assistance from the Federal Aviation Agency.

A Belgian C-130H touches down at Mombasa after a relief flight. The Hercules fleet is used for distributing aid from the main centres at Mombasa and Mogadishu to outlying strips.

Autopsy: The Somali Air Force

Government in Somalia collapsed in January 1991 when the dictator Siad Barre was forced into exile, there to become one of the three major warlords of rival gangs fighting for control of an increasingly desolate and demoralised nation. No less affected by the disintegration of law and order was the Somali Aeronautical Corps (Dayuuradaha Xoogga Dalka Somaliyeed), the aircraft of which were grounded and left to their fate. By far the largest concentration is at Mogadishu, where 28

Right: The single MiG-15UTI enjoys the relative comfort of a hangar.

military aircraft and four civilian are now beyond all hope of economic repair. Looters – more likely local bandits than souvenir-hunting troops – have removed instrumentation and fittings, the transports, most noticeably, being devoid of all internal furnishings and panelling. When the airport was being prepared for Restore Hope traffic, the Somali airframes were dragged

to a corner of the airfield, resulting in further damage.

Those aircraft types present at Mogadishu comprise the following:
MiG-21: Eight examples, comprising two MiG-21UM trainers in greyish-blue overall finish and six MiG-21MFs with brown/

green upper surface camouflage and light blue beneath. First deliveries were made to Somalia in July 1974; trainers appear to be ex-Soviet air force, but single-seat aircraft were specifically built for export, with some labelling in English.
Shenyang F-6: Three F-6Cs and one FT-6 trainer, all with yellow/brown/green upper surfaces and light blue below. Late production aircraft from early 1980s deliveries.
MiG-15UTI: One aircraft, green/brown colours, plus light blue undersides; supplied with MiG-17s.

Left: One of the Shenyang F-6Cs lies in front of an AB 212 and the sole An-24V, the latter featuring a leopard badge on the nose.

Below: Two G222s were delivered to Somalia, this one remaining.

USMC AH-1Ws escorted the first wave of Marines ashore and were again in prominence when troops moved farther inland. Baledogle airfield was secured with the assistance of 12 Cobras on 13 December. The previous day two Cobras were fired upon while flying along the road to Baledogle and made short work of the three 'technicals' which had challenged them. Iscia Baidoa was the next main town to be 'liberated' when US and French troops arrived on 16 December, accompanied by the obligatory Cobras. Local gunmen declined to ask the Cobras for the 'landing fees' which they had extracted from relief aircraft hitherto arriving at the airfield.

Driving inland

It was next the turn of Kisimayu. US Marines and Belgian commandos arrived by sea on 20 December (the first joint amphibious landing since World War II) to secure the town, supported by leaflet-dropping aircraft and USMC helicopters, and with jets from USS *Kitty Hawk* flying low overhead. This replacement carrier, deployed in mid-December, embarked VF-51 and VF-111 with F-14A Tomcats; VFA-27 and VFA-97 with F/A-18C Hornets; VA-52 operating A-6E Intruders and KA-6Ds; VAW-114, the E-2C Hawkeye squadron; HS-4, SH-60F Seahawks and HH-60Hs; VAQ-134 with EA-6B Prowlers; and VS-37 with S-3B Vikings. However, the carrier was not around for long, as the increasing belligerence of Saddam Hussein caused it to be diverted to the Arabian Gulf late in December. Belgians policed Kisimayu airfield, opening it for relief flights into a previously

underserved area of Somalia.

The first food ship for a month entered Mogadishu port on 13 December when the Danish-registered MV *Sea Pearl* arrived with 3,000 tonnes of wheat. However welcome, the supplies were not needed immediately, as 12,000 tonnes (enough to feed one million people for a month) were rotting in a Mogadishu warehouse because road transport was impossible. That was rectified on 20 December when an escorted road convoy left for Baidoa with 300 tonnes of food. Some bandits still attempted to resist the imposition of law and, after aid workers complained of a deterioration in security, USMC Cobras attacked an arms store in Mogadishu on 6 January with TOW anti-tank missiles and machine-guns. This toughening of the peacekeeping operation appeared to have the desired effect and might have helped a meeting of warlords the following day to make a decision to hold a peace conference in Ethiopia during April.

The 10th Mountain Division (Light Infantry) did not bring its dedicated army helicopter units from the USA. Instead, transport helicopters were transferred from the US Army in Europe and placed under control of an HQ team from the 5th Battalion, 158th Aviation Regiment at Giebelstadt, Germany – known in-theatre as Task Force 5/158. The 15 Sikorsky UH-60A Black Hawks of 159th Medical Company from Wiesbaden were ferried to Livorno (Italy) via Nice on 16-17 December and loaded aboard a freighter, together with 16 CH-47D Chinooks of D Company, 502nd Aviation Regiment from Mannheim. A further 15 Black Hawks of 7th and 9th Battalions of 227 Aviation Regiment were flown

from Hanau to Ramstein at about the same time and transported to Somalia in C-5s and C-141s.

Mogadishu airport reached its peak of activity in mid/late December with the arrival of troops direct from the US. It remains a busy base for several nationalities and accepts visiting aircraft of diverse types and origins. Italy, with 2,000 troops in Somalia (Operation Ibis), has a large detachment at Mogadishu and assists the USMC in its armed helicopter patrols of the city. Installation of the Italian force was conducted between 15 December and 9 January, involving 30 flights by Hercules and five by the newly-delivered Boeing 707T/T, as well as four by a chartered Tower Air Boeing 747 which ended on 10 January.

Italian equipment

In its first operational deployment, the army's Agusta A 129 Mangusta helicopter gunship is represented by two from the newly-formed first operating unit, the 49° Gruppo Squadroni at Casarsa, armed with TOW anti-tank missiles. Six Agusta-Bell AB 205As (7.62-mm Minigun or 81-mm grenade-launcher) and four Meridionali-Boeing CH-47C Chinooks from the 1° Regimento at Viterbo provide logistic support. Two Agusta-Sikorsky HH-3F Pelicans of the air force's 15° Stormo, equipped with chaff/flare dispensers, have been used for armed patrols since 12 January, armed with a door-mounted heavy machine-gun. Italian warships are off shore, resulting in a naval detachment of seven Agusta-Bell 212ASs and three Agusta-Sikorsky SH-3H Sea Kings operating from the helicopter carrier *Vittorio Veneto* and its escorts, *San Giorgio*

Above: One of two MiG-21UMs at Mogadishu – these provided training for the six-aircraft MiG-21MF force.

Right: Italian relics – the fuselage of a SIAI-Marchetti SF.260T lies in front of a Piaggio P.166DL3 on the Mogadishu dump.

MiG-17: Three 'Fresco-A' variants dating from mid-1960s. Two coloured as MiG-15UTI, one grey overall with winged leopard badge.

Antonov An-24V: One aircraft with winged leopard badge. Remains from three delivered.

Piaggio P-166DL3: Three aircraft from four originally with civil registrations for defence ministry (one) and transport ministry (three), delivered from 1981. One in chocolate and sand camouflage; two with light blue tops and dark blue undersides.

Agusta-Bell 212: Three, remaining from four delivered in 1981; green/brown/sand camouflage. Two wearing the same serial number (60220).

B-N Islander: Three in chocolate and sand camouflage, plus light blue undersides. Remain from four received from Abu Dhabi air force in 1983.

SIAI-Marchetti SF.260T: One camouflaged military aircraft (green/brown; light grey below), plus one white overall

Above: In among the MiG-21MFs are three BN-2 Islanders, including this badly-damaged example.

with civil registration; delivered 1979-80. Six civil and six military received, the latter marked 'SF 260W' despite being 260Ts.

Alenia G222: One remaining from two delivered in 1980. Grey and green camouflage; light grey below, plus winged leopard badge.

Elsewhere on the airfield are wrecked civilian examples of Partenavia Victor, Piper

Navajo and Piper Aztec. The only aircraft which have survived more or less intact are a hangared Dornier Do 28 (one of the two police aircraft) and what appears to be a Super Cub. Identification of both proved less than easy as they are used to support Marines' tents and are festooned with waterproof sheeting and washing lines. In other parts of Somalia, Hargeisa holds

Above: One of the three MiG-17s at Mogadishu carries the same leopard badge as the Antonov An-24.

Shenyang F-6s and Mil Mi-8s; Kisimayu has HS Hunters (transferred from Abu Dhabi in 1983) and a defected Ethiopian BAC Canberra.

and *San Marco*. Resupply of the Italian garrison at Gialalassi is by 46ª Brigata Aérea Alenia G222.

Among a dozen countries offering troops for Restore Hope, France was well placed to deploy an initial 2,100 via nearby Djibouti, where it has a major air base. The resident Transall C.160F of ETOM 88 was augmented by a C.160NG from ET 64 at Evreux and a C-130H Hercules detached from ET 61 at Orléans. Operation Oryx began on 9 December when these three aircraft began ferrying paratroops and legionnaires to Mogadishu. By 14 December, 466 passengers and 307 tonnes of freight had been delivered to Somalia. Later flights brought 10 Pumas and 12 Gazelles of Aviation Légère de l'Armée de Terre (ALAT – Army Light Aviation) to Oddur, where France established a security base, similar to the Italian unit at Gialalassi and the USMC and US Army detachments at most of the other southern Somalian airfields.

In contrast to all the other aircraft at Mogadishu, the New Zealand air contingent of three Andover C.Mk 1s is directly attached to the UN, and so operates in overall white (two aircraft) or VIP colour schemes. The No. 42 Squadron aircraft arrived at Mogadishu on 7 January, having routed from Whenuapai through Auckland, Brisbane, Townsville, Darwin, Surabaya, Singapore, Butterworth, Colombo and the Seychelles. Duties are carriage of UN personnel and leaflet dropping to keep the local population

The international effort has brought a wide variety of aircraft to Somalia, including the Andovers of the RNZAF's No. 42 Sqn. These fly passenger shuttles, light cargo flights and leaflet-dropping sorties.

advised of developments, there being, of course, no radio, TV or newspapers. While the main famine relief effort is in the south, the Andovers fly throughout Somalia, operating a northern and a southern passenger run. In the first month of operations, the aircraft flew 221.5 hours in 65 sorties, carrying 1,660 passengers and 58,000 lb (26319 kg) of mixed freight.

Also assigned to the UN, Russia has two white Antonov An-32Bs (a new variant of 'Cline') based at Nairobi, Kenya, together with a further two of the same type in civilian markings. Canada has contributed 900 troops to Restore Hope and uses two No. 435 Squadron Lockheed CC-130 Hercules for resupply missions into Mogadishu. The USMC element is mostly 'up country', leaving only a couple of AH-1Ws and UH-1Ns from HMLA-369 based at Mogadishu airport for armed patrols, assisted by an

MH-53E. US Navy visitors include SH-2F Seasprites from warships off the coast. Army residents by early February had been reduced to a single medevac UH-60A, although at least three C-12Ds (including two in a 'VIP' colour scheme) were operating a shuttle from Mombasa.

The target date of 20 January for a US withdrawal is long passed. Rumours of a two-year commitment by the Americans may or may not be true, but *some* authority will have to stay in shattered Somalia for at least that time in order that the nation can be rebuilt from the ground up. Premature departure will only hand back the initiative to the warlords, starting the cycle of famine and intimidation once again. Exponents of air power note with satisfaction that it recently liberated Kuwait from a foreign invader; they may yet be able to add that it rescued Somalia from itself.

BRIEFING

Westland Lynx
Second-generation cats

Available both with a skid undercarriage for army use and in wheeled form for operation from ships' rear platforms, the Westland Lynx has become a familiar sight in NATO countries and farther afield since it first flew in 1971. Progressive improvements have been made in each basic variant during the intervening years, but perhaps the greatest single step forward has been as a result of the Lynx capturing the world helicopter speed record in 1986. Significantly contributing to this feat were aerodynamically-improved main rotor blades with increased chord tips – memorably, if unfortunately, known by the acronym BERP: British Experimental Rotor Programme. With these and other refinements, the Lynx has been reborn in the guise of Battlefield Lynx and (naval) Super Lynx.

The above are export names for similarly improved helicopters now being delivered to the British Army and Royal Navy as AH.Mk 9 and

Powered by the same Gem 41-1 engines as first fitted to the Mk 5, the Lynx AH.Mk 7 has a further improved rotor system. It is the British Army's standard battlefield attack/assault helicopter.

HAS.Mk 8, respectively. All four may be readily distinguished by the swept-tip, composites main rotor blades which offer increased speed and reduced vibration. The tail rotor is now also made from composites materials and, like the AH.Mk 7, rotates (clockwise, viewed from port) in the opposite direction to earlier marks for improved low-speed controllability. With a diameter of 7 ft 9 in (2.36 m), it is 6 in (15 cm) larger than on earlier Lynx. Rotors connect to two Rolls-Royce Gem Mk 42-1 turboshafts, each with a maximum rating of 1,135 shp (846 kW). This is no higher than Gem Mk 41 in later production 'standard' Lynx, although the Mk 42 boasts greater reliability and power retention. The last-mentioned permits maximum take-off weight to be raised to 11,300 lb (5125 kg) from the earlier limits of 10,750 lb (4876 kg) for the AH.Mk 7 army helicopter and 10,500 lb (4763 kg) in naval versions.

Thus far, only the British Army has acquired Battlefield Lynx. The latest land-based model differs from all its predecessors in having a wheeled landing gear, comprising twin nose-wheels and single mainwheels. Struts

Above: This is the first Lynx AH.Mk 9 after conversion by Westland. The new rotor blades give it a top speed some 20 kt faster than the AH.Mk 7. The Mk 9 has no TOW capability.

Below: The AH.Mk 5 was an interim variant of which only four were built before the AH.Mk 7 was adopted as standard. All four served with UK test agencies, this example being from the RAE.

supporting the fixed undercarriage differ in design from the naval Lynx and obstruct the position used for mounting Hughes TOW anti-tank missiles on the AH.Mk 1 and AH.Mk 7. There is thus no roof sight above the port seat, but Westland has undertaken to design a revised mounting for TOW (or Euromissile HOT or Rockwell Hellfire), if customers desire. Optional weapons include two GIAT 20-mm cannon pods; two FN Herstal pods with a pair of 7.62-mm machine-guns in each; or two M.159C pods

containing 19 70-mm rockets each. Similarly, anti-helicopter missiles could be attached on new mountings each side of the forward fuselage. AH.Mk 9s are fitted from the outset with the box-type exhaust diffusers introduced to AH.Mk 7s from early 1989 and will gain the GEC Ferranti ARI 23491 AWARE radar warning receivers ordered for the Army Air Corps (AAC) Lynx fleet in 1992.

Company demonstrator G-LYNX, the world record holder, was modified to Battlefield standard by Slingsby Aviation for static exhibition at the 1988 Farnborough air show. Later, it received a pair of LHTEC T800 turboshafts (as intended for the Boeing/Sikorsky RAH-66 Comanche) and returned to the air as the Battlefield Lynx 800 on 25 September 1991. However, relegation of the RAH-66 to only a development programme resulted in the planned series of private-venture testing being curtailed early in 1992 after only 17 hours.

The first true AH.Mk 9, converted trials installation Lynx XZ170, flew on 29 November 1989. An order had been placed in April 1987 for 16 new-build AH.Mk 9s, plus eight to be produced by direct conversion from AH.Mk 1 (most of the other AH.Mk 1s being meanwhile modified to AH.Mk 7s). Serials ZG884-ZG889 and ZG914-ZG923 were assigned to the new helicopters, of which ZG884 flew at Yeovil on 20 July 1990 and was delivered to the Aeroplane & Armament Experimental Establishment at Boscombe Down on 22 May 1991. Most of the remainder went initially to Wroughton for short-term storage, ZG923 arriving there on 30 June 1992.

Lynx AH.Mk 9 is used both for tactical transport support and as a forward command post on behalf of the rapid deployment unit, No. 24 Airmobile Brigade. Plans for service entry on 30 November 1991 with No. 9 Regiment, AAC, at Dishforth were

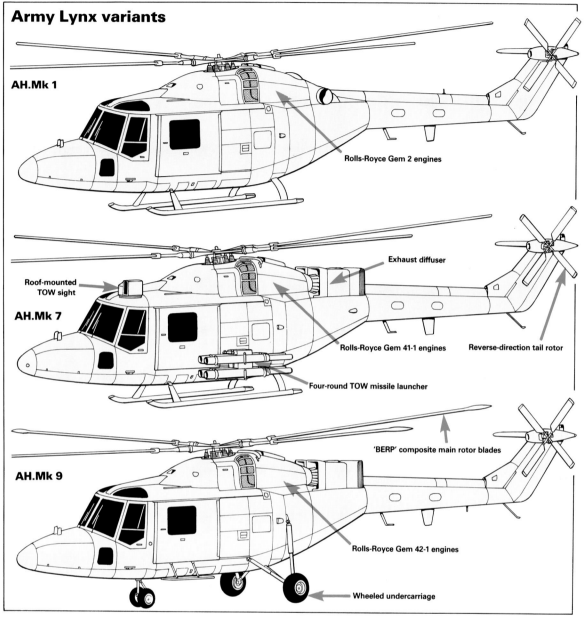

Army Lynx variants

AH.Mk 1

Rolls-Royce Gem 2 engines

AH.Mk 7

Roof-mounted TOW sight

Exhaust diffuser

Rolls-Royce Gem 41-1 engines

Reverse-direction tail rotor

Four-round TOW missile launcher

AH.Mk 9

'BERP' composite main rotor blades

Rolls-Royce Gem 42-1 engines

Wheeled undercarriage

cancelled due to delays with obtaining Controller (Aircraft) clearance through A&AEE, although two helicopters did participate in Exercise Certain Shield in Germany during September 1991. Formed at Topcliffe in January 1990, No. 9 Regiment moved to nearby Dishforth 13 months later, comprising No. 657 Squadron (Lynx AH.Mk 7 and Gazelle) and No. 672 Squadron (Lynx AH.Mk 7). The latter had adopted earlier versions due to delays with the AH.Mk 9 programme and was due to have been joined by newly-formed No. 673 Squadron, also with AH.Mk 9s. In the event, 672 Squadron began receiving Mk 9s in April 1992, at which time Gazelle-equipped No. 664 Squadron arrived from Germany to join No. 9 Regiment in place of No. 673. By June 1992, when No. 672 had received half its assigned 12 AH.Mk 9s, No. 664 had just taken delivery of its first and was anticipating regaining operational status before the end of the year.

The wheeled undercarriage is the main identification feature of the Lynx AH.Mk 9, but of greater significance are the advanced performance 'BERP' rotor blades with paddle tips.

Development of the Lynx HAS.Mk 8/Super Lynx has been a more protracted process because airframe upgrading is combined with considerable changes to the avionics. The Royal Navy plans to obtain 65 HAS.Mk 8s entirely by conversion of HAS.Mk 3s (some of which began life as HAS.Mk 1s) and has operated some of the new equipment in its existing fleet to gain operational experience. Phase 1 of a three-stage upgrade to HAS.Mk 8 was embodied in the last seven new-build RN Lynx, which were designated HAS.Mk 3S and equipped with GEC Marconi AD

3400 secure-speech radios and an improved version of the Racal MIR-2 Orange Crop ESM. Marked by a large spade aerial beneath the tailboom, they were delivered between November 1987 and November 1988 and augmented from April 1989 by 23 conversions at RN Aircraft Yard, Fleetlands.

More profound is the increase in operational capability brought about by Phase 2 fitment of a Racal RAMS 4000 central tactical system which eases the two-man crew's workload by centrally processing sensor data and presenting mission information on a multi-function CRT display. Installation of RAMS 4000 began with XZ236, flown on 25 January 1989 as the predecessor of six 'production' HAS.Mk 3CTS helicopters, conveniently identifiable by the simulta-

Carrying a maximum of four Sea Skua anti-ship missiles, this is a Lynx HAS.Mk 3, the current Royal Navy standard version.

neous fitment of flotation bags to the mainwheel sponsons and nose (as well

as the spade aerial). The six were issued to the Operational Flight Trials Unit at Portland from April 1989, this becoming 700L Squadron on 6 July 1990. Three of the complement were assigned to sea trials, beginning when ZF562 embarked HMS *Newcastle* on 3 December 1990. Operational clearance of the CTS was issued in August 1991.

The full HAS.Mk 8 augments the above-mentioned equipment improvements with a GEC Sensors Sea Owl thermal imager, CAE AN/ASQ-504(V) MAD and Racal RNS252 'Super TANS'. Mounted in a nose turret, Sea Owl is a passive target acquisition aid with ×5 or ×30 magnification, a 240° horizontal travel and the ability to look between 20° upwards and 30° downwards. The turret was first tested in Lynx ZD267 from 30 March 1989 onwards and the system ordered into production the following October. Revised nose de-

sign increases fuselage length by 9.25 in (23.5 cm). The MAD, also used by RN Westland Sea Kings, is a new design which does not need to be deployed behind an aircraft (either in a tail boom or on a trailing wire) and is therefore much simpler and more versatile in its use. Finally, Super TANS is an adaptation of the Lynx's original Tactical Air Navigation System to include a TNL8000 global positioning system receiver for increased accuracy. Avionics testbed for the HAS.Mk 8 programme was former HAS.Mk 3 ZD266.

By late 1992, Sea Owl testbed ZD267 had received all HAS.Mk 8 modifications to become the first to full production standard. Seven conversions were ordered from Westland in February 1992, but all others will be undertaken by the RN's own workshops using Westland-supplied kits. Installation of Sea Owl requires the nose radar to be repositioned under the helicopter, and it had been hoped to upgrade the Lynx's GEC Ferranti ARI5979 Sea Spray Mk 1 during this process. Prime requirement was for 360° scan, but Sea Spray Mk 3 and the preferred MEL Super Searcher were ruled out early in 1988 as too costly. As a result, the HAS.Mk 8 merely has its 180° radar repackaged in a half-redundant circular radome. Lynx HAS.Mk 8 will enter operational service in 1994.

Already in use are first export Super Lynxes, although those ordered so far lack the Sea Owl turret. South Korea signed a contract in 1988 for 12 Super Lynx HAS.Mk 99s to be equipped with Sea Spray Mk 3 radar, Bendix Oceanics AN/AQS-18 'dunking' sonar and TANS-N/Doppler 71 navigation equipment, the first of which (90-0701, temporarily ZH219) flew on 16 November 1989. The initial two were handed over for crew training in the UK on 26 July 1990 and now serve with No. 627 Squadron from Chinhae and aboard 'Sumner'- and 'Gearing'-class frigates.

The second customer is Portugal which, in 1988, requested the US to supply it with Kaman SH-2 Seasprites for three MEKO 200PM 'Vasco da Gama'-class frigates. Late in 1989, the SH-2 was abandoned in favour of five Super Lynx HAS.Mk 95s, including two rebuilt ex-RN HAS.Mk 3s, to be delivered to Montijo in 1993. Illustrating the equipment options available, the Portuguese navy helicopter has 360° scanning Allied Signal (formerly Bendix-King) RDR 1500 radar, RNS252 Super TANS, Racal Doppler 91 and a datalink. Super Lynx HAS.Mk 95 took to the air on 27 March 1992 in the form of ZH580 (to become PN 1001) – previously an HAS.Mk 3S ZF559.

Of 380 (including 13 prototypes)

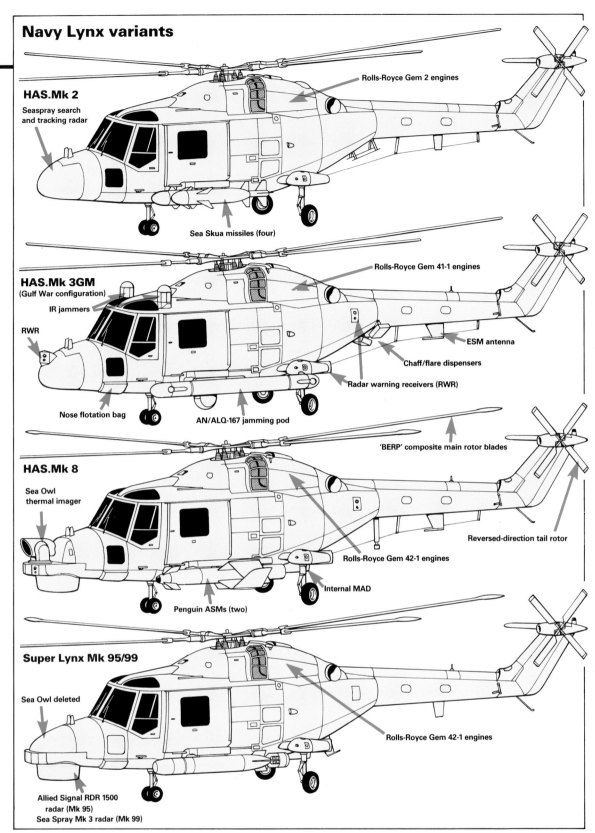

Navy Lynx variants

HAS.Mk 2
Seaspray search and tracking radar
Rolls-Royce Gem 2 engines
Sea Skua missiles (four)

HAS.Mk 3GM
(Gulf War configuration)
IR jammers
RWR
Nose flotation bag
Rolls-Royce Gem 41-1 engines
ESM antenna
Chaff/flare dispensers
Radar warning receivers (RWR)
AN/ALQ-167 jamming pod

HAS.Mk 8
Sea Owl thermal imager
'BERP' composite main rotor blades
Reversed-direction tail rotor
Rolls-Royce Gem 42-1 engines
Internal MAD
Penguin ASMs (two)

Super Lynx Mk 95/99
Sea Owl deleted
Rolls-Royce Gem 42-1 engines
Allied Signal RDR 1500 radar (Mk 95)
Sea Spray Mk 3 radar (Mk 99)

Lynx on order by 1992, new-build second-generation machines account for just 33, with the prospect of five more, plus rebuilds, being ordered by the Brazilian navy. Lynx have accumulated over 500,000 flying hours during 750,000 sorties and will remain in service with 10 countries, including six NATO navies, until well into the next century.

South Korea's 12 Super Lynx Mk 99s are now in service, with Sea Spray 3 radar but no thermal imager. Note the dipping sonar in the centre of the fuselage undersides and the nose flotation bags.

BRIEFING

Fuerza Aérea Venezolana

Coup attempt splits Venezuelan AF

Delivery of 18 surplus USAF Rockwell OV-10A Bronco aircraft to the FAV was completed in April 1991, allowing Escuadrón 152 'Avispones', within the structure of Grupo Aéreo de Operaciones Especiales No. 15 at Base Aérea General En Jefe Rafael Urdaneta, Maracaibo, Zulia, to re-equip from the EMB-312 A-27 Tucano.

The displaced A-27 Tucano aircraft were in turn relocated within the structure of Grupo 13 at Base Aérea Teniente Luis del Valle Garcia, Barcelona, which had been devoid of aeroplanes since the withdrawal of the EE Canberra some 12 months previously. The counter-insurgency (COIN) role was at this time dropped in favour of the unit becoming a Tactical Instructors School, presumably taking on the title Escuadrón 131 'Avispones'. Escuadron 152 has been renamed 'Zorros'.

Operation of the two variants of the Bronco within Grupo 15 is mixed with both units, Escuadrón 151 'Geronimos' and 152 'Zorros', operating the remaining 11 OV-10E and 18 OV-10A airframes. Differences between the two variants are limited, although the former USAF aircraft are reputed to have better avionics and higher airframe hours and they lack the 7.62-mm machine-gun armament of the export version. Unfortunately, one of the 'new' OV-10A aircraft, 0690, was lost in a crash at Santo Domingo on 22 October 1992 following an engine fire, the pilot ejecting safely.

This injection of 'new' equipment within the FAV followed a long period of limited funding which had ultimately left a number of units in a non-operational state, including Escuadrón de Caza No. 36 at Base Aérea Teniente Vicente Landaeta, Barquisimeto. No. 36 had reluctantly ceased

flying the surviving 13 Canadair CF-5A/R and one CF-5D 'Freedom Fighter' through fatigue problems in May 1990. These 14 airframes had been placed in open storage pending funding to return them to flying condition. This programme had two stages, the first including the signing of a contract with Singapore Aerospace in June 1990 to refurbish and upgrade the airframes, two pattern aircraft, (CF-5A 9124 and CF-5D 5681) being dispatched in May 1991, with a scheduled return to service in May 1993. The second phase saw the purchase of six ex-KLu Canadair-built NF-5s, one 'A' and five 'B's. The first of these, 1711 (ex K-4018), flew in its refurbished state during February 1992, and had been delivered to Venezuela by November 1992, along with NF-5A 6324 (ex K-3057) and NF-5B 1721.

Following completion of the two aircraft dispatched to Singapore, funding exists for a further seven airframes to receive similar treatment. These seven aircraft, CF-5A/Rs 6018, 5276, 3318, 3274, 9538, 9456 and 9348, will be updated in Venezuela with the aid of Singapore Aerospace technicians. At present there are 10 FAV personnel working on the programme in Singapore and three Singaporean personnel in Venezuela.

A decision on the remaining five airframes, CF-5A/R 6719, 7200, 8707, 8792 and 9215, all of which remain stored at Barquisimeto, is still awaited and was not expected to be made until the initial phase was almost complete.

Another update programme also left the FAV lacking teeth. A deal to upgrade the surviving FAV Mirage IIIEV/5V and 5DV fighters to Mirage 50 standard had been made with Dassault in March 1988. Withdrawal of the fighters had, however, been staged with the surviving Mirage 5Vs and 5DVs being the first to be returned to Bordeaux. This left three surviving Mirage IIIEVs (0624, 4058, 6732) to keep the aircrew current.

The purchase of additional airframes to bring the operating total back to 18 had been included in the deal, although the subsequent loss of 0624 during 1992 may have seen the final total reduced. The first of these additional aircraft test flew during mid-1990 and delivery of the first modified aeroplane, 0160, occurred in October 1990. Three further airframes, Mirage 50EVs 0155 and 2473, along with Mirage 50DV 7512 have followed. The surviving two Mirage IIIEVs have been returned to France.

Late 1992 therefore saw the FAV well on the road to becoming a fully operational and integrated force again, with Grupo de Caza 16 and its General Dynamics F-16A Fighting Falcons having been invited to participate in the demanding Red Flag exercise in recognition of their professionalism. Venezuela thus became the twentieth country to do so, and the

Left: This aircraft is one of the ex-KLu NF-5Bs recently refurbished for service with the FAV. In the background are T-2D Buckeyes.

Below: Staying loyal to the president during the coup were the F-16s of Grupo 16.

first from the South American continent.

In spite of this seemingly progressive situation within the air force, a failed coup attempt was made by the paratroopers of Grupo de Parcaidistas 'Aragua' led by Lieutenant Colonel H. Chavaz on 4 February 1992. Although quashed, feelings within the air force apparently remained high and at dawn on 27 November a further attempted coup was made by elements of the FAV led by Brigadier General Visconti, the Air Force Logistic Service Inspector. Under the cover of the Air Force Day preparations, Visconti had contrived to move assets sympathetic to Chavaz to the El Libertador Air Base, Palo Negro, Aragua. These assets included one NF-5B, five T-2Ds, three OV-10Es, six OV-10As and a pair of A-27s, which, together with units stationed within the complex, gave him a very commanding situation.

Actual details of the coup attempt are still somewhat sketchy, with many reports conflicting. It is believed that at the forefront of the aerial activity were the Bronco aircraft of Grupo 15. Initially, Visconti and his supporters seized control of El Libertador Air Base at 0330 on the morning of 27 November, supported by the bulk of the 10th Special Operations Group which operates most of the FAV's helicopter assets, and Grupo de Caza 11.

The crews from the FAV's F-16 wing, Grupo de Caza 16, refused to join the rebellion and managed to scramble the two 'QRA' aircraft which fled to Barquisimeto. This base appears, in the main, to have remained loyal to the President. The re-

Broncos fought with the rebels during the coup attempt, as did A-27 Tucanos. Above is an OV-10E from the original batch supplied to Venezuela, while right is an OV-10A from surplus USAF stocks.

mainder of Grupo 16 were either captured or managed to retreat under fire to the administrative compound.

At the same time as action commenced at El Libertador, other personnel took control of nearby Base Aérea Mariscal Sucre, in Boca Del Rio, Maracay, which is home to the Escuola Techinica, Grupo de Policia and Escuola Elementaire d'Avions Militare. This has the attendant flying unit of the Grupo Aéreo de Entrenamiento which operates the EMB-312 Tucano and Beech T-34A Mentor. Four T-2D Buckeyes were also thought to have been present, detached from Barquisimeto.

At first light the three Mirage 50EV fighters of Grupo 11 strafed army barracks in Caracas while a mixed formation of a dozen aircraft including Broncos, Tucanos and a single Buckeye attacked the Presidential palace, the Presidential Guard barracks, the Foreign Ministry and police headquarters.

The two F-16s that had escaped to Barquisimeto returned over the city at around 0700 and began pursuit of the Broncos and Tucanos that were strafing positions loyal to the President. The F-16s also strafed El Libertador with 20-mm cannon fire. Meanwhile, troops who had also remained loyal at both Sucre and El Libertador were subjected to repeated attacks by rebel helicopters and aircraft. In the process one Bronco, reported to be OV-10A 1103, was downed by small arms and AAA fire although the crew ejected safely.

Mirages and Broncos in turn attacked the air base at Barquisimeto to prevent further sorties being flown in support of the government. In the

process they attacked the small apron, destroying three stored CF-5As (believed to be drawn from 6719, 7200, 8707 and 8792). A civilian MD-80 airliner was also hit by 30-mm cannon fire.

Grupo de Caza 12 managed to scramble its sole NF-5A, and one of the F-16s got airborne to shoot down two of the attacking OV-10s, with one pilot managing to eject while the other was killed. The few defending fighters kept up the struggle against the rebel forces but the only other kill to have taken place was an A-27 Tucano brought down by an F-16. A further Bronco was lost over Caracas when it was either hit by small arms fire or suffered an engine problem. The two crew ejected safely, the aircraft crashing to the left of the La Carlota runway.

By 1300 La Carlota air base was secured against the remaining limited resistance and both El Libertador and Sucre followed shortly afterwards when tanks and paratroops entered the bases. This followed the departure of Brigadier General Visconti and 92 officers in a Grupo 6 Lockheed C-130H Hercules to Peru, where they sought asylum. Two of the four Grupo 11 Mirages escaped to the Dutch island of Aruba and an OV-10 Bronco flew to Curaçao. One thousand officers and NCOs were reportedly arrested, which no doubt created a major setback to the FAV in its struggle to become an integrated front-line force once again.

Grupo 11's Mirage 50EV fighters took part in the coup attempt, and two escaped to Aruba after its failure. The Mirages have recently been upgraded by Dassault from 5V standard with Atar 9K-50 engines and canard foreplanes.

C-17 Globemaster III

Next Generation Airlifter

Although it bears the same configuration as the C-5 and C-141 transports currently in USAF service, the McDonnell Douglas C-17 is a thoroughly modern design, incorporating a host of state-of-the-art features. After a lengthy and costly development, the Globemaster III is set to revitalise the US strategic airlift effort, adding its muscle to the ever more crucial rapid deployment capability.

A walk-around check of a Douglas C-17 Globemaster III is one way to reach an understanding of the US Air Force's next-generation airlifter, but it is not likely to get the adrenaline pumping or to stir up electrifying emotion, particularly when contrasted to the 'Black Jets' and 'Stealth Bombers' which will surround the airlifter at its 'open day' debut this year. Even on close scrutiny, not every air show visitor is likely to be awed by the C-17's wealth of high-technology features or, for that matter, to be reminded of the controversy behind the longest-running aircraft development programme in US history.

The C-17 is a high-wing, four-engined, T-tailed transport. That means very little is new on the outside, but pilots can confirm that the Globemaster III is a whole new world on the inside. It boasts an ergonometric flight deck (that is, one optimised for pilot comfort) with digital displays. Its two pilots sit side by side and the flight deck also provides two additional crew members' seats behind the pilots in recognition of the fact that extra crew personnel often accompany long-range missions. The C-17 is flown with a control stick instead of the traditional yoke on transports. It is the first cargo aircraft with a head-up display.

To keep the crew's workload within reasonable limits, the C-17's flight deck includes mission computers and an integrated radio management system. Its quadruply redundant FBW control system with mechanical backup handles 29 control surfaces. A trimmable horizontal stabiliser, four elevators and two articulated rudders are located on the tail; two ailerons, eight spoilers, four flaps, and eight slats on the wings.

The C-17's cavernous interior was designed with real-life cargo sizes in mind, and includes a feature first tested on the YC-15 prototype of the 1970s, this being a palletised load/unload system which the Air Force insists can be handled by a single loadmaster. In the forward fuselage interior, provision is made for 102 permanent side-wall passenger seats which can be folded out of the way, and for up to 12 four-litter stanchions for medical evacuation duties. The C-17's ground-level, roll-on/off ramp is located at the rear of the fuselage. A 68-ft 1½-in (21.11-m) long cargo compartment with powered rollers accommodates up to 18 standard 463L pallets. When closed, the C-17's rear ramp can hold cargo of the same weight as the cargo floor; the ramps of other airlifters can accommodate only light loads.

The airlifter's 165-ft (51.08-m) wing is swept at 25° with a supercritical airfoil and has winglets for fuel efficiency. Almost one-third of the aircraft's structural weight is in the wing.

The four 41,700-lb (185.5-kN) thrust Pratt & Whitney PW2040 turbofan engines are known by the military designation F117-PW-100. The PW2037/2040 engine was FAA-certified in December 1983 and began commercial service on the Boeing 757 in December 1984, and is expected to have six million hours of flying time by the time the C-17 enters service. The engines are suspended well forward and below the wings by cantilevered pylons. Each pylon contains multi-membered forged aluminium stub structures integrated into the wing so that the attachment to the wing has continuous load paths. The pylon box structure is primarily titanium because of its close proximity to the engine.

Valuable thrust reversers

The C-17 employs an engine thrust reverser: the cowling of the engine slides backward, exposing an opening in the cowling itself. Engine exhaust is directed upward and forward through this opening. The reversers are designed to operate at zero forward speed without ingestion or excessive-temperature problems. Because the reverse thrust is aimed upward (and 45° forward), engine running, offloading, and other ground operations can continue while this feature is in use. This permits a new kind of ground performance, namely the ability to complete a 180° turn on a 90-ft (27.86-m) wide runway and the ability to back up a two per cent slope at maximum 2.25g.

Above: Although the proposed purchase of C-17s has been cut from 210 to 120, the **Globemaster III** has the full backing of politicians and military commanders alike. **T**esting is in full swing at Edwards AFB.

Below: The old hand welcomes the new kid on the block: a **C-141B** visiting Edwards AFB provides an excellent comparison with its replacement. **T**he StarLifter is from the 17th Airlift Squadron, 437th Airlift Wing, which is to be the first C-17 unit.

Above: On 15 September 1992, on the first anniversary of the C-17's maiden flight, the test unit put up this four-ship formation led by the first prototype (T-1). After troubles in the development/ procurement stage, the flight test and initial training programmes have progressed very smoothly.

Left: P-1 (88-0265) was the second aircraft from the line, completed in Air Mobility Command's new overall grey scheme. Behind the flight deck is the inflight refuelling receptacle, marked in black.

The C-17 employs a rugged corrosion-resistant T-tail assembly consisting of a 41° swept-back vertical stabilizer with a variable-incidence horizontal stabilizer mounted on top. An intriguing feature of the aircraft is a tunnel which enables a crew member to climb inside the vertical fin to the height of the T-tail for stabilizer maintenance.

The C-17 employs propulsive lift technology, in which air from the engines is forced under the wing, through the flap hinge, and down both sides of the single, split flap, which is itself nearly the size of a DC-9 wing. Based on technology tested in the YC-15, this blown-vane flap system allows a steep, low-speed final approach and low landing approach speed (116 kt with a 15 ft/second descent rate). The flap system features a simple, fixed-hinge, slotted vane flap that is deflected into the exhaust stream to produce re-action-lift and circulation-lift augmentation through the formation of a jet sheet (the engine exhaust), which exits the flap trailing edge at deflection angles related to the flap deflections. A full-span leading edge slat is tailored to provide maximum lift and stall characteristics. Spoilers are drooped with the flap deflection through a simple gearing mechanism to maintain the desired vane gaps.

Above: A view inside Douglas' Long Beach plant shows the first three production C-17s under assembly, together with the two static test aircraft.

Left: The PW2040 is designated F117 by the military. In addition to powering the C-17, it is best known as a powerplant for the Boeing 757. Engines of this family are also being tested on the Ilyushin Il-96 and Tupolev Tu-204.

Below: T-1, the first C-17, eventually got air under its wheels on 15 September 1991. After this take-off from Long Beach, it flew to Edwards to launch the test programme.

Four-engined fighter

Unlike the C-141B it will replace, the C-17 can make an assault landing, if necessary, on an unfinished strip. As for its flight characteristics, Lieutenant Colonel George London, test pilot with the 417th Test and Evaluation Squadron at Edwards AFB, California, (and co-pilot of T-1 on its first flight) says the C-17 is far easier to handle in the airfield pattern than its predecessors. "In current airlifters we would fly around in the pattern at base speed plus 20 kt. At the threshold you would add 10 kt and at touchdown drop 10 kt below that speed. In the C-17 we fly at one speed from turn top final, final, over threshold, and touchdown. We fly angle of attack all the way down and land it just like a fighter. We land it straight down to the ground."

Illustrating Douglas' re-emergence as a builder of transport aircraft for the US Air Force, a KC-10 Extender from the 22nd Air Refueling Wing at March tanks the first C-17. T-1 was the only aircraft completed in a European One style camouflage.

As for its undercarriage, the C-17 features a non-steerable, six-wheel-per-side main landing gear that retracts into low-drag gear pods and a steerable dual-wheel nose gear that retracts into the fuselage.

Behind the C-17's appearance as the next-generation strategic airlifter for the US Air Force's Air Mobility Command is a long and complex story. Developing any new military aircraft takes time and money; developing the C-17 has taken more time than any other aircraft in history and (with just a pair of exceptions) more money. By the time the seventh C-17 (89-1192), known as P-6, joins AMC's 17th Airlift Squadron at Charleston AFB, South Carolina, next year, the American taxpayer will have spent enough on the C-17 to make it the third most expensive aircraft in history, outpriced only by the E-3 Sentry AWACS and the B-2 'Stealth Bomber'.

Globemaster genesis

The Globemaster III's roots can be traced to 1971. Management of the programme has been controversial and doubts about the structural strength of the aircraft wing persist. The C-17 does, however, introduce new capabilities and technology to the sorely neglected strategic airlift mission, so few critics would go as far as *Newsweek*'s Colonel David H. Hackworth, who calls it "the trouble-prone C-17 transport jet which is far more costly and carries no more troops than current models that work."

The need for the C-17 cannot be disputed. The New World Order of which today's leaders speak was ushered in by Saddam Hussein and reaffirmed when the United States moved hundreds of thousands of troops halfway around the world using strategic airlift. In the past decade, strategic airlift has played a role in 40 outbreaks of violence and 50 natural disasters. AMC's fleet of 265 C-141B StarLifters is approaching a 45,000-hour service-life ceiling and is hamstrung by wing spar cracks and cockpit window frame cracks which impose flying restrictions. A Lock-

heed proposal for a service life enhancement programme for the C-141B has merit, as does Lockheed's interest in reopening the C-5B Galaxy production line, but neither reflects staunchly pro-C-17 Pentagon policy.

Inflight refuelling tests were completed with both KC-10 and KC-135 tankers – here a 4950th Test Wing NKC-135E provides the gas. The view serves to show the large size of the fuselage, despite the compact overall dimensions of the new airlifter. Noteworthy are the distinctive vortex generator vanes on the engine nacelles.

Today's C-17, though intended as a C-141B replacement, traces its heritage to 1971's AMST (Advanced Military STOL Transport) requirement for an airlifter able to deliver outsized cargoes directly to the battlefield. The AMST programme produced the Boeing YC-14 and Douglas YC-15, both intended to carry 150 troops or 81,000 lb (36740 kg) of payload and to operate from a runway no longer than 625 yd (570 m). Both aircraft employed STOL technologies and a supercritical wing developed from NASA research by Dr Richard Whitcomb.

The Boeing YC-14 made its first flight on 9 August 1976: it was powered by two 51,000-lb (226.87-kN) thrust General Electric CF6-50D turbofan engines and used blown air for low-speed STOL characteristics. The Douglas YC-15 first flew 26 August 1975, and was powered by four 16,000-lb (71.17-kN) thrust Pratt & Whitney JT8D-17 turbofans with the option of employing other engines, and used externally blown, double-slotted flaps for powered lift.

T-1 approaches a tanker over California's Mojave Desert. The first machine was the only C-17 to fly with an instrumented nose probe for accurate airflow measurements. Small vanes were also attached to T-1's wingtips.

McDonnell Douglas C-17 Globemaster III

1 Radome
2 Weather radar
3 ILS aerial
4 Downward vision window
5 Rudder pedals
6 Control column
7 Instrument panel, four full-colour multi-function displays
8 Head-up displays
9 Overhead systems switch panel
10 Co-pilot's seat
11 Pilot's seat
12 Two observer's seats
13 Nosewheel hydraulic retraction jack
14 Forward-retracting nose undercarriage
15 Underfloor equipment bay
16 Static ports
17 Combined entry door and airstairs
18 Cargo winch
19 Loadmaster's station on starboard lower deck
20 Pitot heads
21 Portable water tank
22 Crew rest bunks
23 Inflight-refuelling receptacle
24 Escape hatch

25 Avionics equipment racks
26 Miscellaneous equipment stowage lockers
27 Sidewall-mounted folding troop seats, 27 each side

28 Formation lighting strip
29 Stowable centreline troop seats, 48 seats back to back
30 Cargo compartment deck
31 Roller conveyors and tie-down points
32 Auxiliary power unit (APU) in starboard fuselage sponson
33 Air system ducting
34 Litter stanchion stowage
35 Starboard wing integral fuel tankage
36 Starboard engine nacelles
37 Leading-edge slats

38 Starboard navigation light
39 Winglet
40 Tail navigation and strobe lights
41 Starboard aileron
42 Fuel jettison
43 Double-slotted flap
44 Four-segment spoiler panels
45 External flap hinges
46 Communications and navigation antennas
47 Starboard paratroop door
48 Toilet
49 Anchor cable supports
50 Ramp door actuators

51 Parallel chord tailfin
52 Tailplane actuator
53 Anti-collision light
54 All-moving tailplane
55 Starboard two-segment elevator
56 Tailplane pivot bearing
57 Port two-segment elevator
58 Elevator hydraulic actuators
59 Two-segment double-acting rudder panels
60 Formation lighting strip
61 Rudder hydraulic actuators
62 Rear fuselage strake
63 Rear ramp door
64 Parachute deployment mechanism
65 Formation lighting strip
66 Ramp jacks
67 Ramp folding toe-plate
68 Cargo loading ramp

69 Tow release unit
70 Port paratroop door
71 Retractable blast deflector
72 Fuselage sponson fairing
73 Flap hydraulic jacks
74 Spoiler jacks
75 Port spoiler panels
76 Port double-slotted flap
77 Fuel jettison
78 Aileron hydraulic actuator
79 Port aileron
80 Static dischargers
81 Port winglet

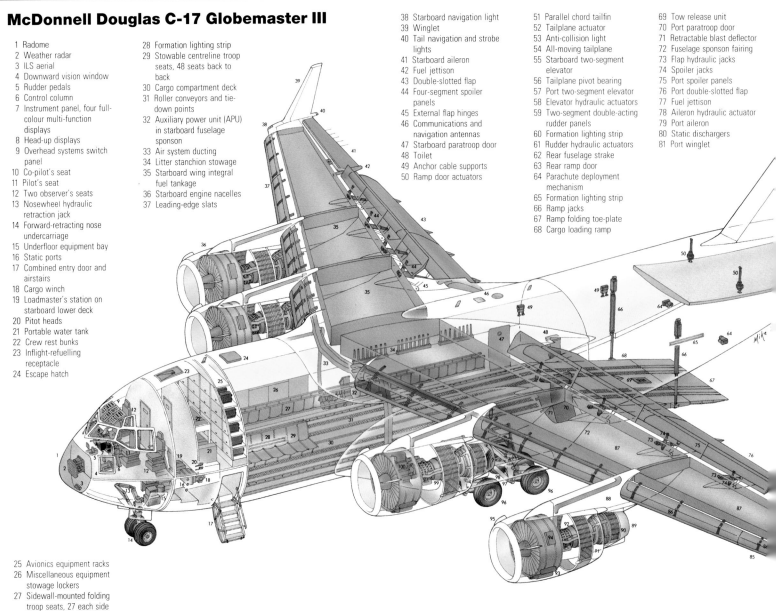

Satisfied to keep the C-130 Hercules in production, the US Air Force elected not to produce either AMST candidate. The YC-15, however, gave Douglas a 'leg up' when the CX requirement came along.

CX first steps

A draft RFP (Request For Proposals) for a CX heavylift cargo transport was issued in February 1980 and was followed in October by a formal RFP. The new airlifter was to be intended for the strategic airlift role, supplanting C-5 and C-141 transports and eventually replacing the C-141; however, it was to be capable of short-field landings like the tactical C-130. The RFP required a fuselage cross-section able to carry outsized loads, including the M1 Abrams main battle tank; undercarriage and high-lift devices to enable the CX to operate from runways 3,000 ft (915 m) long and 90 ft (27 m) wide; and thrust reversers to manoeuvre the aircraft in and out of congested parking areas and to back up a 5° slope.

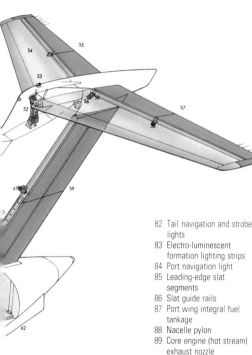

82 Tail navigation and strobe lights
83 Electro-luminescent formation lighting strips
84 Port navigation light
85 Leading-edge slat segments
86 Slat guide rails
87 Port wing integral fuel tankage
88 Nacelle pylon
89 Core engine (hot stream) exhaust nozzle
90 Hot stream thrust reverser
91 Fan air thrust reverser
92 Pratt & Whitney F117-PW-100 turbofan engines
93 Engine accessory equipment gearbox
94 Full-authority digital engine control (FADEC)
95 Nacelle strakes
96 Tandem three-wheel main undercarriage units
97 Mainwheel door
98 Levered suspension leg strut
99 Inboard Pratt & Whitney F117-PW-100 turbofan
100 Sponson-mounted air conditioning pack

CX designs were proposed by Boeing and Lockheed, in addition to Douglas. The Boeing proposal was for a three-engined design with two of the engines mounted atop the wings in the manner of the builder's YC-14. Lockheed's submission was similar in appearance to the C-141B StarLifter.

Though the Lockheed Georgia Company had far more recent experience building transports, the four-engined, blown-flap Douglas proposal was selected as the CX aircraft, and an announcement to this effect was made on 28 August 1981. The ink was hardly dry on the announcement in September 1981 when Lockheed, seeking a way around its loss of this CX contract, argued – more correctly than it knew, as things turned out – that it could produce 44 new-build C-5 Galaxies more quickly and at less cost than a C-17 fleet. The company's reasoning was without fault, but it did no harm (just as it has done no harm to production prospects for the C-130 Hercules) that the idea was supported by the chairman of the Senate armed services committee, also of Georgia. While being debated, the proposed new Galaxies were referred to by the designation C-5N, with the N suffix meaning 'new'.

In 1982, the US Air Force ordered a new production run of 50 C-5Bs, as the new Galaxy was renamed. Longer-term airlift needs were to be assessed on the basis of a Congressional study, a sop to Capitol Hill legislators, each of whom was a stalwart proponent of airlift so long as it was manufactured in his district. In part to salve feelings at Douglas, and partly out of common sense, design work on the Douglas CX aircraft (soon designated C-17) went ahead while the Air Force procured the C-5Bs and 60 Douglas KC-10A Extender dual-role tanker/transports.

The Congressional examination of airlift needs concluded that by 1986 the US armed forces would require a strategic airlift capacity of 66

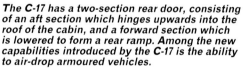

The C-17 has a two-section rear door, consisting of an aft section which hinges upwards into the roof of the cabin, and a forward section which is lowered to form a rear ramp. Among the new capabilities introduced by the C-17 is the ability to air-drop armoured vehicles.

The most prominent of the C-17's aerodynamic refinements are the large winglets, which cut the bleed of high pressure air around the wingtip. Also noticeable is the supercritical aerofoil section.

million ton-miles per day (MTM/D). Military Airlift Command's strategic airlifters, including its added C-5Bs and KC-10As, as well as Air National Guard, Air Force Reserve, and CRAF (Civil Reserve Air Fleet) aircraft, would only be able to transport 46 MTM/D. A future C-17 would make up the 30 per cent shortfall.

Congressional politics kept intervening. With the slump in airline revenues, Capitol Hill legislators wanted to help US air carriers dispose of older Boeing 747s. Given Washington's readiness, during the Reagan years (1981-1987), to spend profligate sums on anything for military

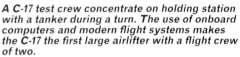

use, the military airlift community was the obvious dumping ground. Plans were formulated to equip the 105th Military Airlift Wing, New York Air National Guard (then operating the Cessna O-2 Skymaster) with used 747 airliners. The designation C-19 was applied. In the Pentagon, the disgruntled Air Staff argued that no 747/C-19 could land near a battlefield or carry an outsized cargo. The 105th eventually received C-5As instead and work continued, slowly, on the C-17.

The essential design of the C-17 was finalised by early 1984. The new aircraft was to be powered by four Pratt & Whitney PW2037 turbofans, later uprated to the PW2040.

A full-scale fuselage mock-up, including cargo compartment and flight deck, met with favourable reception. During 11-20 September 1984, a cargo-loading test using active-duty Air Force loadmasters and users from the Army and Marine Corps handled 11 load combinations. Typical loads included **(1)** two armoured personnel carriers, two five-ton trucks with 2½-ton trailers and three Jeeps, or **(2)** three AH-1S Cobra

and three OH-58C Kiowa helicopters. Early on, loadmasters – the same unsung experts who saw the potential for 'stretching' the Lockheed C-141 after the engineers missed it – were sceptical of plans to operate the future C-17 with a crew of two pilots and just one loadmaster, whose primary work station is at the forward end of the cargo compartment. The sole loadmaster is supposed to handle the ramp/cargo door, airdrop, LAPES and CDS (container delivery system), all from this station. The scepticism felt by loadmasters persists today.

Project go-ahead

In February 1985, equally persistent Air Force lobbying yielded a contract to cut metal for a C-17 prototype. The Air Force, caught up in the free-spending Cold War, established a requirement for 210 C-17 aircraft. Of these, 48 were to go directly to the Air National Guard and Air Force Reserve. Douglas (in sharp contrast to the seasoned Lockheed Georgia Company) had not manufactured a military transport since its C-133 Cargomaster of the 1950s. Though Douglas's de-

A C-17 test crew concentrate on holding station with a tanker during a turn. The use of onboard computers and modern flight systems makes the C-17 the first large airlifter with a flight crew of two.

sign and engineering capabilities exceeded many in the industry, this West Coast branch of the McDonnell Douglas Corporation was primarily a manufacturer of airliners; Douglas lacked recent immersion in the new world of military procurement which demanded of a prime contractor not merely the knowledge of how to build aircraft (which Douglas had) but surefootedness at managing a major system (an area where Douglas could not have been weaker).

In the 1950s, when the United States still enjoyed the world's most productive industry, nearly all of the work in building a C-124, C-133, or any other aircraft took place right in the factory. In the new era of the C-17, in order to court as many Congressmen as possible, basic work on a military aircraft had to be 'farmed out' to subcontractors in as many states as possible. No manufacturer produced an entire aircraft any longer.

The new world also demanded that a prime contractor be quick of foot in the minefield of Capitol Hill politics. While corporate giant McDonnell Douglas ranked second to none in its ability to woo Congress – a legitimate exercise of rights under the American system – little of this skill had trickled down to the parent company's Douglas branch in Long Beach. Not until half a decade later, in early 1992, did Douglas shake up its boardroom leadership, slim down its executive roster, and become more effective at the lobbying game. In the mid-1980s, quite mistakenly, the company was still focused on building an aircraft.

Landing at Edwards at the end of its first flight, P-1 demonstrates the eight-section lift-dumper/spoiler arrangement and the full-span leading-edge slats. Combined with the externally-blown flaps, they bestow extraordinary field performance for an aircraft of this size.

Cargo carriage
In addition to outsize loads such as tanks and helicopters (typical load three AH-1s and three OH-58s), the C-17 can carry a maximum of 18 463L freight pallets. The internal loading system is fully mechanised for one-loadmaster operation.

Passenger carriage
For the passenger-carrying role, the C-17 is equipped with 54 tip-up seats along the cabin sides. To these can be added a further 48 along the centreline, or 100 pallet-mounted seats for a maximum of 154. In the medevac role, 48 litters can be carried.

Fuel
Fuel is held in six main wing tanks, situated integrally between the main spars and extending for virtually the full span of the wing. Total capacity is 27,108 US gal (102614 litres).

Airdrop
Through the open rear ramp the C-17 can drop a maximum of 110,000 lb (49895 kg) on multiple platforms, 60,000 lb (27215 kg) on a single platform or 102 paratroops. Eleven 463L pallets can be air-dropped, two of these carried on the rear ramp.

McDonnell Douglas C-17 Globemaster III

One hundred and twenty C-17s are to be procured for the strategic airlift mission. The design was driven by the need to carry main battle tanks such as the M1 Abrams, and other large items such as helicopters, while retaining the ability for tactical delivery profiles, including LAPES and short landings into austere strips. Consequently, the aircraft is very large and capacious, but has outstanding STOL characteristics.

Cargo cabin
The main compartment measures 68 ft 2 in (20.78 m) long, including the rear ramp, and has a volume of 20,900 cu ft (592 m³). The height under the wing is 12 ft 4 in (3.76 m) and the loadable width is 18 ft 0 in (5.49 m).

Specification
Powerplant: four Pratt & Whitney F117-PW-100 turbofans, each rated at 41,700 lb (185.5 kN) thrust
Dimensions: wing span 171 ft 3 in (52.20 m); length 174 ft 0 in (53.04 m); height 55 ft 1 in (16.79 m); tailplane span 65 ft 0 in (19.81 m); wheel track 33 ft 8 in (10.27 m); wheelbase 65 ft 9 in (20.05 m)
Weights: operating empty 269,000 lb (122016 kg); maximum take-off 580,000 lb (263083 kg); maximum payload 172,200 lb (78108 kg)
Performance: maximum cruising speed at low altitude 403 mph (648 km/h); normal cruising speed Mach 0.77; approach speed 132 mph (213 km/h); take-off run with 167,000-lb (75750-kg) payload 7,500 ft (2286 m); landing run with similar load 3,000 ft (915 m); range with 160,000-lb (72575-kg) payload 2,765 miles (4445 km); self-ferry range 5,412 miles (8710 km)

The flight deck of the Globemaster III is a far cry from that of the C-141 or C-5. Two auxiliary crew seats are provided, and each pilot has a head-up display. A control stick is fitted in place of the standard yoke.

Drawn up in the mid-1980s, a schedule calling for a first flight in 1989 proved too ambitious. This milestone was rescheduled for August 1990, then for December 1990, then for June 1991. There was a little grumbling in Congress but in the early days, when the C-17 programme might readily have been reorganised or turned over to another manufacturer, the Globemaster III's teething troubles did not attract enough attention for such a change, a sharp contrast to the situation half a decade later when difficulties with the A-12 attack and P-7 patrol aircraft led to their cancellation.

In the mid-1980s, such a draconian step would have seemed unlikely. Times were good. Dollars were being spent. Never mind that the money was borrowed, mortgaged against a nation's future as American indebtness rose and rose. People were at work: Douglas employment on the C-17 increased by 4,000 jobs in 1986 alone.

Playing it safe

The Pentagon might have saved time and money by dropping its requirement that the C-17 be capable of landing on an unpaved airstrip near the battlefield. This was not done even though no one believes, today, that the costly airlifter will really be taken within close range of an enemy's guns and missiles. Interestingly, by the time the C-17 enters service, no one in the US Air Force below the rank of major general will be a Vietnam veteran. Those who flew airlifters into Tan Son Nhut and Da Nang remember too well the hazard of landing and taking off within range of a guerrilla army's mortars and B-40 rockets, to say nothing of today's farther-reaching battlefield weaponry.

The first metal was cut on the C-17 on 2 November 1987. Two sections of a 68-ft (21.05-m) tiedown rail were joined in a ceremony on 24 October 1988, the first actual 'assembly' in the C-17 building process.

LTV Aerospace in Dallas (renamed Vought on 1 September 1992) won the task of manufacturing C-17 engine nacelles, UARRSI (universal aerial refuelling receptacle slipway installation), and tail sections. In addition, a subcontract worth no less than $18.9 million went to LTV's Sierra Division (renamed Sierra Technologies and separated from LTV/Vought on 1 September 1992) to develop a station-keeping system to provide the flight crew with navigational and positioning information. This system was to make it possible for 18 C-17s to fly in formation, regardless of visibility.

Early on, there were delays with the C-17's electronic flight control system (EFCS) which resulted in a contractor change from Honeywell to General Electric. Soon thereafter, an August 1989 report by the General Accounting Office spoke of further C-17 delays, many related to the management of the programme. "[T]he pro-

gramme faced significant schedule, cost, and performance challenges," the report noted. At that point, the $37.5 billion expended on the C-17 made the programme "one of the Department of Defense's largest." The *Washington Post*'s George Wilson conducted an independent analysis of C-17 costs and concluded that each aircraft would set back the US taxpayer $326 million, roughly the tab for 16 AV-8B Harriers or six EA-6B Prowlers.

Above: Forward (left) and aft (right) views of the bare C-17 interior. Of note in the forward view are the obstruction caused by the wing carry-through structure, the stairway leading to the flight deck, and the loadmaster's work station on the starboard side.

Left: Seen being moved into a test facility, 'Static' was one of two ground-test airframes, the other being designated 'Durability'. This aircraft suffered a wing failure while under test.

In April 1988, Pentagon officials acknowledged that the estimated weight of the C-17 had risen 8.2 per cent over original plans, resulting in the aircraft not meeting one of its contractual performance requirements. With the increased weight, the C-17's ferry range would fall from the 4,914 nm (5,651 miles/9095 km) specified in the RFP to less than 4,700 nm (5,405 miles/8700 km). Officials noted, however, that the C-17 would still be able to meet the RFP requirement to carry a 167,000-lb (75750-kg) load an unrefuelled distance of 2,400 miles (3862 km).

In August 1988, Deputy Defense Secretary William Taft IV rebuffed anti-C-17 forces in Congress and the Pentagon by refusing to 'zero' procurement of the new aircraft. Effectively turning back demands that the programme be slashed or terminated, Taft ordered no change in plans which called for 210 airframes, with production to peak at 29 aircraft per year in 1993. At the time, it was noted that the C-17's IOC date – defined as the day a squadron of 12 aircraft was in operation – had slipped from April 1992 to September 1992. This was the latest of numerous delays: IOC was later to be rescheduled for May 1993, then May 1994.

Also in 1988, Pratt & Whitney confirmed a higher-thrust version of the PW2037 engine, now known as the PW2040, providing 41,700-lb (185.5-kN) rather than the 38,250-lb (170.15-kN) originally foreseen.

Production progress

In September 1989, Douglas Vice President Bob Clepper announced that "our goal is to have the wing, center fuselage, forward fuselage and aft fuselage ready to join together by the end of the year [1989] and . . . first flight of the C-17 in December 1990." Again, projecting future dates for achievement of milestones proved an elusive undertaking.

When the 'downsizing' of the US military began in 1990 – not because the Cold War was ending but in recognition of Washington's growing deficit paralysis – Defense Secretary Richard B. Cheney in April 1990 reduced the C-17 requirement from 210 to 120 airframes. Ironically, the decision came just weeks before the biggest airlift in history, Operation Desert Shield, which punctuated the need for strategic airlift capability.

In May 1990, US Air Force officers acknowledged that they had examined, then rejected, an unsolicited proposal from an Allison/Rolls-Royce team calling for the Rolls-Royce RB211-535E4B to be used on the C-17. The Air Force's analysis had been based on a buy of 210 airframes rather than the new figure of 120 and had concluded with the astute finding that "the [Rolls] engine does not fit the C-17's nacelle." In fact, the RB211 is compatible with the C-17 nacelle's size and shape, and discussion of introducing this powerplant at some juncture in the production run continues today.

Another hiccup in the C-17 programme came in August 1990 when the US Air Force suspended a progress payment after the manufacturer failed to deliver its required, semi-annual Estimate At Completion (EAC) report by the scheduled 1 August deadline. In September 1990, the C-17 prototype (87-0025), known as T-1 for its role as a test ship, and minus engines, was moved out of doors at Long Beach, California,

to undergo pressure testing for the structural integrity of its fuselage. Two other test articles, known as T-2 and T-3 and not assigned military serial numbers, are a 'static article' for load testing to verify structural limits and a 'durability article' which will be 'exercised' through two 30,000-hour lifetimes on outdoor equipment.

The manufacturer's EACs grew dramatically in 1991 and the Air Force held back some $266 million in progress payments caused by the overruns.

In August 1991, the Air Force began training crews from the 17th Airlift Squadron, 437th Airlift Wing, Charleston AFB, South Carolina, which is to be the first operational C-17 unit. A simulator was delivered to Charleston. By the start of 1992, the 17th AS began relinquishing its C-141B StarLifters. The squadron was then scheduled to receive its first aircraft, P-6 (89-1192) in February 1993 (subsequently changed to May). To practise assault landings, something it never did with its C-141Bs, the Charleston wing constructed an unpaved airstrip measuring 90 ft by 3,500 ft (27.86 m by 1067 m) at the oddly-named town of North, South Carolina, and also prepared to practise at the Holland LZ (landing zone) at Fort Bragg, North Carolina. One of the first Charleston pilots, Major Larry Kudelka, was favourably impressed by the C-17 flight test programme. "Once we got this thing into the air, we've been proceeding without a glitch from one milestone to the next," Kudelka claimed. An outside review of the flight test programme by the GAO confirms that it has been remarkably smooth.

Above: Final assembly of the C-17 is entrusted to the Douglas Long Beach plant, although components are manufactured by several subcontractors. Shown outside are P-1 and P-2, the first two production aircraft.

Above: The main undercarriage of the C-17 is housed in low-drag fairings, which preserve as nearly as possible the circularity of the frontal cross-section.

Below: P-1 seen during its maiden flight on 18 May 1992, streaming a calibration cone on a wire from the fin-tip.

On 15 September 1991, after at least the fourth delay, T-1 made its first flight, taking off from Long Beach Airport and flying to Edwards Air Force Base. The C-17's maiden flight was piloted by William Casey, with Lieutenant Colonel George London as co-pilot, Ted Venturini as loadmaster, and Henry van de Gradd as flight test engineer. London was a member of the 6510th Test Wing at Edwards, which formed a C-17 Task Force and has carried out most developmental flying.

A major problem with the C-17 programme emerged on 1 October 1991 when the 'static test article' had a wing structural failure under much less demanding conditions than had been foreseen. The test was a simulation of load conditions with vertical gusts of 55 ft (16.7 m) per second at an altitude of approximately 32,000 ft (9750 m) at a speed of 275 kt (315 mph; 508 km/h) with a heavy weight of 585,000 lb (265350 kg). These were conditions not likely to be encountered often in the real world, if at all, but are at least theoretically possible for a heavily-laden C-17 which has just refuelled in flight.

Structural setback

The structural failure of the wing is by far the most serious problem confronting the Globemaster III today. 437th Airlift Wing Commander Brigadier General Thomas Mikolajcik acknowledged that "we're going to have to see a resolution of the structural problem before we can bring [the C-17] on line." Mikolajcik also said he is pleased with the training of future C-17 crew members of his 17th Airlift Squadron "which has been ticking like a Swiss watch." An industry source confirmed soon after the structural failure that Douglas had started to repair the 'static test article' and will add 600 to 700 lb (272 to 317 kg) to the structure of the aircraft wing (aluminium stinger segments and steel strap reinforcements), and stiffen ribs and spars in several areas of the wing. This will add one per cent to the wing's total weight of 60,000 lb (27215 kg) and seems unlikely to raise new questions about the C-17's weight.

As part of a series of range/payload demonstration flights, six USMC LAVs were carried, including one on the full-strength rear ramp.

On 17 October 1991, the C-17's FBW system failed on the 11th flight of the T-1 test aircraft. The mechanical backup system functioned. The incident pointed to a need for software changes, which were made.

On 17 January 1992, T-1 reached the 100-hour flight test milestone on its 35th mission at Edwards. During its first 100 hours, the C-17 had reached a maximum speed of Mach 0.83 and an altitude of 35,000 ft (10670 m). Flying qualities were demonstrated as low as 4,000 ft (1220 m) and at air speeds as slow as 83 kt (95 mph; 153 km/h). Simulated engine-out approaches and go-arounds were performed by shutting down an engine on approach and restarting it in the air, using both JP-4 and JP-8 fuel.

T-1 was the only C-17 painted in Europe One, or 'lizard green', the camouflage colour used by Military Airlift Command (which became Air Mobility Command on 1 June 1992) until the time of its flight test programme.

The first production C-17 (88-0265), which was also the second aircraft built, known as P-1, made its first flight from Long Beach to Edwards

on 19 May 1992. Painted in the new 'AMC proud grey' colour scheme, P-1 was assigned to developmental work on the C-17's ability to operate from unpaved airstrips.

The cargo door and ramp of the C-17 were opened in flight for the first time at Edwards on 17 June 1992. The door was opened and closed smoothly at 10,000 ft (3050 m) and airspeed of 200 kt (230 mph; 370 km/h). This and subsequent tests have validated the Globemaster III's capability for airdrop and LAPES work.

Soon afterward came the maiden flight of the second production aircraft (88-0266), or P-2, on 20 June 1992. The only C-17 painted in a high-gloss version of 'MAC proud grey' rather than the semi-gloss adopted by AMC, P-2 carried additional avionics as compared to T-1 and P-1 and was thus a genuine production aircraft.

Following this flight, there began a flight test programme which has been carried out with remarkable efficiency. The 6510th at Edwards began a step-by-step exploration of the C-17's flight capabilities. Unlike the development programme which preceded it, the flight test programme has met virtually every scheduled milestone.

Programme milestones

Aircraft P-3 (89-1189) made its first flight on 7 September 1992. One of the Edwards' runways was closed for repairs over the holiday (Labor Day) weekend, so Douglas obtained permission to land on the dry lake bed for the first time.

In late 1992, an M60 main battle tank became the first tracked vehicle to be loaded on a C-17 in tests at Edwards. The 91,000-lb (41280-kg) vehicle was tied down aboard P-1, which had tufts on the aft end of its fuselage to analyse airflow patterns. Flights were carried out with the M60 on board. A few weeks later, in early 1993, P-4 went to Fort Hood, Texas, for a prolonged demonstration of loading capabilities which included some flights with heavy cargoes.

The fifth C-17 Globemaster III, and fourth production ship, P-4 (89-1190), made its maiden flight on 9 December 1992. P-5 (89-1191) followed with its first flight on 31 January 1993, and is scheduled to go to NAS Patuxent River, Maryland, for lightning and electromagnetic interference tests. By the time this account appears in print, P-6 will also be flying.

The Globemaster III name, honouring the earlier C-74 and C-124 manufactured by Douglas, was applied to the C-17 on 5 February 1993 by AMC chief General Ronald R. Fogleman. The christening occurred days after a C-17 completed a 2,750-mile (4425-km) non-stop, non-refuelled west-to-east crossing of the United States followed by a 2,500-mile (4025-km) leg with a 160,000-lb (72580-kg) payload. The appellation may be fitting, but even the naming of the C-17 was not without its moments.

Although strategic airlift is the principal mission of the C-17, the aircraft's ability to operate into austere sites is welcome in many scenarios. Demonstrating a lakebed landing is P-3 at the completion of its first flight. Note the split rudder arrangement.

P-1 passes over the Rogers Dry Lake landing strip used by the Shuttle. Central to the STOL ability of the C-17 are the flaps, which are blown with exhaust to produce a vectored stream of jet thrust.

In 1983, Douglas quietly named the future C-17 the Loadmaster. This nickname fits Douglas's style for naming transports (C-5 Skymaster, C-118 Liftmaster, C-133 Cargomaster, etc.). It would also have provided tribute to the superb enlisted men and women who work behind the flight deck on AMC's airlifters, among the most important people in the Air Force and the least recognised. Nobody was going to get away with naming history's third most expensive aircraft after an enlisted person, particularly not in the 'me' 1980s, and, as an AMC officer acknowledges, "the generals (none of whom had ever been a loadmaster) didn't like the idea, so eventually [it] died."

AMC's predecessor Military Airlift Command then held a couple of 'name the plane' contests which got nowhere, although MAC commander General Duane Cassiday wanted to name the C-17 Champion. His successor, General H. T. Johnson, wanted to call it the Pegasus (a name which already belongs to the US Navy's Beech T-44A but, because of its obvious handicap, is rarely used) but was warned of possible copyright infringement with the commercial rocket used to launch satellites dropped from a B-52. There was also a concern that it was too close to the Lockheed tradition of using constellations and characters from Greek mythology. When Fogleman replaced Johnson, the US Air Force had just embarked on its 'global reach, global power' theme (AMC airlifters use the radio callsign REACH), so Globemaster III became inevitable. One colonel at AMC headquarters supported, in vain, Loadmaster II. "The 'real' name will be selected by the crews who fly the C-17," this colonel points out. "I suspect that the same spirit that brought us 'Aardvark' and 'Warthog' will be evident. I hope it is more flattering than 'Fat Albert' [an unofficial handle for the C-5]!"

The first three production C-17s make their way to the Edwards runway. Such a scene will become commonplace as the Globemaster III becomes operational from 1994 onwards.

As the US embarks on further force reductions in the 1990s, while at the same time intervening in locations as disparate as Bosnia and Somalia, the C-17 Globemaster III will benefit from the fact that President Clinton supports the programme. Except for the wing structural problem, most of the C-17's difficulties have been solved or have become history. The deterioration of the C-141 fleet and the absence of any visible alternative to the C-17 are convincing reasons why the planned buy of 120 aircraft will probably continue.

Five years ago, Douglas invested heavily in a planned EC-17 airborne command post to replace the Air Force's EC-135 Stratotanker fleet. This and other specialised versions of the C-17 are now unlikely to materialise (the EC-135s are being replaced by surplus E-6A Mercuries). While Douglas believes there is some potential for further sales, including some export sales, it is unlikely that the C-17 will ever appear in the same numbers as its predecessors.

Serial numbers

T-1 87-0025 first flight 15 September 1991; Edwards AFB

P-1 88-0265 used for structural tests at 100 per cent load prior to first flight; made first flight 19 May 1992; used for flight tests in which manoeuvres conducted to create loads measured by instrumentation on the aircraft; Edwards AFB

P-2 88-0266 first flight 20 June 1992; additional avionics compared with T-1, P-1; different grey than AF adopted; Edwards AFB

P-3 89-1189 first flight 7 September 1992; to Eglin for climatic hangar tests

P-4 89-1190 first flight 9 December 1992; to Fort Hood, Texas, in February 1993 for loading demonstrations

P-5 89-1191 first flight 31 January 1993; in February 1993 on ramp for electromagnetic testing, to go to Patuxent River for lightning tests

P-6 89-1192

Third production lot:
P-7 90-0532
P-8 90-0533
P-9 90-0534
P-10 90-0535

Fourth production lot:
P-11
P-12
P-13
P-14

General Dynamics F-111

The 'Earth Pig'

Much of the F-111's career has been surrounded by controversy, but in its 'middle age' it has proved to be the king of the low-level strikers, unmatched in its combination of blistering speed, long range, terrain-hugging ability, smoothness of ride, sturdiness, heavy warload and accuracy of delivery. Happiest with its characteristic snout right down in the mud, the 'Aardvark' remains a key element in the offensive capabilities of the United States and Australia.

Often criticised, or at best misunderstood, by politicians, military commanders and journalists alike, the F-111 has nevertheless engendered a huge amount of respect from the ground and air crew who fly and maintain the aircraft. It has certainly commanded more than passing respect from the group who matter the most: enemy defences.

Left: F-117 'Stealth Fighters' claim to own the night, but the F-111 crews would dispute that. The nature of the F-111's impressive avionics suite suits it perfectly to nocturnal activities, one of the very few aircraft to be able to operate to its full capability no matter what the weather or time of day.

Main picture: There are few more awe-inspiring experiences than witnessing an 'Aardvark' pulling g at low level and high speed. An air show favourite for many years has been 'torching' – dumping fuel from the tailcone fuel vent into the hot jet gases, as demonstrated here by an F-111E of the Edwards-based 6510th Test Wing.

Left: Breathing new life into tired airframes, the Raven programme provided the USAF with a unique jamming platform that can fly the same mission profiles as the strike aircraft it is assigned to protect. Few USAF combat operations would now be contemplated without the protective umbrella of the 'Spark Vark'.

General Dynamics F-111

Bottom: The third aircraft graphically displays the unique and revolutionary arrangement of the world's first swing-wing combat aircraft.

Below: The prototype rolled out at Fort Worth a few weeks ahead of the 'official' date of 16 October 1964. Its first flight was on 21 December, with Dick Johnson and Val Prahl.

Last of the Century Series fighters, the F-111 is one of the oldest tactical aircraft in the US Air Force inventory. As it reaches the twilight of its career, 25 years after entering operational service in July 1968, surprisingly few people, even within the Air Force, understand its capabilities and limitations. Designed to combine the range and payload of the B-66 with the speed and (relative) manoeuvrability of the F-105, the F-111 remains unmatched in its ability to deliver large bomb loads at long range, high speed and low altitude, at night and in any weather. Because of these attributes, current plans call for it to remain in service for perhaps another 20 years.

In the late 1950s it was discovered that most aerodynamic problems encountered by experimental variable geometry aircraft, such as the Bell X-5 (based on the German P.1101 design) and Grumman XF10F-1, could be alleviated by using dual pivot points placed outboard of the fuselage. Rather than build another experimental aircraft to explore the practical aspects of this theoretical breakthrough, the Air Force used it as the basis for Specific Operational Requirement (SOR) 183 (issued on 14 June 1960), calling for a tactical fighter specialising in nuclear strike missions. This new design was to have an unrefuelled range of 3,300 nm (3,795 miles; 6107 km), the ability to dash for 400 nm (460 miles; 740 km) at Mach 1.2, and be capable of using 'unprepared' airfields.

At the same time, the Navy was developing a new fleet air defence fighter. The fixed-wing Douglas F6D Missileer was to be a subsonic aircraft with good loiter capability which would rely on its Eagle missiles to engage the enemy. Partly because its large radar dictated a wide fuselage, it was to feature side-by-side seating similar to the Douglas F3D Skyknight. As the Eisenhower administration ended in December 1960, the F6D was cancelled because the design was seen as a step backward from the F-4 it was intended to replace.

The new Kennedy administration's Secretary of Defense, Robert Strange McNamara, saw an opportunity to save money by using the same airplane to fulfil both the Navy and Air Force missions. Three weeks after taking office, on 14 February 1961, he ordered a study to determine the feasibility of using a design based on SOR 183 to perform close air support (CAS), air superiority, and long-range interdiction missions. By May 1961 the CAS mission was split off into a separate programme which resulted in the LTV Corsair II, while the remaining requirements were to be satisfied by a single bi-service design (led by the Air Force) which was called the tactical fighter, experimental (TFX).

McNamara ordered development of the TFX on 7 June 1961, Air Force and Navy attempts to dissuade him proving

unsuccessful. The two services could not agree on compatible requirements, which resulted in McNamara himself setting the design's basic characteristics in September 1961, with a request for proposals (RFP) being issued in October 1961, calling for initial operational capability (IOC) to be reached by October 1965.

There followed four design competitions, all of which were won by Boeing. Howls of protest were heard in the Pentagon on 24 November 1962 when McNamara overruled everyone and decreed that the team of General Dynamics (GD) and Grumman would build the TFX. The main stated reason was the greater commonality of GD's design, although the political benefits of having it built in then-Vice President Johnson's home state probably did no harm.

After its award, the TFX became known as the F-111. On 21 December 1964 the Air Force's F-111A flew for the first time from GD's Fort Worth, Texas, plant. The Navy's F-111B followed on 18 May 1965 from Grumman's Bethpage, New York, facility. What followed was one of the most painful and controversial development programmes ever endured by the American military: not only were the aircraft overweight and over budget, they did not work.

Today, one of the more readily visible results of McNamara's involvement with the programme is the fact that the F-111 never received an official name (although for a while it was derisively known as 'McNamara's Folly'). While the public has grown fond of the name 'Aardvark' (the nocturnal African mammal with a long snout and heavy tail), the F-111 is generally known to crews as 'Earth Pig', 'Vark', or simply 'One-Eleven'. Despite several 'name-the-plane' contests, no other name was ever adopted and the Air Force leadership seems resigned to these monikers. The EF-111A, which did receive the official name 'Raven', is commonly called the 'Spark Vark'.

Navy interceptor

The F-111 introduced a number of radical innovations to combat aircraft, including variable-geometry wings, terrain-following radar, and afterburning turbofan engines. Three features were insisted upon by the Navy: the crew escape capsule, side-by-side seating and the weapons bay. Including these made the F-111B so big that the Navy was able to extricate itself from the programme after spending $238 million on seven airframes (in its day, this caused every bit as big a stink as today's B-2). In the process, the design went through four weight reduction programmes which reduced its vaunted commonality with the Air Force version from 80 per cent to less than 30 per cent.

Like the Douglas F6D Missileer it replaced, the F-111B was not designed for classical air-to-air combat, but rather to engage the enemy from up to 100 nm (115 miles; 185 km) away with AIM-54 Phoenix missiles. Its targets would be tracked by the AWG-9 radar system (which could track up to 24 at a time), with missiles being launched against as many as six. After the demise of the F-111B programme on 10 July 1968, several of the seven completed aircraft served as testbeds for

the AWG-9/AIM-54 weapon system. Three of the seven F-111Bs crashed, with the loss of four lives. The last aircraft were retired in May 1971.

Congress gave the go ahead for the Navy fighter, experimental (VFX) programme, which became the Grumman F-14 Tomcat, simultaneously with cancelling the F-111B. It used the F-111B's AWG-9/AIM-54 armament and TF30 engines in an airframe which was smaller and lighter by virtue of its use of ejection seats and tandem seating, as well as the deletion of the weapons bay.

Air Force 'Aardvarks'

From the outset, the F-111 was really an Air Force aircraft. The F-111A emerged powered by the TF30-P-3 engine and a basic avionics package (described later). The FB-111A version for Strategic Air Command was tailored for the long-range nuclear penetration role, and had long-span wings for extra range, strengthened undercarriage and partially revised avionics. The next Tactical Air Command variant was the F-111E, which was essentially similar to the F-111A apart

Above: No less than 28 pre-production F-111As undertook the massive and frustrating evaluation process. Despite the problems, the F-111 showed its enormous promise, as evidenced here by a test-drop of 16 Mk 82 low-drag bombs.

Left: The long-span wings of the Navy's F-111B version are readily apparent, as is the much shorter nose radome. Carrier trials took place aboard USS Coral Sea in late 1968.

Below: The F-111B was surprisingly well-suited to carrier operations, posing no problems during launch, approach or deck/hangar handling. However, by the time of the trials the programme was virtually dead, and the aircraft redirected to AWG-9/AIM-54 testing for the forthcoming F-14 programme. Finally retired in May 1971, the four survivors languished on Navy dumps (below left).

Above: On daylight missions, the F-111 has occasionally been used as a bomb-leader, taking along less sophisticated aircraft on bombing missions and supplying drop commands to increase firepower. Here a 366th TFW machine leads a pair of F-4Ds.

Right: As applied to the F-111, the three-tone South East Asia camouflage proved highly effective, as demonstrated by this 4427th TFRS D model. 'Aardvarks' skipped the European One generation of schemes, progressing straight to all-over grey in the early 1990s.

from modified air inlets and some minor improvements to the nav/attack system. Next came the F-111D, which featured uprated TF30-P-9 engines and a completely new and far more capable avionics system. Finally, the F-111F introduced the very powerful TF30-P-100 engine, but was reduced in its avionics capability compared to the D model. However, it was this model which proved the most attractive in terms of updating, and is now the principal operational variant.

Crew escape capsule

Two of the three requirements the Navy had insisted upon were embodied in the side-by-side seating crew escape capsule. Another radical departure from the traditions of fighter design, the capsule has an undeserved reputation for not working. While it may not always work exactly right, it does not fail at a greater rate than ejection seats, and has many advantages. F-111 crews never wear parachute harnesses or the dreaded anti-exposure ('poopy') suit, much to the envy of

Below: A desert affair – F-111As from the 366th TFW at Mountain Home close on a Utah ANG tanker high over the Great Basin. In terms of optimum refuelling speeds, the F-111 is one of the fastest receivers in the Air Force at over 300 kt.

other fighter pilots. The capsule floats, and even has a bilge pump (operated by pumping either stick fore and aft) for use in the event of a leak. The capsule contains a large quantity of survival gear. However, recognising the need to get away from the capsule in a hurry in a combat situation, a 'hit-and-run' mini-survival kit was included. This was contained in a small, triangular-shaped box located above the WSO's seat in the F-111D/F and above the AC's seat in other versions.

Operating in the high-speed, low-level regime exposes the F-111 to very high aerodynamic pressures, known to engineers as 'high-Q'. To bail out at high-Q using an ejection seat usually leads to what are politely known as 'flailing injuries', which can (and have) resulted in death by traumatic amputation from wind blast. The escape capsule protects the F-111 crew from this grisly fate. Perhaps the most remarkable escape from a 'Vark' was a Cannon-based F-111D crew on a functional check flight (FCF). When the jet started rolling uncontrollably at Mach 2, they 'punched out' and lived to fly another day.

The down side of the escape capsule concept is landing. Ejecting the whole cockpit means slowing a very large mass to an impact velocity compatible with human survival. Over the years the capsule has increased in weight, meaning that hitting the ground in one is equivalent to jumping off a two-story building sitting in a kitchen chair – not something to be contemplated lightly. As the weight increased, so did back injuries (compression fractures), until it became necessary to improve the parachute design. The first choice was a triple-chute design, similar to that used by Apollo spacecraft. Unfortunately, these parachutes tended to open (and rip apart) in succession. To preclude damaging aircrew morale, the design was changed to a single parachute made of Kevlar allowing it to be thinner (and larger) yet still fitting into the same space as the old one. This design promises to cut back injuries by reducing the impact to the equivalent of jumping off (only) a one-and-a-half storey building in a kitchen chair.

Another complication with the capsule is the necessity of requalifying its ejection characteristics whenever a change of equipment causes a significant change in centre of gravity. This requires ejecting a capsule from a rocket sled to make sure it still works, an expensive proposition not suffered by ejection seats. Also, the combined and differential weights of F-111 crews are limited to ensure the capsule ejects as it should.

Operationally, the side-by-side seating arrangement enhances crew co-ordination during task-saturated portions of the mission, such as night/in-weather low-level navigation and target attack. The canopy frame is very robust, with the centre frame between the seats a collection of handles for the escape system, lights and air vents. The combination of side-by-side seating and extensive canopy structure has obvious visibility disadvantages, the most notable being a 'blind cone' behind the jet from the 5 to 7 o'clock position. Instead of 'Checking Six' like other fighters, F-111s 'Check 4:30 and 7:30'.

Despite the F-111's primarily nocturnal mission, daytime operations are practised extensively. These have proved convincingly that the mutual support provided by tactical formations is vital in offsetting the visibility and manoeuvrability limitations of the aircraft. Typical formations include line-abreast and wedge. Line-abreast provides optimum mutual support by allowing each aircraft to check behind the other for enemy aircraft. (Two line-abreast elements in trail are known as a battle box.) The wedge formation trades mutual support for better element manoeuvrability. Both formations are practised first as two-ship elements, then in three- and four-ship flights. During exercises like Red, Green and Maple Flag, these formations form the heart of mixed 'gorilla' packages (incorporating dedicated fighter-escort, electronic jamming, and defence suppression aircraft) to practise the best overall solution to the problem of daytime survivability.

The unimportance of the daytime mission to the F-111 as viewed by the decision-making levels of the Air Force is best illustrated by the failure to fund a modern HUD, or a programme to calibrate each HUD/ODS for distortions in its aircraft's windscreen, as was done with the F-16. In practice, F-111s have rarely been employed in daylight except in low-threat situations with nil threat from enemy fighters. For the most part, this beast only comes out at night.

Swing wings and fancy flight controls

The F-111 was the first operational aircraft to employ variable-geometry, or swing, wings. With 20/20 hindsight, it has been convincingly argued that the aerodynamic location of the wings was incorrect (something that an 'X' aircraft might have discovered). Certainly, the interaction between the wings, fuselage and air inlets caused serious developmental problems.

Variable geometry is ideal for an attack aircraft, having several advantages over fixed wings. Fully spread, they shorten take-off and landing rolls while improving low-speed handling qualities. Intermediate positions reduce drag and maximise range, while providing a rock-solid bombing platform. In the fully swept position, they offer high-speed flight with minimal fuel consumption and good supersonic handling characteristics. Unlike the later F-14A which has an auto-sweep capability, all F-111 wing sweeping is initiated manually by the AC, through use of a pistol-grip control which slides forward and aft under the left canopy railing.

Despite the aerodynamic benefits of swing wings, there were natural suspicions about this radical innovation. These increased dramatically in late December 1969, when a wing separated from an F-111A during recovery from a dive bomb

Above: Flying in the 'soup' presents no difficulties to the experienced F-111 crew, such are the capabilities of the avionics suite.

Left: Strategic Air Command's FB-111s were immediately recognisable by virtue of a unique camouflage, long-span wings and the characteristic blister on the nose forward of the cockpit, which housed the astro-tracker.

Far left: This view of a Pakistani Shenyang F-6 running an intercept on an F-111E serves to illustrate the restricted rearwards view in the F-111. In a combat situation at this altitude, the One-Eleven would open the taps and be in a different country from the MiG by now!

Below: For a period during the gear retraction cycle, the F-111 fights the drag of the wheel well door.

Right: An F-111F from the 48th TFW approaches a KC-10 tanker. The refuelling receptacle is located behind the cockpit, to port of the centreline. KC-10s were used to support Lakenheath 'Varks' during the 1986 raids on Libya.

Below: A feature of the swing-wing design is the glove vanes, which angle downwards in the high-lift regime to improve airflow over the wing/glove region.

attack. The entire F-111 fleet was grounded for seven months while the problem (eventually determined to be shoddy sub-contracting) was located and fixed. Although wings have been known to unintentionally depart fixed-wing aircraft, because the F-111's wings were designed to move, it gained an undeserved reputation of having 'wings that fall off'.

With roughly the same wing area as the F-15, but nearly twice its weight, F-111 wing loading is far higher than any other modern fighter, resulting in relatively low instantaneous and sustained turn rates. Because of this, it uses raw speed as its primary defence. An Iraqi 'Fulcrum' pilot discovered during Desert Storm just how effective this defence can·be as he tried to convert on (get behind) the leader of a four-ship of 'Varks' in a trail formation. He ended up as 'number five' in a futile tail-chase of the last of the F-111Fs.

The wings have full-span slats and double-slotted flaps. They sweep back into the top of the fuselage and are covered by large panels called 'overwing fairings'. These fairings are hinged at the front, lifting up during supersonic or high-*g* flight to equalise air pressure within the fuselage/wing cavity.

Flight control

Roll control is provided by two sets of fly-by-wire (having no mechanical backup) spoilers, another F-111 operational 'first'. The inboard set is 'locked down' when the wings are swept past 45°, while the outboards are locked at 47°. As the spoilers are locked down, the all-moving tailplane assumes more responsibility for roll control. Because the tailplane is not nearly as effective as the spoilers at the speeds associated with most attack profiles, the wings are seldom swept past 44°. In the early 1980s, one crew learned the hard way how important the spoilers are. While participating in an exercise at the Otterburn bombing range in northern England, they performed a 'pop-up' manoeuvre to position themselves for an angular bombing pass. With their speed still high, they rolled inverted and 'pulled down' to their desired dive angle. Having 'bled off' airspeed as they aligned themselves with the target (and forgetting that the wings were swept past 45°), when they tried to roll upright the airplane responded very sluggishly, while continuing toward the ground at an alarming rate. Proving once again the old fighter pilot axiom that "I'd rather be lucky than good," they pulled out of the

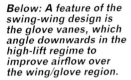

Scotland bomber! F-111s from both Upper Heyford and Lakenheath were active most days over the bombing ranges of northern England and Scotland, notably Tain range on the banks of Dornoch Firth and Spadeadam electronic warfare range in Northumberland. On their way to and from the ranges, the low-level art was practised through the fells and mountains. Lakenheath produced a patch for veterans of these realistic training missions (above).

bombing run 4 ft (1.2 m) from the ground (based on a ground observation). Shaken, but alive, they never again forgot to check their wing sweep.

The F-111 was designed with very sophisticated flight controls (for the 1960s). Contained in five separate computers, not only were commands from the terrain-following radar and navigation computers incorporated to permit hands-off low-level penetration, the changes in trim caused by sweeping the wings were automatically compensated for by a

Above: A flight of F-111s graphically demonstrates the variable-geometry wings in a party-piece fly-past. Note that the weapons pylons also change angle to match the wing-sweep.

Above left: With wings in the most common mid-sweep position, an F-111F barrels in on the photo-ship, illustrating the considerable area of the Triple Plow II intakes.

Left: A 'red-tail' from Lakenheath's 494th TFS banks over during a transit flight at medium altitude. On the inner pylon it carries a baggage pod, a converted napalm canister with side-loading door.

General Dynamics F-111

'parallel trim' system. Because of this system, there was no sensation of wing movement. The flight controls were so effective at compensating for changes in configuration that F-111s have lost pieces of airframe and suffered damage (such as accidentally cutting power lines with their wings), without the crew even noticing. The flight controls had to be manually checked on the ground, unlike the later F-14A, which had automatic checks. These time-consuming but vital checks could be disconcerting for the uninitiated, as they made the aircraft shudder and shake.

All F-111s were constructed with provisions for four pylons fixed for carriage at 26° of wing sweep. Of these, only the inboard fixed pylons were used operationally, and only by FB-111As for carriage of two extra 600-Imp gal (2727-litre) external fuel tanks (explaining the 'pigeon-toed' appearance of some FB-111A fuel tanks on take-off). Other versions only used the four movable inboard pylons, with external tank carriage being limited to F-111Cs, F-111Es and F-111Fs (and only from the outboard pylons). Operationally, fuel tanks would probably only be used in conjunction with AGM-69A SRAMs (on FB-111As only) or B61 nuclear weapons on the inboard pylons. As training aircraft, FB-111As modified as F-111Gs no longer carried any tanks (although they did retain the FB-111A pylons, which were pointed at the front and more sharply angled at the back than those found on other F-111s).

The FB-111A, F-111B and F-111C featured wingspans extended by 7 ft (2.1 m) which improved aircraft aspect ratio (and therefore range) at the price of somewhat reduced manoeuvrability. These aircraft had longer wing spars than the tactical F-111s, which had provisions for bolt-on ferry wingtips to provide similar improvements to their range. Although the ferry tips looked like the longer wings, since they had no spar they imposed severe manoeuvrability constraints. In any event, they never appear to have been used operationally.

Wing settings

When parked, the F-111's wings are usually either swept back to 54° or forward to 16° with the flaps at 35° and slats extended (the stabilizers 'droop' until supplied with hydraulic pressure during engine start). The wings are set to 16° during the ground checks, and normally to 54° for taxi. Prior to take-off they are again put to 16° with the slats down and the flaps at 25°. At this time the 'ground roll spoiler' switch is activated, raising the spoilers whenever both throttles are in idle. This feature kills lift and shortens the ground roll during landings or take-off aborts. Take-off is at about 160 kt (183 mph; 295 km/h), and the wings are quickly 'cleaned up' and swept to 26° for climb-out, initial cruise and/or air refuelling. The most common sweep settings for low level are 35° or 44°, with the latter being standard for 'toss' weapon deliveries. Depending on the amount of fuel remaining, landing approaches are normally flown at slightly lower speeds than take-off, with the sweep set at 16-20°, slats down and flaps at 35° (25° if single engine). After landing, the ground roll spoiler switch is deactivated and the wings swept to 54° for taxi back to parking. (Incidentally, the anti-collision lights are turned on and off at the same time as the ground roll spoiler switch. While normally used throughout the flight, they are turned off prior to combat, automatically retracting into the top and bottom of the fuselage.) Also turned off prior

to night combat are the electro-luminescent 'strip-lights', fitted during the early 1980s to provide better visual references for night formation flying.

The FB-111A/F-111G, F-111C, F-111D and F-111F had stronger undercarriages than earlier models. The FB-111A/F-111G also had much larger brakes (which made the depth of their wheels much shallower) in anticipation of carrying much larger payloads than the tactical versions. The interior of the speedbrake door on all versions was gloss red with black anti-skid strips over the areas rounded out for the tyres. The aft main gear door was originally designed to align parallel to the fuselage when extended. In 1975 this door was attached to the gear strut, thus making it mount perpendicular to the fuselage when the gear was extended. To do this, the back of the door was cut off, making it only 28.5 in (72 cm) long.

Increased speed

The F-111's Pratt & Whitney TF30 engines give it superior fuel efficiency in the low-altitude, high-speed regime (better than the F-15E's F100 engines). When flown with stable power settings the engines seldom stall, despite their poor reputation in this regard with the F-14A community. However, when they do, it is usually accompanied by a loud bang that is not soon forgotten, and the mission for the day is aborted.

Different versions of the F-111 have had different engines. The earlier F-111A, F/RF-111C, and F-111E versions had a total of about 37,000 lb (165 kN) of thrust (not much more than the much smaller F-4). The FB-111A/F-111G increased this to nearly 41,000 lb (183 kN), the F-111D to nearly 42,000 lb (186 kN), and the F-111F to over 50,000 lb (222 kN), one third more powerful than the original engines. Although the noise level on the ground near an F-111 is deafening, in the cockpit it is no worse than a commercial airliner, with the loudest noise being the cooling fans for the avionics.

As the F-111Es are transferred to Cannon the more powerful F-111D engines will be fitted, as has already happened with the EF-111As. It should be noted that the value of increased thrust in the later versions is seen in take-off, acceleration and air-refuelling performance, rather than in range, speed or payload. The FB-111A/F-111G had a different boattail fairing from the other variants mounted between the

engine exhausts.

As mentioned earlier, the stalls caused by the interface between the wing, fuselage and inlets caused one of the biggest design challenges of the F-111 programme. Operational F/EF-111As, F/RF-111Cs, the first FB-111A (67-0159) and the cancelled F-111Ks were fitted with Triple Plow I inlets, which featured 20 vortex generators inside the inlets and hydraulically translated cowls. The second FB-111A (67-0160) and some F-111Bs were fitted with Super Plow inlets, which replaced the translating cowls with double 'blow-in' doors. The remaining FB-111A/F-111Gs, as well as all F-111D/E/Fs, were fitted with Triple Plow II inlets, which featured triple 'blow-in' doors, increased the inlet area by 10 per cent, increased the separation between the inlets and fuselage, removed the external splitter panel, and featured inlet spikes 18 in (46 cm) longer than those of the Triple Plow I. The increased frontal area and slightly less efficient blow-in doors gave the Triple Plow II aircraft a slightly slower top speed than those equipped with Triple Plow Is. However, the operational implications of this were nil when compared with the advantages of having more powerful engines with fewer compressor stalls, especially considering how seldom the aircraft used their supersonic capability. The fuselage of

Above: . . . but with power on, the well-known torch effect is created. US crews are banned from this wasteful and potentially hazardous pastime, but the Australians continue to produce the spectacular party trick at selected air shows.

Below: An evening take-off highlights the burner tail of an F-111F, which features a bright plume from the bottom of the jetpipe. The aircraft is configured with GBU-15s and correspondent AXQ-14 datalink pod.

Top: The broad slab-like back of the 'Aardvark' is readily apparent as this thirsty FB-111A approaches the tanker.

Above: A change to the camouflage scheme gave rise to the 'Dark Vark' nickname for the FB-111s. Here an aircraft accompanies an F-16 during an exercise in Korea.

Right: During their long career in Europe, the F-111Fs of the 48th TFW visited and exercised from air bases throughout NATO. This aircraft is seen during an exercise at Incirlik in Turkey.

Triple Plow II aircraft angles back ever so slightly at the inlets to create more room between the two structures. These aircraft also feature a small, round inlet between the engine inlet and the fuselage. Finally, the F-111D/E/F and FB-111A all have a pattern of grey and/or fibreglass-brown panels of radar-absorbing material (RAM) on the interior of their inlets.

Although primarily known for its performance at low altitude, clean F-111s have exceeded at least Mach 2.5 (with tales of Mach 2.7) above 40,000 ft (12190 m), though this is not realistic with a combat load. Flying supersonically at low level is rarely done, although it is very impressive. There is not any indication that the jet has gone supersonic other than the Mach indicator, and the fact that things are going past very quickly. Normally, the aircraft is only flown supersonically at medium altitudes during air combat training. Sustained high-speed runs are only accomplished during periodic FCFs, which have been known to blister paint and sometimes rip small pieces of skin or antennas from the aircraft. To illustrate just how clean the F-111 is aerodynamically (despite how it looks on the ground) F-111Fs with about one-third of their fuel remaining and no pylons have been 'super-cruised' (i.e., flown supersonically without using afterburner) quite nicely at sea level, with the wings swept all the way back.

No one really knows how fast a clean F-111 will go, its limit speed being determined by surface heating. Each F-111 has a timer which starts automatically when the aircraft surface temperature reaches a certain level. When the timer reaches 300 seconds, it is time to slow down or melt the canopy. Very few crews have ever started the timer; none have seen it get even close to its limit, or seen the aircraft stop accelerating. The F-111 is capable of Mach 1.2+ at low level, and one unofficial study indicated that a formation of supersonic 'Earth Pigs' could cause more damage by sonic boom over-pressure than they could by dropping bombs (this tactic is not used because it would amount to targeting civilians). Practically speaking, typical ingress and attack speeds for a combat-loaded F-111 range from 510-570 kt (585-654 mph; 942-1053 km/h). At its normal, peacetime training speed of 480 kt

(551 mph; 886 km/h), the F-111 compares to the typical family car by travelling over 9 miles (14.5 km) per minute at 0.3 miles per gallon (0.1 km/litre).

Prior to engine start, the blow-in doors/movable cowls are closed, opening as the engines power up and suck them open. They remain open until after take-off, when sufficient air can be provided by the intakes alone. After landing they again open to increase the air available to the engines during ground operations. The nozzle of the engine shut down first will remain fully open, while the other will partially close. This is because the engine shut down last loses hydraulic power too fast to open the nozzle.

Deeper penetration

The F-111 has an internal fuel capacity of over 5,000 US gal (19000 litres). At 32,500 lb (14742 kg), the fuel load alone weighs more than a combat-configured F-16. The internal fuel can be augmented on selected versions with pairs of 600-US gal (2271-litre) external fuel tanks, plus another 585 US gal (2214 litres) split between two rarely used weapons bay, or 'Tokyo', fuel tanks. Optimum cruise altitude with a combat load is about 25,000 ft (7620 m). When necessary, in-flight refuelling is accomplished nearer 20,000 ft (6100 m). When it is necessary to 'top off', minimum afterburner is usually selected on one engine to keep the jet from 'falling off the boom' (inadvertently disconnecting from the tanker). Refuelling is followed by low-level ingress, target attack, low-level egress, and climb-out to return to base at around 30,000 ft (9140 m).

Its fuel capacity gives the F-111 a range unmatched by any other tactical aircraft. With internal fuel only, an unrefuelled combat sortie about 2.5 hours long is possible. Using a high-low-high mission profile, with half the mission being flown at low level, this results in a combat radius of between 500-600 nm (575-690 miles; 925-1110 km). When carrying higher-drag weapons, like cluster bombs, mission radius decreases to about 400 nm (460 miles; 740 km).

During Red Flag-type exercises, F-111s always launch first and hold at low altitude (where fuel consumption is highest), waiting for the other fighters to take off and inflight refuel before the 'push' (beginning of the attack). They then ingress at speeds which are excruciatingly slow for 'Varks' to stay back with the package, attack the most distant targets, egress near the back of the pack, and return to base while many of the other fighters inflight refuel again. Another peacetime example is the use of ranges in the United Kingdom. F-111s based in southern England would routinely fly at high level to southern Scotland for a 15-20 minute low-level flight en

Left: Unlike other jamming platforms, the EF-111A Raven is able to accompany high-performance strike aircraft as they penetrate hostile airspace at low level. In addition, the aircraft undertakes a stand-off barrage jamming task to saturate enemy defences prior to and during friendly air raids.

Above: For most of its career the 'Earth Pig' had two homes – one was the desert climes of the American West, the other being in the 'clag' and rain of Europe. 'Aardvarks' such as this 20th TFW F-111E held the balance in central Europe, possessing the chilling ability to strike deep at the heart of the Warsaw Pact war machine with tactical nuclear weapons.

Left: In Europe the standard electronic protection for the F-111 was provided by the shallow AN/ALQ-131 ECM pod, usually carried on the aft station between the ventral strakes.

Above: Despite being optimised for the strategic nuclear mission, the FB-111A retained impressive conventional bombing capability. Here a 'Dark Vark' lays down a pattern of Mk 82 AIR ballute-retarded bombs.

Top: With Pave Tack pod deployed to provide laser range-finding information to enhance 'dumb' bombing accuracy, an F-111F lets fly with 12 Mk 82 AIRs over the Bardenas Reales bombing range in northern Spain. Released virtually simultaneously, the bombs will produce a carpet of destruction on the ground suitable for covering a large area of soft targets.

route to bombing ranges near Inverness (Tain) or Aberdeen (Rosehearty), then climb to medium altitude, return to let-down for a short low-level flight into Spadeadam range in northern England for a radar bomb scoring attack before climbing out to return to base. In the United States, F-111s from Cannon often fly unrefuelled as far as north-eastern Arkansas or south-western Arizona to fly low levels and attack bombing ranges before returning home. They also can fly at low level for as long as an hour when transitting to and from West Coast bases, and have flown non-stop and unre-fuelled to Langley AFB, Virginia, with 24 inert 500-lb (227-kg) bombs. If all this strikes the reader as relatively ho-hum, ask an F-16 pilot about the last time he contemplated a 700-nm (805-mile; 1300-km) low-level sortie.

In combat terms, an F-111 can go half again as far as an F-15E with the same payload and, during the Cold War, could have ranged farther into Eastern Europe from England than the Panavia Tornado from West Germany, all at higher speeds. Because of this, F-111s were the long, sharp teeth of NATO's Cold War planning, slated to attack targets that would have otherwise required strategic systems to reach.

In the end, the value of the F-111's range was proven in the crucible of the south-west Asian scenario, played out during the 1991 Gulf War with Iraq. F-111Fs flying from Taif, in south-western Saudi Arabia, initially flew the classical

'high-low-high' mission profile, inflight refuelling once before crossing into Iraq, and again before returning to base. Tactics were changed to strictly medium-altitude bombing after the first night or two, when it became evident that the greatest threat was the masses of barrage-fired anti-aircraft artillery (AAA). This change in tactics usually negated the need for post-strike inflight refuelling. Unfortunately, some-one forgot to tell the tankers, who called to complain after they had dumped several million gallons of jet fuel on about the third night because the expected hordes of 'Aardvarks' failed to appear.

Bigger payload

Since the mission of F-111s is to attack targets deep in enemy territory (for a tactical scenario), maximum range is usually a mission requirement. Once an F-111 gets to the tar-get, it can deliver a large variety and quantity of ordnance. Each of the four pivoting pylons can carry stores attached directly to them or suspended from bomb release units (BRUs), which are more aerodynamic versions of the multi-ple ejector racks (MERs) carried by other fighters.

Each BRU-3 can hold up to six 1,000-lb class bombs, in theory allowing for carriage of 24 bombs. In practice they are almost always carried on the outboard pylons only, with the inboard pylons left empty. Actual combat employment has shown that loads of eight high-drag 750-lb cluster bombs or 12 low-drag 500-lb bombs offer the most reasonable trade-off between combat range and firepower. (If the bottom BRU stations are empty, the load is called a 'flat four'; when the inboard BRU stations are empty, it is a 'slant four'.) Weapons carried on BRUs have included the SUU-30, Mk 20, Mk 82 (LDGP, SE, or AIR), M117 (LDGP, D or R), or the BLU-107 Durandal, and the F-111C's Karinga cluster bomb unit (CBU).

Up to four pylon-mounted stores can be carried, including the Mk 84 (LDGP or AIR), SUU-64 and SUU-65 tactical munitions dispenser (TMDs), GBU-10, GBU-12, and GBU-24. (Both Mk 84 and BLU-109 warhead versions of GBU-10/24s are used.) After the early 1980s, Paveway I ver-sions of the GBU-10/12 were used occasionally for training missions, but only Paveway IIs and IIIs have been used in combat.

Only two GBU-15s are carried operationally, always on

Left: During a test flight, a pre-production F-111A totes 24 M117 bombs using all eight potential wing hardpoints, with cameras faired under the wingtips to record separation. In practice, the F-111 has only used the four inboard positions for ordnance carriage.

Left: In test configuration, the FB-111A could carry a SRAM on each wing pylon, plus a further pair in the internal weapons bay. In practice, the largest load was four – two in the bay and two on the inner pylons.

the outboard pylons to prevent inadvertently breaking the bombs' wings by sweeping the aircraft wings too far back (the same restriction applies to the rocket-boosted AGM-130 version). GBU-15 and Pave Tack are not related *at all*; the latter is not required to deliver the former, which uses electro-optical (EO) or imaging infra-red (IIR) guidance, not the laser guidance provided by Pave Tack. Only F-111Fs fitted with the AXQ-14 or improved (but externally identical) ZSW-1 datalink pods on the aft ECM pod station can guide these weapons. When this happens the ECM pod is carried on the forward station.

F-111s were designed as Cold Warriors of the first degree, and carriage of nuclear weapons was a vital part of that mission. B43 weapons were available until the mid-1980s, and B57s until the late 1980s. B61s entered service in the late 1960s and B83s in the late 1980s. All of these weapons have been qualified for use with F-111s, with the B61 being of primary importance. In addition, the AGM-69 SRAM was qualified for use on the FB-111A. With the end of the Cold War, this capability has become progressively less important. F-111Cs never carried nukes.

Sidewinders are considered optional equipment because they are primarily daylight weapons, and F-111s prefer to work at night whenever possible. Starting about 1983, AIM-9 launchers were loaded on stations 3A and 6A, mounted halfway up the outside of the outboard pylons. Although modifications to allow carriage of AIM-9L/Ms from these stations have been studied, due to clearance prob-

lems with the aircraft wings only short-winged AIM-9P-3s can be carried there; AIM-9L/Ms must be carried on launchers mounted on the bottom of the pylons. Except for GBU-12s, precision-guided munitions (PGMs) preclude use of stations 3A and 6A for AIM-9 carriage. During Desert Storm, Sidewinders were only carried on the first night by a few aircraft. AIM-9P-3s were fitted on inboard pylons when two GBU-24s or GBU-15s were mounted on outboard pylons, or on 3A and 6A with loads of four pylon-mounted TMDs.

Stateside F-111s carry the SUU-20 practice bomb dispensers. Typically, these are carried on the inboard pylons, with BRUs loaded outboard. Europe-based F-111s substituted SUU-21 dispensers, which helped prevent inadvertent releases by enclosing the bombs between releases.

EF-111As normally fly without pylons unless carrying MXU-648 baggage pods (old BLU-1 napalm tanks with a door fitted in the side) or the airborne instrumentation

Left: Instant sunshine! An F-111D carries the sinister yet distinctive shape of the B61 tactical nuclear free-fall bomb under its wing. B61 training 'shapes' were frequently dropped, proving to possess excellent ballistic properties which allowed very precise aiming. If the unthinkable had occurred, such accuracy would have been somewhat academic.

system (AIS) pods used during exercises like Red Flag. They carry no operational stores.

Weapons bay

Another 'Navy requirement', the F-111 weapons bay, is not used for tactical missions except to store the Pave Tack pod. There are five types of interchangeable F-111 weapons bay doors. The original doors are used with an internal luggage rack, nuclear weapons, and/or 'Tokyo' fuel tanks. An M61A1 20-mm gun was optional equipment for F-111A/D/E and pre-Pave Tack F-111C/F models (the FB-111A/F-111Gs

never used guns). The gun installation replaced the two bay doors on the right side of the aircraft and extended just slightly over the centreline. It was installed on all aircraft used in Vietnam, but never used. The guns were removed about 1983 when AIM-9P-3s began to be carried for self-defence. The gun ports were faired over and the fixed right side of the installation used as a luggage rack on F-111As and F-111Ds, although F-111Es and non-Pave Tack F-111Fs reverted only to the original weapons bay doors. F-111Cs and F-111Fs usually carry a Pave Tack pod in the bay on a rotating cradle. Although usually installed, the cradle can be removed and replaced by the normal weapons bay doors in about an hour. Both the gun and Pave Tack installations can mount ECM pods. EF-111As have a special cradle hinged on the right side of the fuselage to hold their ALQ-99 jamming system. The RF-111C's reconnaissance pallet is similar, but only as wide as three of the four weapon bay doors, leaving the left-most door in its original configuration, except for the addition of a single camera window.

Normally, the weapons bay is opened after the airplane taxis to its parking spot and not closed until after the engines are started. The only times this does not happen is if the WSO forgets to follow his checklist, an ECM pod is fitted in the forward position, or during the Cold War when 'Varks' sat nuclear alert (when no weapons were being carried in the weapons bay). EF-111As and RF-111Cs only open their bays for maintenance of their special systems.

The AVQ-26 Pave Tack pod was the first laser designation system to provide the capability to autonomously deliver LGBs at night. LGBs were first used during Vietnam, but their employment had always been limited to daytime, and the pods used put the aircraft designating the target in a vulnerable position. Pave Tack not only permitted round-the-clock attacks but, since it was integrated with other aircraft sensors, far more aggressive attacks were possible. Between 1981 and 1984 all F-111Fs were modified to carry Pave Tack; Australian F-111Cs were also modified beginning in the late 1980s.

Natural night fighters, the F-111F community used Pave Tack to great effect during the 1991 Gulf War, delivering the majority of LGBs employed by the USAF. During the first night or so, the tactic developed for the Paveway III GBU-24 was used. Called the 'Ramp-Level', or 'Mini-Toss', the AC pulled up only enough to impart an upward vector to the bomb before releasing it. Only a few hundred feet higher than when he started, the AC then rolled into 90° of bank for a like amount of turn, rolling out gradually to allow the WSO to designate the target until bomb impact. By the third night of the war this risky manoeuvre was deemed unnecessary, and all future attacks were conducted from medium altitude using level deliveries.

The Gulf War attacks differed from the tactic developed for the earlier Paveway II LGBs. Used during the 1986 Libya raid, the F-111F pulled up to a much higher altitude before releasing the bomb. As the AC pulled the aircraft away from the target in a 135° bank (making it descend back towards the ground), the WSO concentrated totally on designating the target.

Pave Tack was originally intended to equip 180 F-4Es and 60 RF-4Cs. However, because of a protracted and difficult development programme, the actual number of F-4s equipped with it was substantially lower. A practical drawback to using the 1,385-lb (628-kg) pod with the Phantom was its large size, which required carriage on the centreline station, replacing the 600-US gal (2271-litre) external fuel tank. In the end, F-4 crews referred to the AVQ-26 as 'Pave Drag'. About 150 pods were built, with all eventually being used by F-111s.

Pave Tack mounting

In contrast to its F-4 installation, F-111C and F-111F Pave Tack pods are mounted on a rotating cradle in the weapons bay, thereby minimising the pod's impact on aircraft performance. For this, the outer weapons bay doors are modified with a 'cut-out' section towards the rear, while the inner ones are replaced by the cradle. The doors are left open while on the ground, but closed prior to taxi. They are not normally opened in flight. Looking forward, the cradle rotates clockwise to stow the pod and counterclockwise to expose it. The pod is stowed prior to take-off, and usually kept that way for most of the mission until nearing the target area, when it is used by the WSO to find and designate targets for LGBs. It is extended prior to landing, with the turret tucked away in the 'stowed' position to protect the gallium-arsenide forward-looking infra-red (FLIR) window. (This window is a milky amber colour, while the two smaller laser windows are clear but have a distinct bluish tint.) Extending the pod is a habit that is hard to break, even when the pod is not installed; more than one WSO has earned the dreaded nickname 'Bags' after rotating the cradle prior to landing during a cross country when it only held the crew's personal baggage.

The cradle is a metal frame covered with a thin, aerodynamically shaped fibreglass fairing. To allow uninhibited

A little known facet of the F-111 is its limited reconnaissance capability, provided courtesy of the KB-18 strike camera mounted under the forward fuselage, offset to starboard. This is a panoramic-style camera, but sweeping fore and aft rather than side to side. Thus, one frame shows the aircraft's nose at the top and the tail at the bottom. A typical result is shown left, also serving to provide some idea of the excitement of flying at low level in a 'Vark' through the moonscape of the Utah desert.

Far left: Apart from carriage of sensors or guns, the weapons bay has rarely been used operationally by F-111s. However, the strategic FB-111A utilised the space for the carriage of SRAMs or free-fall nuclear weapons. In long-range configuration only one weapon is carried, the remainder of the bay being taken up by an auxiliary fuel tank.

General Dynamics F-111

movement of the pod head, there is a 'box' cut out of the rear of the cradle on the pod side. The pod head rotates about the longitudinal axis of the barrel, while the turret rotates at right angles to the head. This wrist-like movement allows the pod to view virtually the entire hemisphere beneath the aircraft. The 4-in (10-cm) 'hump' exposed when the pod is stowed in the weapons bay is smoothly faired, with no 'hard' lines. Two sets of bolt holes, with 30-in (76-cm) spacing, are visible on the 'hump' side of the cradle and are used to mount the pod to the cradle. On aircraft using Vietnam paint schemes, the pod was overall 34087 olive drab with predominantly black markings, while the cradle was overall black, except for the cooling duct inlets, which were white. However, both cradles and pods (gradually) are being painted to match the new 36118 grey scheme.

While the pod was mounted on the RF-4C and F-4E so the equipment access doors opened downward on the left-hand side, on the F-111 the barrel of the pod is rotated 90° so that the doors open when the pod is rotated out of the bay. Cooling on the Phantom's installation was by ram air through an inlet

on the right-front portion of the pod. With the F-111 installation, this inlet is located on top of the pod (hidden by the cradle) and fed with aircraft-supplied cooling air through ducts mounted in the weapons bay and fed through the cradle. Finally, the nosecone used with the F-4E is removed for F-111 use.

Australian 'Aardvarks'

After initially selecting the North American Aviation A-5 Vigilante to replace their Canberras, in October 1963 the Australians finally decided on the F-111A in an agreement which also offered the free lease of two squadrons of B/RB-47E Stratojets until the F-111s could be delivered (an option not exercised, although three B-47s did visit Australia in November 1963). This agreement called for 18 F-111As to be delivered beginning in late 1967, to be followed by six RF-111As two years later.

In April 1966 it was decided to take advantage of extended wingtips and strengthened landing gear of the new FB-111A design (although F-111C avionics remained virtually identical to those in the F-111A). This change delayed initial delivery until July 1968 and resulted in the new designation of F/RF-111C. However, when the vital wing carry-through box (WCTB) structure failed during static testing in September, deliveries of F-111Cs were suspended until Australian concerns about airframe structural integrity were satisfied. This entailed static testing an F-111C WCTB to 32,000 hours and delayed projected deliveries until the spring of 1970. When an F-111A lost its wing while pulling out of a dive bomb pass on 22 December 1969, six days after the first F-111C entered the WCTB modification programme, the programme was put on hold once again. Until the fate of the F-111C programme was determined the Australians were leased 24 F-4Es, which arrived in 1970. It was not until June of 1973 that the first of 24 F-111Cs was actually delivered. The

Left: Four Australian 'Pigs' were modified in 1979-80 to RF-111C standard for service with No. 6 Squadron. These have a pallet-mounted recce suite comprising various high- and low-altitude cameras, radar altimeter and infra-red linescan. The windows for the panoramic sensors are set in a characteristic fairing which projects below the weapons bay doors.

last F-4E was returned to the US in June of 1974.

Although F-111A 63-9776 had been modified and successfully flight tested as an RF-111A between December 1967 and October 1968, high overall programme costs led to the cancellation of all USAF reconnaissance versions. Still requiring a reconnaissance aircraft, and now on their own, the Australians modified four F-111Cs to RF-111C standard in 1979-80 by installing a unique pallet in the weapons bay and a control panel in the cockpit. (While A8-126 was modified and tested by GD, A8-134, 143 and 146 were modified in Australia.)

By late 1980 the transfer of four USAF F-111As to Australia as attrition replacements had been agreed. These arrived between May and August of 1982, and were flown for a time as F-111As before being modified with the longer wings and strengthened landing gear of the F-111C (however, they retained the F-111A WCTB). Using numbers corresponding to their USAF serials (A8-109, 112, 113 and 114), these aircraft are now considered F-111Cs.

During 1983, F-111C A8-147 was modified by General Dynamics with the same Pave Tack system used by the F-111F. All other F-111Cs were modified in Australia beginning March 1985, with 10 pods being shared by 18 aircraft. At about the same time, the F/RF-111C fleet received other modifications to make them compatible with the GBU-15 glide bomb. The only F-111s that can deliver this weapon are the F-111C and F-111F. Lacking the latter's datalink pod, the F-111Cs are limited to the cumbersome lock-on before launch (LOBL) direct attack mode. Three final weapons which are unique to the F-111C community are the indigenous Karinga cluster bomb, the AGM-84 Harpoon anti-ship missile, and the AGM-88 HARM. No. 1 Sqn is the primary operational unit, with No. 6 concentrating on training and reconnaissance duties.

Despite adoption of Pave Tack and new weapons, it was not until the early 1990s that the F-111Cs received any major avionics update under the AUP programme. The first aircraft, under test in the US, received a mid-grey colour scheme, replacing the three-tone camouflage worn since the F-111Cs were first delivered.

Raven

The October 1973 Yom Kippur War demonstrated the vulnerability of tactical aircraft to the massive, integrated air defence networks favoured by the Soviets and their client states. Tactical Air Command (TAC), having spent as little on electronic warfare as possible, was preparing to retire its ancient EB-66 stand-off jamming aircraft the following year. Recognising the need for a quick solution to this problem, they soon settled on the Eaton/AIL ALQ-99 jamming subsystem (JSS) designed for the Navy's Grumman EA-6B Prowler. However, the Air Force did not believe the Prowler to be fast enough to keep up with its strike packages. Other factors weighing against the EA-6B were its lack of endurance and the need to create a new logistic system to support it.

After some initial compatibility tests were performed, the Air Force awarded Grumman a contract to develop the first two EF-111As on 26 December 1974. While the aerodynamic

prototype flew on 15 December 1975, the 'all-up' aircraft did not take wing until 10 March 1977. As with most electronic warfare systems, the Raven programme was subjected to more than its fair share of scrutiny. By 23 December 1985, 42 F-111As had been converted to EF-111A Raven electronic jamming system (EJS) aircraft. Their ALQ-99E was modified for use by a single electronic warfare officer (EWO). Installing the new jamming system resulted in the right side of the cockpit being extensively modified. All bombing systems (including the AC's ODS), and the right-hand control column were removed to make room for the jamming system controls and displays. Also, the INS and ARS control panels were relocated to allow the AC to control them (freeing the EWO to concentrate on his jamming duties). All provisions for delivering weapons were removed during the EF-111A conversion process, precluding the option of launching AGM-88 high-speed anti-radiation missiles (HARMs) from Ravens.

Defensive avionics

The bullet fairing on the top of the tail of all but the EF-111As originally contained a countermeasures receiver set (CMRS). An infra-red system designed to detect rear hemisphere missile launches, it was removed during the mid-1980s because it was hard to maintain and gave numerous false alarms when it worked. Radar homing and warning (RHAW) gear was installed on F-111s from the outset, the first tactical aircraft to be so equipped. Unlike the CMRS, it was continually updated to detect the latest threats. Experience from the Yom Kippur War, in October 1973, led to the development and installation of the Compass Sail antenna during the late 1970s. It was located under the nose, to the right of centreline and next to the KB-18 strike camera (which had been installed only a year or two earlier) on the F-111D, and on the centreline, staggered slightly in front of the KB-18, on the F-111A, F-111C, F-111E and F-111F. It was also in this location on the FB-111A/F-111G (which had no

Above: Following the lead of the USAF's F-111F fleet, the RAAF modified its F-111C fleet to be compatible with the AVQ-26 Pave Tack pod, to enhance conventional bombing capability and to allow the use of laser-guided weapons. Only 10 pods were purchased, although all strike F-111Cs were modified.

F-111 weapons

From cluster bombs to nuclear missiles, the F-111 can carry just about any air-to-ground weapon. The weapon system allows highly accurate bombing with free-fall weapons in any weather, while the addition of the Pave Tack system allows the F-111C and F to autonomously deliver precision-guided munitions.

F-111 ORDNANCE LOADS

Stn 2/7	Stn 3/6A	Stn 3/6	Stn 4/5	Wpn Bay	ECM Pod	Remarks
F-111A Vietnam War						
not used	not used	6 M117 LDGP	pylon	fwd ALQ-87	aft ALQ-87	
not used	not used	6 Mk 82 SE	pylon	fwd ALQ-87	aft ALQ-87	SE or LDGP
not used	not used	Mk 84 LDGP	Mk 84 LDGP	fwd ALQ-87	aft ALQ-87	
not used	not used	4 SUU-30B/B	4 SUU-30 B/B	fwd ALQ-87	aft ALQ-87	slant 4 load
(Gun installed in weapons bay.)						
FB-111A Cold War (postulated)						
fuel tank	not used	fuel tank	B61 or B43	B61 or B43	none	fuel cell in rt. bay
fuel tank	not used	fuel tank	AGM-69A	B61 or B43	none	fuel cell in rt. bay
fuel tank	not used	fuel tank	fuel tank	2 AGM-69A	none	
fuel tank	not used	fuel tank	AGM-69A	2 AGM-69A	none	
(B83 probably not operational, based on FB-111A drawdown and Cold War's end.)						
F-111D/E/F Cold War (postulated)						
not used	optional	6 Mk 82	pylon	optional	aft ECM	LDGP, SE or AIR
not used	optional	6 Mk 20	pylon	optional	aft ECM	
not used	optional	Mk 84	Mk 84	optional	aft ECM	LDGP or AIR
not used	optional	4 SUU-30H/B	pylon	optional	aft ECM	slant 4 load
not used	optional	6 BLU-107	pylon	optional	aft ECM	from mid-1980s
not used	not used	pylon	B57 on 4 or 5	not used	aft ECM	one bomb only
not used	not used	pylon	B61 or B57	not used	QRC 80-01	F-111D only
not used	not used	fuel tank	B61	not used	aft ECM	
not used	not used	fuel tank	B61	B61 or B43	aft ECM	fuel cell in rt. bay
(Gun optional in weapons bay until early 1980s. Pave Tack pod normal on F-111Fs thereafter. ECM pods were ALQ-87 in early 1970s, medium-length ALQ-119 until early 1980s, then shallow ALQ-131.)						
F-111F Operation El Dorado Canyon						
not used	not used	6 Mk 82 AIR	pylon	AVQ-26	aft ALQ-131	Tripoli Airfield
not used	not used	GBU-10C/B	GBU-10C/B	AVQ-26	aft ALQ-131	HQ and Terr. Camp
F-111E Operation Proven Force						
not used	AIM-9P opt	6 Mk 82 AIR	pylon	not used	aft ALQ-131	
not used	AIM-9P opt	1 CBU-87	1 CBU-87	not used	aft ALQ-131	CEM
not used	AIM-9P opt	1 CBU-89	1 CBU-89	not used	aft ALQ-131	Gator
F-111F Operation Desert Storm						
not used	AIM-9P opt	6 Mk 82 AIR	pylon	AVQ-26	aft ALQ-131	493 acft-1st night
not used	AIM-9P opt	1 CBU-87	1 CBU-87	AVQ-26	aft ALQ-131	CEM
not used	AIM-9P opt	1 CBU-89	1 CBU-89	AVQ-26	aft ALQ-131	Gator-1st week
not used	not used	GBU-15	pylon	fwd ALQ-131	aft AXQ-14	(V)-1/2/21/22
not used	not used	GBU-10E/B	GBU-10E/B	AVQ-26	aft ALQ-131	sta 4/5 opt
not used	not used	GBU-10J/B	GBU-10J/B	AVQ-26	aft ALQ-131	sta 4/5 opt
not used	not used	GBU-24/B	GBU-24/B	AVQ-26	aft ALQ-131	sta 4/5 opt
not used	not used	GBU-24A/B	GBU-24A/B	AVQ-26	aft ALQ-131	sta 4/5 opt
not used	not used	GBU-24	GBU-10	AVQ-26	aft ALQ-131	bad weather
not used	not used	GBU-24	AIM-9P opt	AVQ-26	aft ALQ-131	/B or A/B
not used	not used	GBU-10	AIM-9P opt	AVQ-26	aft ALQ-131	E/B or J/B
not used	not used	GBU-12D/B	GBU-12D/B	AVQ-26	aft ALQ-131	sta 4/5 opt
not used	not used	GBU-28 left	pylon	AVQ-26	aft ALQ-131	Mk 84 LDGP right
F-111A/C/D/E/F/G training						
not used	optional	6 Mk 82	SUU-20/21	optional	optional	LDGP, SE, or AIR
not used	optional	Mk 84	SUU-20/21	optional	optional	LDGP or AIR
not used	optional	6 Mk 20	SUU-20/21	optional	optional	
not used	optional	GBU-10	SUU-20/21	optional	optional	Paveway I or II
not used	optional	GBU-12	SUU-20/21	optional	optional	Paveway I or II
not used	optional	GBU-24/B	SUU-20/21	optional	optional	
(AIM-9E or P-CAP common on 3A or 6A; if at a Flag exercise AIS pod on the other shoulder station. SUU-20 used in US and by F-111C, SUU-21 used in Europe. Pave Tack normal for F-111C or F-111F, while others use bay doors or gun, except for F-111G, which only used bay doors. ECM pods were as per war loads, none for F-111C or F-111G.)						
F-111C						
not used	not used	AGM-84	AGM-84	optional	not used	
not used	not used	fuel tank	AGM-88	optional	not used	
not used	not used	AGM-88	AGM-88	optional	not used	
not used	AIM-9B opt	6 Karinga	4 Karinga	optional	not used	Australian CBU
not used	AIM-9B opt	6 Mk 82	6 Mk 82	optional	not used	LDGP or SE
not used	AIM-9B opt	Mk 84 LDGP	Mk 84 LDGP	optional	not used	
not used	not used	GBU-10C/B	GBU-10C/B	AVQ-26	not used	Paveway II
not used	not used	GBU-12B/B	GBU-12B/B	AVQ-26	not used	Paveway II
not used	not used	GBU-15	pylon	optional	not used	(V)-1
(Pave Tack normal after mid-1980s.)						

Above: Australian F-111Cs carry the widest ordnance range of any variant. In addition to the normal USAF range, they carry the Harpoon anti-ship missile (closest to aircraft nose) and the Karinga cluster bomb (in front of AGM-84s).

Below: Weapons of the FB-111: although the front row of iron bombs would cause considerable damage, the back row is far more serious. In the centre are two SRAMs, outside of which are B61 and B83 nuclear bombs.

BRUs were used by F-111Fs only once during Desert Storm, early in the war, by a Freedom aircraft to deliver 12 Mk 82s (probably AIRs). The war ended before they could be used with previously untried loads of 12 GBU-12s (three per BRU) or flat-eight TMDs.

Loads of four pylon-mounted TMDs were employed by F-111Fs, with 530 CBU-87 combined effects munitions (CEMs) being delivered. However, the similar CBU-89 'Gators' were only used for the first week, when 212 were dropped, and then conserved in case of a prolonged ground war.

A total of 70 GBU-15 stand-off weapons was expended. Despite a formal decision to only use long-chord wings with Mk 84 and short-chord wings with BLU-109 warheads, during Desert Storm both kinds of wings were used with Mk 84s (BLU-109 warheads were

not used). GBU-15(V)-1, -2, -21 and -22 versions were all employed (with 62 IIR against only eight EO seekers, and slightly more short than long-chord wings being used). While only 493rd TFS aircrew were qualified to employ GBU-15s, aircraft from all teams but Independence were used to deliver them. An aircraft carrying the AXQ-14 pod controlled the bomb, which was usually launched from another aircraft.

The F-111Fs' primary weapons were LGBs. A total of 469 GBU-10E/Bs, 389 GBU-10J/Bs (GBU-10Is), 270 GBU-24/Bs and 924 GBU-24A/Bs was used against a wide variety of targets. It was very common, especially during the early part of the war, for aircraft to only carry two LGBs, using the outboard pylons.

During periods of bad weather, a mixed

load of either GBU-10s or -24s and Mk 84s was used. If the weather was good, the GBUs would be dropped on pinpoint targets; if it was bad the Mk 84s would be employed for area bombing (146 Mk 84s were delivered). Apparently using the same logic, some aircraft used mixed loads of GBU-10s and GBU-24s on the outboards.

A total of 2,542 GBU-12D/Bs was used to attack Iraqi tank and artillery concentrations. When it was discovered that 60-odd F-111Fs had destroyed 10 times as many tanks as 250 F-16s, the F-16s were directed to cease attacks by mid-afternoon each day to allow the dust to settle before the 'Varks' went to work at night. The F-111F LGB attacks were the 'improved tactics' about which military briefers very coyly avoided talking.

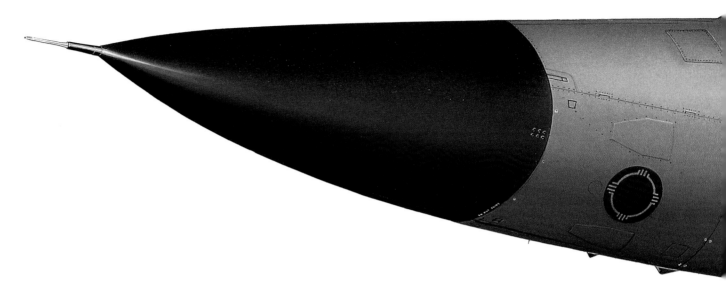

General Dynamics F-111F
524th Fighter Squadron
27th Fighter Wing
Cannon AFB, New Mexico

Since 1969 Cannon AFB has been the USAF's 'Vark City', having by 1993 established an unbroken 24-year association with the F-111, which is set to continue into the next century. Indeed, if USAF plans are adhered to (an unlikely event in the face of an ever-shrinking budget and increasing force draw-downs), the 'Earth Pig' will have shattered the calm of the local town of Clovis for 46 years! Along the way, the resident 27th Fighter Wing will have operated every USAF variant of the type. F-111As were initially assigned, followed by F-111Es. These paved the way for the vastly-improved D model, which remained the 27th's primary type for many years. Towards the end of the 'Dog's' reign at Cannon, the remnants of SAC's FB-111 force were assigned to the base, reworked for essentially a training role as the F-111G. These did not last long, for in the massive reshuffle of USAF air assets, both Ds and Gs were retired. At the same time, deliveries of F-15Es to the premier strike unit in Europe, the 48th Fighter Wing at RAF Lakenheath, released the F-111F fleet for continued service back in the warmer climes of New Mexico. Although inferior in terms of avionics when compared to the D model, the F-111F

was nevertheless simpler to fly and maintain, featured far more powerful engines, and sported the all-important Pave Tack pod. Some 25 F-111Es also left behind the rain of England, moving from Upper Heyford to take over the training role from the F-111Gs. To further consolidate the remaining 'Aardvark' assets, EF-111 Ravens began to be reassigned from Upper Heyford and Mountain Home, and in 1993 all active F-111s had gathered at Cannon, greatly easing the maintenance effort. Regular detachments were maintained at Incirlik in Turkey (Operation Provide Comfort II – F-111F, EF-111A) and Dhahran in Saudi Arabia (Operation Southern Watch – EF-111A).

The loss of three out of four F-111 wings may have appeared to signal the beginning of the end for the 'Aardvark', but the type's prowess at long-range strike in all conditions remains unmatched in the Air Force structure. Although the force is considerably leaner than two years ago, the F-111 is a hard act to kill off, and the 100 or so remaining aircraft are having their capabilities further enhanced through the EF-111A/F-111E AMP and F-111F Pacer Strike upgrade programmes.

Precision-guided munitions

Although retaining excellent accuracy in the conventional bombing role, the F-111F's forte is laser-bombing, using the Pave Tack pod in conjunction with various laser- and electro-optical-guided bombs. Laser-guided weapons are the most important, the F-111F employing the Paveway families of weapons. There are three families, each signifying different seeker heads and tail fins. Paveway I is rarely used now (principally for training), these early weapons having a gimbal-mounted seeker head and fixed rear wings. The Paveway II family retains the earlier seeker, but has pop-out rear wings. F-111s use the 500-lb (GBU-12) and 2,000-lb (GBU-10) versions, the latter available in either standard Mk 84 or BLU-109 penetration warhead varieties. The principal member of the Paveway III family is the 2,000-lb GBU-24, again with either Mk 84 or BLU-109 warheads. These introduce much larger rear pop-out fins that give better range. This in turn allows the bomb to be launched from lower altitudes than Paveway IIs. The fixed seeker head is considerably revised, and the forward control fins are much larger. They operate across a range of deflections, as opposed to the 'bang-bang' fins of earlier variants, which could only be fully deflected. Mid-course guidance keeps the bomb on track prior to target acquisition, and a variety of terminal attack modes is available for the optimum angle of arrival at the target. A further member of the family is the 4,800-lb GBU-28, but this retains Paveway II-style fins. Depicted on this aircraft are GBU-24A/B Paveway IIIs, with BLU-109 warhead.

Propulsion system

All F-111s have been powered by versions of the Pratt & Whitney TF30 two-shaft turbofan with thrust augmentation. This engine has proved troublesome over the years, notably in its susceptibility to compressor stall. Triple Plow I intakes were fitted to the production F-111A, these being distinguished by a large splitter plate next to the fuselage. Triple Plow II was introduced by the F-111E, this intake dispensing with the splitter plate but being moved further from the fuselage and being of greater area. However, the TF30-P-3 engines of the F-111E were not powerful enough to take advantage of the more efficient intakes, and it was the F-111D which introduced a more powerful engine (TF30-P-9), the increase being achieved by uprating the rotational speed. The TF30-P-100, which powers the F-111F, was a completely new engine, with rotational speed raised to a maximum of 14,870 rpm, gas temperature raised to 1260°C and new components throughout to cater for such extra demands. A new afterburner was fitted, complete with a 'soft-light' function which prevents rapid changes of pressure in the aft section. A primary variable nozzle was fitted with iris segments, while downstream the characteristic jetpipe 'tail-feathers' were allowed to 'float'. Thrust of the new engine was vastly increased compared to earlier models, while the tolerance to airflow distortions was much greater. A further engine development, the JTF10A-39, would have introduced yet greater thrust at reduced weight, and would have been interchangebale with the P-100. However, this engine was cancelled, just as the TF30's troubles had finally all been ironed out.

Pave Tack pod

Allowing the F-111F far greater operational effectiveness than other variants, and the ability to autonomously launch laser-guided weapons, the AN/AVQ-26 Pave Tack pod is mounted in the former weapons bay, with the sensor turret at the rear. This can be rotated and retracted for minimum drag in the cruise and to protect the sensor windows. Contained within the turret is a Texas Instruments FLIR and an International Laser Systems laser designator/rangefinder. The base unit forward of the turret contains a digital aircraft interface unit which provides direct inputs into the central weapons computer, a CRT interface to provide images on the WSO's cockpit display, environmental control systems, stabilisation and drive equipment.

By rotating and swivelling the turret, the Pave Tack provides hemispherical coverage beneath the aircraft. When locked forward, the pod can be used as a terrain-following aid. Target acquisition is undertaken using the FLIR in its normal, wide field-of-view mode, taking cues for direction from the aircraft's radar. When the target has been acquired, the WSO can change to a narrow field-of-view image which provides greater magnification for the accurate designation of the target. The laser is bore-sighted with the FLIR sensor, and can be used as a range-finder for conventional bombing, or as a designator for the delivery of LGBs. For the latter, the turret must remain manually directed at the desired mean-point of impact (DMPI) until bomb impact. Providing the target remains within the hemispherical coverage beneath the aircraft, the turret can remain aligned on the DMPI. Bombs are released from a suitable stand-off distance in the general direction of the target, the laser designating the DMPI with reflected laser energy for the bombs. The laser provides coded designation so that weapons do not inadvertently track other designated points. The precision attained by this system was amply demonstrated during the 1991 Gulf War, as was the ability to immediately assess bomb damage.

Ford Aerospace was the prime contractor for Pave Tack, the initial development award having been let in 1974. Flight testing began in 1976, initially for the RF-4C and F-4E Phantom fleet. The F-111F began test flying with the pod soon after. Initial operating clearance was granted in late 1980 for the Phantom and early 1981 for the F-111F. US Air Force acquisition totalled 149 pods, of which 75 were initially for the F-111F force. Ten pods were supplied to the Royal Australian Air Force for its F-111Cs, while other pods were supplied to the USAF (70 for use on Phantoms) and South Korea (eight for use on F-4Es).

Paint schemes

Tactical F-111s were delivered in the three-tone South East Asia camouflage, the A models initially featuring grey undersides, although the Harvest Reaper aircraft had olive drab undersides. Subsequently, black undersides were adopted – more in keeping with the 'Aardvark's' nocturnal habits. F-111A and D aircraft had hard-edged patterns, while Es and Fs featured soft-edged demarcation. FB-111As were delivered in a unique SAC scheme, while EF-111As emerged from conversion in a light grey scheme.

Although FB-111As were repainted from May 1984 in a European style camouflage, the tactical 'Varks' retained the SEA camouflage until the early 1990s, crews finding it more effective than the European One scheme applied to most other tactical aircraft. Beginning in 1990, the painting of F-111s switched from Sacramento to Cannon for a time because of environmental concerns. At the same time a new scheme was introduced, consisting of all-over 36118 Gunship Gray, the priority being the F-111Gs transferred from SAC. F-111Ds, Es and Fs then followed. Some aircraft had the area between the ventral strakes left in the old black as an accumulation of oil in this region affected paint adhesion. In 1990 an FB-111A (68-0294) and an F-111G (67-7194) were tested with a 36081 grey radome, but the black radome remains standard. F-111Cs were delivered in three-tone SEA camouflage, but may change to grey when undergoing AUP upgrade.

Squadron colours have traditionally been carried on the fin, consisting of a coloured band high on the fin (TAC) or on the fin-top bullet fairing (USAFE). The 27th Fighter Wing now adds the squadron nickname to the fin-band. The wing's aircraft also traditionally carry the New Mexico 'Zia' insignia on both sides of the nose.

HOUNDS

CC

AF
70 396

pler
xciters

e' rad
ons ba

Self-defence
In addition to its main system receivers and jammers, the EF-111 has a comprehensive defensive avionics suite. Receivers and jammers are located in the rear of the football fairing, in the tailplane trailing edges, tailbooms and in the small bullet fairings mounted over the wing glove section.

Jammers
The 16-ft (4.9-m) canoe fairing covers the main jamming equipment housed in the weapons bay, which consists of 10 transmitters, five exciters and six digitally-tuned receivers. Seven frequency bands are covered by the equipment. At the rear of the bay are two air-water heat exchangers which act as a spill for hot air.

Radar
The nose radome houses the APQ-160 attack radar, used for accurate mapping, and the terrain-following radar which allows low-level penetration in the ECM escort role.

Grumman/ General Dynamics EF-111A Raven

Universally known as the 'Spark Vark', the EF-111 provides the US Air Force with non-lethal defence suppression. The aircraft can operate in both stand-off and escort modes but, unlike the Navy's Prowler, cannot fire the AGM-88 HARM anti-radiation missile. This machine is shown in the markings of the 430th Electronic Combat Squadron, based at Cannon AFB as part of the 27th Fighter Wing.

Above: An underview of a 366th TFW EF-111A reveals the ghostly shape of the Raven. All of the jammers are housed in the ventral canoe fairing.

Receiver antennas
Hostile radar emissions are detected by antennas in the SIR (System Integrated Receiver) pod, otherwise known as the 'football' fairing. These face forwards, sideways and rearwards, and are augmented by further receivers lower down the fin and blade antennas on the fuselage sides under the wing. Receivers provide information for the central computer, which then analyses and prioritises the threats for display in the cockpit and automatic operation of the jamming system.

The canoe fairing hinges open to allow rapid access to the jammers for maintenance. Note the Triple Plow I intakes inherited from the aircraft's previous incarnation as the F-111A.

KB-18). The EF-111A has neither Compass Sail antenna nor KB-18.

Chaff and flares are carried in the aircraft's internal countermeasures dispenser set (CMDS), located in the bullet fairings. In theory, the CMDS could be linked with the CMRS and RHAW to automatically dispense chaff and flares, but in practice this was never done. The older ALE-28 dispensers were gradually replaced between 1990 and 1992 by the USAF-standard ALE-40 (but fewer than 10 Desert Storm aircraft had this modification).

All F-111s were fitted with the ALQ-94 internal electronic countermeasures (ECM). Designed to counter most threats of the Vietnam era, they gradually became less effective. The ALQ-137 upgrade programme proposed during the late 1980s was abandoned because of high costs.

In addition to self-contained deception jammers, most

F-111s could also carry ECM pods. Over the years, these pods gradually assumed a greater responsibility for the electronic protection of the F-111. ALQ-87 ECM pods were first used by F-111As based in Thailand during the Vietnam War. Two were mounted on the forward (weapons bay) and aft fuselage stations. These pods were also mounted on F-111Es and F-111Fs, but normally only from the aft fuselage station.

The short version of the ALQ-119 (and, later, the externally similar QRC 80-01) replaced the ALQ-87 in the late 1970s. Used by the F-111A, F-111E and F-111F, they were the only ECM pods with which the F-111D was ever operationally equipped.

The shallow version of the ALQ-131 was introduced on F-111Fs, and then F-111Es during the early 1980s. While normal carriage was on the aft fuselage station, F-111Fs sometimes carried it on the Pave Tack cradle when the GBU-15's

Far right: 66-0049 was the first prototype of the EF-111 but, although aerodynamically representative of the Raven, did not have a full electronics suite.

Right: Preliminary work on the 'Electric Fox' began in late 1975 with the first of 29 flights by this F-111A modified with the EF's intended belly canoe fairing. The aircraft continued to wear its 'NA' tailcodes, but had the Air Force Systems Command badge on the fin.

Above: 66-0041 was the first 'full-up' EF-111A, complete with electronic suite. This first took to the air at Grumman's Calverton plant on 17 May 1977. It became the first Raven delivered to the Air Force, handed over to the 366th TFW in November 1981.

Right: A dramatic underview of 66-0041 during testing reveals the size of the canoe fairing. To either side of the rear end of the fairing are large exhausts for hot air generated by the powerful jamming system.

AXQ-14 datalink pod was carried on the aft station. On rare occasions ALQ-131s were used on F-111Ds.

Relying totally on internal jammers, the FB-111A/F-111Gs had a large UHF radio antenna at the aft fuselage station location and lacked capability to carry ECM pods. EF-111As and F-111Cs do not carry ECM pods either. Staying with antennas, the large tactical air navigation (TACAN) antenna just behind the escape capsule on all versions began to be replaced by a smaller one from the spring of 1991. Also, during 1989, some F-111Fs were observed with raked-back lower front UHF antennas.

Offensive avionics

The most important difference between operational versions of the F-111 was their mission avionics. The initial 159 F-111As had Mk I analogue avionics systems having about the same level of sophistication as early F-4Cs. The inertial navigation system (INS) had an uncorrected drift rate of about 7 nm (8 miles; 13 km) per hour. It displayed present position and destination co-ordinates in windows; the co-ordinates had to be manually adjusted by turning knobs beside the windows. When the aircraft arrived at the destination, the weapon systems officer (WSO) would tell the aircraft commander (AC) the initial heading for the next destination. While the AC began the turn, the WSO would turn the knobs on the INS control panel to enter the next destination's co-ordinates. Co-ordinates for two offset aim points (OAPs) along the route could be loaded into a mechanical box about the size of a half dozen compact disc boxes stacked atop one another. The OAPs were radar significant landmarks used to help locate the targets with the attack radar system (ARS). (The analogue ARS used a cathode ray tube (CRT) display which could be shielded from sunlight by an optional rubber hood.) If more than two OAPs were required, more of the multi-thousand dollar boxes had to be brought along. These boxes were also fragile; dropping one would (at best) modify the co-ordinates, but more usually break it.

Weapon delivery from the F-111A was done manually. On the ground the crew determined the manner in which the weapons were to be delivered. Considering a variety of factors including weather, delivery tactic, target altitude, air-

craft weight, speed and wing sweep, they would determine from large manuals how the bombs should be delivered to hit the target, with the results of these calculations being fed into the stores management system's (SMS) ballistics computer unit (BCU) and weapons control panel (WCP). This system required considerable skill to compensate for any unforeseen changes to the original plan. Like most F-111s, the F-111A had an optical display system (ODS) bombing sight on the AC's side of the cockpit to aid visual weapons delivery. Although the ODS looked like a head-up display (HUD), when used with the F-111A it only provided the AC with a reference to his manually-entered depression angle for use in aiming the 20-mm M61A1 cannon or dropping bombs. Use of these stone age systems made the first-place finish by Mountain Home's F-111As in their last-ever Long Rifle bombing competition (triumphing over F-111Ds, F-16Cs, A-10As and F-15Es), a real tribute to the crews of these ancient war horses.

The F-111's terrain-following radar (TFR) is integrated with the ARS, INS, navigation computers and autopilot. This linkage of systems has formed the cornerstone of the F-111's ability to deliver a wide variety of weapons under the cover of night and/or weather for the last quarter century. This is an important distinction, because until the low altitude targeting and infra-red for night (LANTIRN)-equipped F-15E and F-16C/D fleets are fitted with this level of systems integration, they are limited to 'good weather' operations only. The A-6E and B-52G/H also require the pilot to hand fly night, low-level missions – vastly increasing workload, but retaining some capability in poor weather. This leaves the Rockwell B-1B and Panavia Tornado as the only other all-weather-capable combat aircraft.

TFR descent to low level is normally started from cruise altitude. Engaging the system results in an abrupt push-over to a 10° dive, which becomes even steeper when the radar

determines the aircraft is within 5,000 ft (1524 m) of the ground. As the aircraft descends to 2,000 ft (609 m) above ground level (AGL) it begins to level off, stopping at 1,000 ft (305 m). Once the crew is satisfied everything is working 'as advertised', they begin the process of 'stepping down' to six progressively lower terrain set clearance planes (SCPs), from 1000 ft (305 m) to as low as 200 ft (60 m). In a way, this is easier to do at night when concentration on monitoring the instruments allows a certain amount of detachment; during daylight one is confronted with the reality of the situation. Within seconds the F-111 is flying at tree-top level, where the high wing loading usually gives a ride so smooth that it almost seems like the earth is moving beneath the aircraft, rather than the other way around. Neither words nor videos can describe the almost other-worldly experience of rocket-

General Dynamics F-111

Above: An F-111A from the 429th TFS taxis out at Takhli on 27 December 1972, at the height of the Linebacker II campaign. The aircraft is armed with 500-lb Mk 82 SE (Snakeye) retarded bombs for a low-level delivery. The ALQ-87 ECM pod provided protection against SAMs.

ing along in the full moonlight at 200 ft (60 m) at 9 miles (14.5 km) per minute. The experience is somewhat less enjoyable, but no less impressive, in the weather.

Flying low level in a straight line would not be very practical; it is also necessary to turn, which requires the TFR to 'look into' the turn. The original system used by F-111As during Vietnam was limited to only 10° of bank, but this limitation was overcome later, making all F-111s capable of automatic 30° bank turns.

For all F-111 crews embarking on their type conversion course, terrain-following flight takes some getting used to. In the initial stages, the desire to fly hands-on in the fast, low-level environment is strong, but after a few exhilarating rides all pilots become confirmed converts to the capabilities of the system. In South East Asia, the dramatic karst limestone terrain provided the new technology with the sternest of tests, and it performed well. Diving down the face of a steep mountain before sweeping up the next obstacle gave rise to the term 'skiing', also an allusion to the TF radar itself, which projects a ski-shaped radar lobe out ahead of the aircraft. If no terrain is detected within the area above the 'ski', the aircraft is pushed-over, but if terrain breaks the theoretical line of the 'ski', then a pull-up is commanded.

While Australian 'Aardvarks' and the F-111E had an avionics system similar to that of the A model, it was the F-111D which ushered in far greater automation.

The F-111D was intended as the definitive version, but became a classical case of the engineers 'biting off more than they could chew'. Known for years as the 'Dog', the F-111D's problems need to be seen in perspective to be appreciated; some of the features attempted with it 25 years ago are only now becoming practical. While all F-111s had more or less similar capabilities, the F-111D's systems were almost always unique; the engineers knew what they wanted to do, but the technology of the late 1960s just was not able to deliver. For example, when the F-111D was contracted for in 1968, its digital computer complex (DCC) was formed by two '4π' 8K computers, which were jammed into boxes about the size of night stands (at a time when typical 8K computers were the size of an American deep freeze). It is not surprising that developmental problems should arise from an attempt to build an entire avionics structure using this level of technological push. In the end, its Rockwell-developed Mk II digital avionics delayed the F-111D's introduction to squadron service until 1971, and only 96 of the originally planned 315 were built (including the cancellation of 60 proposed RF-111Ds).

Computer capabilities

The DCC computers had some redundancy, but one specialised in navigation while the other's primary function was weapon delivery, replacing the BCU. Incorporation of weapons' ballistic equations increased the flexibility of deliveries by sensing actual flight parameters and continuously updating the release point. Up to 150 navigational data points were loaded on the ground from a punch tape and could be manually altered by the WSO. (The punch tape was generated by a cantankerous analogue computer about the size of an American refrigerator. Theoretically designed to be deployed to forward locations and used by any WSO, in reality they were carefully babied in fixed locations and only used by a few, patient specialists.) These points could be used as either turn points (TPs) or OAPs, allowing for nearly 100 TPs. A data point was one set of latitude, longitude (entered to the nearest hundredth of a degree, or about 60 ft/18 m), and elevation. A sequence point was a data point the airplane could fly to. Each sequence point could have up to two OAPs to verify and update the navigational accuracy of the INS, and help build an 'air data' navigation model should the INS fail.

The F-111D's DCC also introduced the integration of multiple navigation sensors through use of 'Kalman filtering'. This process determined position by comparing and weighting INS, Doppler radar, ARS, and even long-range aid to navigation (LORAN), with all but the latter eventually being made to work. The Mk II INS was based on that used by the Apollo lunar landing programme. It had an average drift rate of 2370 ft (722 m) per hour. While this was better than the stated performance of many modern inertial platforms, its reliability was so poor that actual performance was seldom as good as advertised. It also required about 15 minutes to align, compared with four minutes for the F-15E's longest alignment time.

play (VSD), multi-sensor display (MSD), two HUDs and a mode select coupler (MSC). The F-111D also had a moving map, known as the horizontal situation display (HSD), until it became unsupportable in the mid-1980s and was removed. The VSD and MSD were television, rather than CRT displays. The VSD displayed heading, attitude, TFR and ARS information to the AC, while the larger MSD provided the same information to the WSO. The MSD was unique in that its display was deemed bright enough not to need a hood to shield it from sunlight. While it was always bright enough to see, when the sun came from over the WSO's right shoulder the glare could make it nearly impossible to interpret. The HUDs were primarily for visually-aided weapon deliveries, but could also be used to aid navigation. The VSD, MSD, and HUDs had filters to darken them for night use. The MSC configured displays for various navigational modes.

The F-111D's SMS was a stroke of engineering genius which made it by far the easiest of all F-111s from which to release a weapon. By pressing a single button on its WCP, it communicated through the DCC to properly configure all

Above: Twenty-four Mk 82 LDGPs rain from a 366th TFW F-111A. Even at the end of its career, the A model was still winning bomb competitions, despite its archaic avionics.

Far left: A Constant Guard F-111 heads north with a load of Mk 82s during Linebacker II.

Below: WSO's eye-view of a TFR ride through Laos in 1972, the jungle canopy barely disguising the aircraft's proximity to uncompromising limestone. The karst terrain provided crews with a wild experience, known as 'skiing'.

With its multi-mode radar, the F-111D was intended to combine improved ground mapping with air-to-air capabilities using the AIM-7G Sparrow (something not achieved in a practical sense until the introduction of the F-15E). More powerful, and with greater resolution than other F-111 radars, it also had features called terrain-following backup (TFBU) and moving target indicator (MTI). TFBU used the TF radar antennas as a backup transmitter when the main ARS transmitter failed, while MTI used Doppler inputs to show only moving radar returns (e.g. trains), making them easier to attack. The force-stick radar control handle (RCH), or 'goat-turd' (because of its shape), is said to have served as the model for the F-16's control stick. Although technically superior to other F-111 radars, the positioning accuracy provided by Navstar global positioning system (GPS)-aided INSs of current avionics systems has made brute ARS power less important.

The F-111D's instrument display system (IDS) was the first attempt to integrate displays from multiple sensors into a coherent format for the crew, something that did not really come of age until the Tornado and F/A-18 were introduced about 10 years later. It consisted of the vertical situation dis-

Above: Top Dog – the F-111D ruled the roost at Cannon for 21 years. In terms of weapons delivery, the D model was far more capable than any other variant, but the system design goals were over-ambitious, and the 'Dog' was plagued by maintenance problems throughout its career.

Right: Taxiing for a Red Flag mission, an F-111D carries practice bomb carriers, live Mk 84 AIRs, a Sidewinder on the port shoulder pylon and an AIS pod on the starboard.

Below: The unmistakeable profile of the Aardvark's snout, in this case an F-111E. The blade antenna serves the nav/comms system, the angular fairing is for the KB-18 strike camera and the forward fairing is the Compass Sail.

the various avionics and displays needed to perform a given weapon delivery task, including radar level deliveries (RLD), visual level deliveries (VLD), toss and visual deliveries. Angular deliveries included both the low-angle bomb (LAB – 10° or less dive angle), and the low-angle low-drag (LALD – greater than 10° dive angle). All could be performed in either DCC-aided or manual backup modes. When the DCC aided visual deliveries, a continuously computed impact point (CCIP) was displayed on the HUD.

The increased cooling requirements of the Mk II avionics led to the installation of four air-water heat exchanger vents between the back of the weapons bay and the beginning of the speed brake on F-111Ds. (Also found on F-111Fs, these vents were similar to those used by the EF-111A, which has two larger vents in the same general area.)

When it became apparent that the F-111D was going to be seriously delayed, 94 F-111Es were built as an interim measure. Delivery of these aircraft was interrupted for seven months following the previously mentioned crash in December 1969. After deliveries resumed in August 1970, most of the new F-111Es were delivered from General Dynamics to Cannon AFB, New Mexico, where they spent a few months before being sent on to their final destination at RAF Upper Heyford, England. Most aircraft were delivered to England between September 1970 and July 1971, with final deliveries occurring by August 1973. In terms of avionics, F-111Es were virtually identical to F-111As, except that they introduced a new, more capable SMS (but not as good as that on the F-111D).

The FB-111A developed for Strategic Air Command (SAC) was initially viewed as an interim aircraft to ensure SAC's ability to penetrate Soviet defences until the B-1A was fielded. With this in mind, the order was reduced from 263 to 76 (with most of the airframes coming from the F-111K programme for the United Kingdom, cancelled in January 1968 partly because of the difficulties with the Mk II avionics). The FB-111A used those parts of the Mk II avionics that worked (INS/DCC), and replaced troublesome items with Mk I parts. The product, called Mk IIB, resulted in the AC's side of the cockpit looking like the older Mk I aircraft while the WSO's 'office' changed substantially. The main practical difference between Mk II and Mk IIB was integration; while the former system tied the various avionics systems together to simplify the task at hand, the latter required much greater human involvement. Because its navigation control panel was different than that used by the F-111D, the FB-111A could have up to four OAPs linked to each turn point.

The FB-111A also added some items for its unique strategic mission. These were the astrotracker navigation system (ANS), located in front of the canopy, provisions for the AGM-69 short-range attack missile (SRAM), incorporation of an Air Force satellite communication (AFSATCOM) capability, and an SMS optimised for its mission as a nuclear

bomber. One feature unique to the FB-111A was that it had
no provision for manually releasing weapons – all releases
had to initiate from the system computers, with the AC's
depressing of his 'pickle' button only acting as a consent to
the computer's actions.

The 106 F-111Fs combined the tactical WCP from the analogue F-111E with the Mk IIB avionics system. In combination with much more powerful engines, the F-111F was
close to what the Air Force had in mind when it began the
TFX programme. The F-111F first flew in August 1971, and
deliveries to Mountain Home AFB, Idaho, began one month
later (the new engines having to be retrofitted to the first 49
aircraft). Although the F-111F was much easier to maintain
than the F-111D, it was much more difficult to employ.

Upgrade programmes

Aside from the introduction of the Pave Tack system on
F-111Fs in the early 1980s, no performance-improving
avionics upgrades were ever approved for F-111s. Instead,
upgrades were approved for their reliability and maintain-
ability (R & M) benefits alone, with any performance improvements resulting as the unavoidable fallout of technological progress. Efforts to perform a co-ordinated avionics
facelift, like the multi-staged improvement programmes
(MSIPs) for the F-15 and F-16, were always rejected as being
too expensive, as were state of the art improvements like the
F-15E's synthetic aperture radar (SAR). However, co-ordination of the various piecemeal programmes resulted in increasing similarities between the different variants over the
years.

With the cancellation of the B-1A in 1977, the FB-111A's
importance increased dramatically. The Carter administra-
tions initially proposed an extensive modification of 67 existing FB-111A airframes to FB-111H standard, to be followed
by 98 new builds. However, this proposal was rejected by
Congress to preserve the B-1 programme. SAC then initiated a comprehensive avionics modernisation programme
(AMP) for its existing fleet of aircraft. With TAC selectively
adopting some features for its aircraft, AMP resulted in vary-
ing levels of modification to all USAF versions of the F-111
during the late 1980s. It was responsible for new TFRs being
fitted to all USAF F-111s, and also provided new 64K

Above: 63-9776 was modified to RF-111A standard with a bay-mounted recce pallet. This version was scrapped, as was the later RF-111D version based on the D model bomber.

Right: The FB-111H (upper) was an ambitious project for reworking the FB-111A airframes as strategic bombers with F101 engines and carriage for up to 10 SRAMs, the latter possible by incorporating a tandem undercarriage. When this was cancelled, GD proposed reworking FB-111As and Ds to FB-111B and C models respectively (lower), similar to the FB-111H.

Below: Rear view detail of a 48th TFW F-111F.

weapon/navigation computers (WNCs) for the FB-111A, F-111D and F-111F DCCs. Both the FB-111A and the F-111F received extensive ARS modifications which resulted in a re-designation of that system. The FB-111A alone received dual, state-of-the-art INSs (along with a new control panel), a new TV-type ARS control and display panel (with a rectangular-shaped hood which included a 'peep hole' for the AC), a second UHF radio, and two multi-function displays (MFDs) like those used by the F-16C/D. The FB-111A AMP prototype was 68-0247, with kit-proofing of the production modification being performed on 68-0272.

The new WNCs were the same physical dimensions as the old computers, but contained only two circuit boards. (A decision by the Air Force not to accept a contractor recommendation to double memory to 128K resulted in future programming being restricted to the older Jovial language rather than switching to the new USAF standard, Ada. Modification of the computers after they were built would have cost 10 times what it would have when they were being built.) Unlike the old 4πs, WNCs were essentially redundant. The software programme for these computers varied between different models, with the FB-111A and F-111F being programmed by General Dynamics, while the F-111D used Rockwell. For the FB-111A, WNCs increased the available navigation points from about 100 to 350. For the F-111D they increased to over 800, and the F-111F to 1,000. Turnpoints available increased to three sets of 100 for the FB-111A, one set of 1,000 for the F-111D, and 20 sets of 100 for the F-111F (the differences being driven by hardware limitations on the control panels and competing software requirements). Also, the analogue punch-tape data loader was replaced by a digital computer system, called the mission data terminal (MDT), which utilised data transfer modules (DTMs) to load the information into the aircraft. In the FB-111A, the DTMs were loaded by the WSO in the cockpit, while the tactical aircraft had to be loaded from an external piece of flight-line equipment, called the mission data loader (MDL).

TFD updates

The 1960s technology of the original TFR system was so outdated that vendors were no longer interested in supplying parts for them and the system had become hopelessly unreliable. On occasion, visibly shaken crews returned from daytime missions after the supposedly 'fail-safe' TFR had tried to fly them into the side of a hill. The new system featured better overall capabilities, especially in terms of reliability, all-weather performance, and susceptibility to electronic jamming. At the same time, another part of the TF system, the low-altitude radar altimeter (LARA) was replaced with the similarly updated combined altitude radar altimeter (CARA).

During the early 1980s all F-111Fs were modified with the Pave Tack system which enabled the WSO to visually acquire targets 24 hours a day using high-quality infra-red video, and self-designating them with a laser for attack with laser-guided bombs (LGBs). Integration of this system required additional cockpit controls and displays, the most significant of which was the virtual image display (VID). The VID permitted simultaneous display of both radar and Pave Tack video by use of two small TV displays (the bigger of the two mounted above the smaller) located behind a magnifying glass to make them look larger. So, although the F-111F's radar appears to have a hood similar to that used by other models, it is really quite different. The F-111F's ability to autonomously deliver LGBs at night was a major factor in its selection to participate in the counter-terrorist attack against Libya in 1986. (When other F-111s delivered LGBs, either another aircraft or ground-based lasing was required.)

During 1979/80 four F-111Cs (A8-126, 134, 143, and 146) were modified to RF-111C standard by the installation of a unique pallet in the weapons bay and a control panel in the cockpit. During the mid-1980s, the other surviving F-111Cs were modified with the same Pave Tack system used by the

F-111F. At about the same time, F/RF-111Cs received other modifications to make them compatible with the GBU-15 glide bomb (another F-111F weapon), and (unique to the F-111C community) the AGM-84 Harpoon and AGM-88 HARM.

During the mid-1980s, when it appeared the Cold War would continue indefinitely, the decision was made to update the F-111As and F-111Es with digital avionics. A/E AMP used the FB-111A AMP's cockpit and computer hardware. However, while its software was based on the FB-111A's, it was rewritten in Jovial programming language so it could be maintained by the Air Force instead of contractors. This software was intended as the baseline for all future F-111 software. Another variance from the AMP programme was the use of a single ring laser gyro (RLG) INS with a 7,000 ft (2133 m) per hour drift rate, but updated with GPS inputs through Kalman filtering. (GPS-equipped F-111s are identifiable by an antenna in front of the canopy, where the FB-111A's ANS was located.) The hardware installation and software design contract, awarded to Grumman, progressed slowly on all fronts, with flight testing of the new software being especially troubled. Prototype work was done with F-111A 66-0050 and F-111E 68-0040. The latter effort was considered a failure, and the aircraft was then used as the kit-proof aircraft. The end of the Cold War struck just as the conversion programme was getting underway, and the programme was changed to modify only 25 F-111Es, all of the EF-111As, but none of the F-111As. The first production AMP F-111E was 68-0050, and this aircraft saw action in the 1991 Gulf War.

As the resurrected B-1B was brought on line in the late 1980s, SAC became willing to transfer its FB-111As to TAC. Initial plans called for transferring two squadrons but, as the magnitude of the budget cuts brought about by the end of the Cold War became evident, it was decided to only activate one squadron. F-111G was the designation given to 30 FB-111As after removal of all strategic modifications (except the SMS) and incorporation of the tactical capability to manually initiate weapon release. They were then transferred to TAC at Cannon AFB, beginning in 1990, with the remainder being retired or sold to Australia. As RAF Upper Heyford closes in 1993, its AMP F-111Es will be transferred to Cannon and the F-111Gs retired.

During the early 1990s, the old five-box set of analogue flight control computers will be replaced on all remaining USAF F-111s with a single-computer digital flight control system (DFCS). This modification will be completed either before, or in conjunction with, the F-111F's Pacer Strike modifications as the aircraft undergo depot maintenance. Be-

tween 1993 and 1998, all remaining F-111Fs will be upgraded by Rockwell's Pacer Strike programme to make them very similar to the AMP F-111Es, including the reduced capability of only three sets of 100 TPs and a single 350-data point table. Prototyping is being done with 74-0187, with kit-proofing on 70-2400. The former will be returned to the 27th TFW after completion of testing. The F-111D was originally scheduled for modification with Pave Tack (or even LANTIRN) as part of Pacer Strike, but was removed from that programme in 1990 and retired by 1993. Although they had relatively new airframes and the avionics problems were resolved, F-111Ds had unique equipment and logistic requirements. While many of its features were superior to other F-111s they were also different, and in the post-Cold War days of shrinking defence budgets, different was deadly.

Australian update

The F-111C fleet entered the digital age with Rockwell's avionics update programme (AUP) in the early 1990s to a configuration similar to Pacer Strike F-111Fs. The most im-

Above: AIM-9Ps are the most commonly seen Sidewinder variants on 'Earth Pigs'. This F-111F is in classic 'laser-bomber' configuration, with Pave Tack pod fully deployed, ALQ-131 ECM pod under the rear fuselage and a GBU-10 2,000-lb Paveway II under each wing.

Below: The 'Vark' is more associated with power and speed than manoeuvrability, but the tough airframe can pull g when required. With hard ride selected in hilly terrain, TFR flight can produce gut-wrenching control inputs.

Above: The Harvest Reaper jets were specially prepared for the first deployment to Thailand, equipped with better avionics. However, in the space of 55 missions, three were lost.

Right: An F-111A lands at Takhli after a Combat Lancer mission. Such missions were flown alone, so there was no indication as to what caused the losses of two of the aircraft. However, the aircraft of the one crew to survive was brought down by faulty welding.

Harvest Reaper was the programme codename for upgrading the F-111As sent to Asia.

portant difference between the two will be the substitution of 256K weapon computers for the 64K ones used by the USAF's AMP programme.

With the AMP F-111Es and Pacer Strike F-111Fs having virtually identical avionics, follow-on modifications and software changes will be applied to both. Current plans include a new MFD to replace the ancient SMS, as well as replacing the two WNCs with a single box containing two 640K computers, to be known as the very high speed integrated-circuit computer complex (VCC), which will allow adoption of Ada software programming. These modifications will follow Pacer Strike by about two years. The SMS/VCC prototype aircraft will be F-111E 68-0078 and F-111F 70-2400.

Combat operations

After years of political and technical struggles, and with a real war in progress, there was an overwhelming political need seen to show what this new aircraft could do. The first operational F-111As began arriving at Nellis AFB, Nevada, on 17 July 1967 as part of the initial training programme known as Combat Trident. Six of the early aircraft (66-0017, 0018, 0020, 0021, 0022, and 0023) were chosen to become the first F-111s to be used in combat; these became known as the Harvest Reaper jets, and could be distinguished by their olive drab undersides (at a time when the normal colour was light grey). Only eight months after the first aircraft had arrived, on 15 March 1968 the Harvest Reaper F-111As deployed to Takhli RTAFB, Thailand, as Operation Combat Lancer.

Arriving on 17 March 1968, Combat Lancer was intended to vindicate the much maligned F-111. Instead, this premature and politically motivated deployment quickly began to resemble an attempt to put out a fire by dousing it with gasoline. The first combat sortie was flown successfully on 25 March. However, aircraft 66-0022 was lost on 28 March, followed quickly by 66-0017 on 30 March, with the loss of both crews; because of the low-level profiles being flown, the aircraft vanished without a trace. Two new crews and aircraft (66-0024 and 0025) were sent from Nellis, arriving on 5 April. Missions continued successfully until 22 April when 66-0024 crashed, although the crew ejected successfully. Combat Lancer was suspended and then terminated, following a similar crash at Nellis on 8 May (due to faulty welds in the flight control hardware). The surviving five aircraft finally returned to Nellis on 22 November, having completed only 55 combat missions. Although the potential of the aircraft was evident to those familiar with the operation, the

critics were more vocal than ever.

Several groundings later, the F-111A was again sent into combat. Two squadrons of Nellis F-111As were deployed in late September 1972 back to Takhli as Operation Constant Guard V during the renewed attacks on North Vietnam called Linebacker I. Again unable to resist the temptation to 'hit the ground running', a politically inspired decision was made to preposition a few crews a day early so that missions could be flown as soon as the first six planes to arrive could be refuelled and loaded with bombs. The first missions were flown on 28 September 1972, but resulted in the loss of one aircraft and its crew, one maintenance abort, two successful sorties and two cancellations. There followed a five-day suspension of combat operations while crews were allowed to acclimatise to their new surroundings. This was followed by medium-altitude strikes, beginning on 5 October 1972, with low-level sorties being approached more cautiously.

The F-111 gained the nickname 'Whispering Death' during medium-altitude operations over Laos; Royal Laotian army troops watching it gave it that name because they could not hear anything until the bombs started exploding. In addition to dropping their own bombs, the F-111s also served as 'pathfinders', directing other fighters where to drop their bombs. They also participated in the Linebacker II bombing campaign between 18 and 29 December 1972 (except for Christmas Day). Between 28 September 1972 and March 1973, the 48 Constant Guard V F-111As flew over 4,000 combat sorties while suffering only six combat losses (including 68-0078 on 28 September, 67-0066 on 17 October, 67-0063 on 8 November, 67-0092 on 21 November, 67-0099 on 18 December and 67-0068 on 22 December). There were also two operational losses (67-0072 on 20 February and 67-0111 on 8 May 1973). Its 0.015 per cent loss rate made it the most survivable combat aircraft of the Vietnam War.

Move to Korat

The Vietnam War effectively ended following a January 1973 peace agreement with North Vietnam. By the end of July 1973 F-111 operations shifted from Takhli to Korat RTAFB, north-east of Bangkok, where they remained until returning to the US in mid-June 1975. As a final bit of excitement, F-111As located the SS *Mayaguez* after it was hijacked by Cambodians in May 1975. Vietnam was the only time the F-111A saw combat, although many of those con-

Above: Back in Thailand during Constant Guard V, the F-111As of the 474th TFW were determined to fully demonstrate the capabilities of the F-111. Apart from a disastrous first mission, the aircraft achieved a superb record in the 4,030 combat missions up to 22 February 1973, losing only six aircraft.

Left: A 429th TFS 'yellow-tail' returns from a combat mission. The second SEA sojourn finally dispelled a lot of doubts surrounding the aircraft, proving the accuracy of its weapon delivery and low-level navigation systems. Indeed, it was assigned to some targets in downtown Hanoi which were 'off-limits' to any other aircraft.

Left: Cruising into the sunset, a Constant Guard F-111 sets out on a Linebacker II mission in December 1972. F-111s usually operated alone in South East Asia, using their superb navigation suite and TFR to thread through the terrain unseen by enemy defences. Once in the target area, the radar allowed first-pass blind attacks with highly accurate results. Operating without ECM, Iron Hand defence suppression or fighter cover, the F-111s relied on themselves for defence and swift rescue would have been difficult if the aircraft went down, but crews greatly valued the security of lone missions.

Above: The 347th TFW took over control of the F-111s in Thailand, one of which is seen here with Phantoms of the 4th and 33rd TFWs.

Right: Returning from the Combat Lancer deployment, these F-111As 'torched' Nellis.

Below: EF-111As from Upper Heyford took part in El Dorado Canyon and the Gulf War, while F-111Es flew missions in Proven Force.

verted to EF-111A Ravens were destined for much more action.

Following the Vietnam War, F-111As were relegated to a training role, serving in this capacity at Nellis and Cannon until being transferred to Mountain Home AFB, Idaho, in mid-1977 as part of Operation Creek Swing/Ready Switch. All were retired by the spring of 1992.

EF-111As began arriving at Mountain Home in November 1981. By February 1984 a squadron was based at RAF Upper Heyford. On the night of 14/15 April 1986 five of these aircraft participated in Operation El Dorado Canyon, the counter-terrorist attack on Libya.

Ravens also played a crucial role during the 1991 Gulf War. Five Upper Heyford aircraft were part of Operation Proven Force from Incirlik AB, Turkey, while 20 Ravens from both Upper Heyford and Mountain Home formed part of Operation Desert Storm from Taif AB, Saudi Arabia. The latter flew 875 sorties and 4,401.4 hours. The 390th ECS's 66-0016 scored an unofficial kill on the night of 17 January when a Mirage F1EQ chasing it flew into the ground. The 42nd ECS's 66-0023 (an ex-Combat Lancer F-111A) and crew were lost in combat on 14 February. EF-111As remain in southwest Asia supporting Operations Provide Comfort from Incirlik and Southern Watch from Dhahran AB, Saudi Arabia. Support for the former has gradually shifted from Upper Heyford to Mountain Home to Cannon, while the latter began as the responsibility of Mountain Home, but is now supported by Cannon as well.

Cold War E models

Deliveries of the next variant to enter service, the F-111E, began in late 1969. These were soon interrupted by the F-111A crash which resulted in all F-111s being grounded for the first seven months of 1970. When flying resumed, most F-111Es were delivered to Cannon where they spent several months before being sent to Upper Heyford. Beginning in mid-September 1970, the majority of deliveries to Upper Heyford were completed by July 1971, although an additional 25 aircraft followed in mid-1973. For most of the next 20 years the F-111Es waged the Cold War from their base in Oxfordshire.

F-111Es were deployed on a weapons training detachment at Incirlik when Saddam Hussein invaded Kuwait in August 1990. They remained there, building to a strength of 22 aircraft (including 68-0050 as the sole 'AMP jet') by the beginning of the Gulf War and forming the heart of the night operations staged from Turkey, known as Operation Proven Force. These operations were conducted from medium altitude without loss. Because they lacked the autonomous PGM capability of the F-111Fs, F-111E bombing results were no better than other aircraft with this handicap. F-111Es provided early support to Provide Comfort from Incirlik following the Gulf War. F-111E operations will be reduced throughout 1993, with AMP aircraft transferring to Cannon by mid-July (where they will be used as trainers), and the remainder being retired by December 1993, when Upper Heyford will close.

F-111Fs began arriving at Mountain Home in June 1971. Following the murder of an American officer by North Korean soldiers in what became known as the 'tree chopping incident', F-111Fs were deployed to Taegu AB, Korea, between 16 August and 19 September 1976. Called in on what they believed to be a routine mobility exercise, some airmen were not really prepared to deploy. More than one had packed their mobility bags with crumpled newspapers and were reduced to buying underwear from their better-prepared squadron mates.

After one Reforger exercise (called Cold Fire in the spring, and Central Enterprise in the autumn by the Air Force) in the mid-1970s had such bad weather that only Upper Heyford's F-111Es could fly, it was decided to get more F-111s into NATO as soon as possible. The result was Operation Creek Swing/Ready Switch, which transferred the F-111Fs to

Left: Clutching its load of 12 Mk 82 AIR weapons, 71-0893 launches for El Dorado Canyon on the evening of 14 April 1986. With callsign 'Puffy 11', this aircraft led 'Puffy' and 'Lujac' flights against Tripoli airport. It was the only machine to achieve a hit, destroying two Il-76 transports. The raid launched a new crop of patches, including those shown below left.

Above: 'Remit', 'Elton' and 'Karma' flights hit Al Azziziyah barracks with LGBs, while 'Jewel' hit the Sidi Bilal terrorist training camp. This is 'Remit 31', which damaged Khadaffi's house, preparing to launch for the raid.

Below: Five Upper Heyford EF-111s took part in El Dorado Canyon, with their own special message for Colonel Khadaffi.

RAF Lakenheath, England, in July 1977. This also placed the F-111Fs in NATO before nuclear delivery restrictions were imposed by the strategic arms limitation treaty (SALT I).

Beginning in January 1986, Lakenheath began planning for possible counter-terrorist bombing attacks. Precipitated by the simultaneous machine-gun massacres of airline passengers in Rome and Vienna on 17 December 1985, the planning went through several iterations, awaiting another terrorist incident with a more provable link to the prime suspect, Colonel Muammar Khadaffi's Libya. A 'smoking gun', in the form of the bombing of the La Belle Disco in Berlin, was presented to the US on 5 April 1986. Two basic plans had been generated: an attack of six aircraft flying in international airspace, or one with 18 if overflight permission could be obtained from France. With less than two days to go before the raid the plan was changed to 18 aircraft (plus six spares, which returned after the first inflight refuelling) through international airspace (around Spain), reflecting American and British determination in the face of French reluctance.

Operation El Dorado Canyon occurred on the night of 14/15 April 1986. Nine aircraft were sent against the Azziziyah barracks in Tripoli (where Khadaffi lived), six visited Tripoli's airport, while three others attacked the terrorist training camp at Sidi Bilal, west of Tripoli. Originally the plan had been for six aircraft to go against each target, but this was changed at the last minute by the White House, most probably by a Marine by the name of Lieutenant Colonel Oliver North, who was destined for considerable notoriety a couple of years later. Because the basic plan had been for only two aircraft to attack the barracks complex, and a number of factors made it too difficult to change at the last minute, this attack presented Tripoli's defenders with a succession of targets in single file. They caught on by the eighth aircraft (70-2389) and shot it down, killing the crew. Of greater psychological than military significance, this raid was nonetheless the most successful military action by the United States since the Vietnam War. Its legacy is that it convinced political leaders that the best way to conduct such an endeavour is to define the objectives and constraints, then let the military execute the operation. The fruits of this lesson were harvested during Operations Desert Shield and Desert Storm.

Following the Iraqi invasion of Kuwait on 2 August 1990, the United States initiated Operation Desert Shield to protect Saudi Arabia. The first USAFE wing to deploy was from Lakenheath, with the initial contingent of 19 aircraft leaving for Taif on 25 August, composed of portions of both the 492nd TFS and 494th TFS. A second group of 14 followed on 2 September, which was essentially the 493rd TFS. Mean-

while, the elements of the 492nd TFS and 494th TFS remaining at Lakenheath had been reorganised as the 492nd TFS; this 'new' 492nd TFS was deployed with 12 aircraft on 29 November. A final contingent of 11 aircraft, with most of the 495th TFS instructors, was sent on 11 December. Another six aircraft were transferred piecemeal, bringing the total to 66 aircraft in place at start of Operation Desert Storm on 17 January 1991. These were distributed among named maintenance teams with 18 aircraft each to Justice (492nd AMU) and Freedom (493rd AMU), 17 to Liberty (494th AMU, 74-0183 having been lost with its crew on 10 October during training at Askr bombing range, near Taif), and 13 to Independence (495th AMU). Mission totals for these units were 658, 651, 650 and 458 respectively.

General Dynamics F-111

On the first night of the war aircraft 70-2384 was severely damaged in a collision with a KC-135 and repairs were not completed until after the ceasefire. The first F-111F to drop bombs on Libya, 70-2391, also led the first Desert Storm mission. One aircraft returned with a bullet hole in its tail on the first night, but no aircraft were lost in combat. Only four aircraft and a very small training contingent of 495th TFS personnel remained at Lakenheath, with virtually no flying taking place there between 12 December and the return of most of the wing on 11 and 14 March, with the 492nd TFS remaining at Taif until 11 May.

The F-111F, with its ability to deliver a wide variety of PGMs, was one of Desert Storm's most effective aircraft. Of 2,598 sorties scheduled, 2,417 took off and 1,919 reached the target area (others aborting because of various problems). Total combat hours flown were 9,381.2, meaning that each mission lasted about four hours. The 66 deployed F-111Fs (out of a total of 84, only 70 of which were actually in the wing's possession) dropped 5,576 bombs weighing 3,650 tons and costing nearly $95 million. They destroyed 2,203 targets, including confirmed direct hits on 920 tanks and armoured personnel carriers (one seventh of the total destroyed during the war), 252 artillery pieces, 26 vehicles, 67 troop and munition assembly areas, 245 hardened aircraft shelters (HASs), 113 bunkers, 13 runways, four aircraft in the open, 13 hangars, 19 warehouses, 158 buildings, 23 logistics sites, nine lines of communications (LOCs), 25 surface-to-air missile (SAM) and AAA sites, 11 'Scud' missile sites, five pumping stations, four mine entrances, 32 chemical facilities, nine towers, two ships and 12 bridges destroyed (with another 52 seriously damaged by a total of 160 bomb hits). These attacks resulted in 321 secondary explosions. Of more than 8,000 PGMs delivered by the USAF, F-111Fs delivered 4,666.

The F-111Fs' primary weapons were LGBs which were used against a wide variety of targets. A prime use of the BLU-109-based GBU-10J/Bs and GBU-24A/Bs was the destruction of HASs. While attack packages at the beginning of the air war sent only six aircraft against a given airfield, later raids often had 20-24 aircraft. Targeted against various structures on the airfields, they accounted for 245 of the 375 HASs destroyed during Desert Storm (it is believed that 141 aircraft were destroyed in their shelters). On 24 January F-111Fs carried out the first attack on a 'super HAS', which housed Iraq's most advanced aircraft, but failed to destroy it. They returned two days later and succeeded, prompting the beginning of the exodus to Iran the following morning of the cream of Iraq's air force, including Mirage F1s, MiG-29s, Su-22s and Su-24s. Iraq's air and air defence force commanders were executed the same day.

Staunching the flow

On 27 January, two GBU-15(V)-2/Bs were used to destroy oil manifolds at the Al Almadi pumping station which were feeding an Iraqi-created oil slick in the Persian Gulf. Four 493rd TFS aircraft were launched, all configured with two bombs, datalink and ECM pods. One aircraft was forced to turn back because of maintenance problems. Two of the remaining aircraft (the first flown by Captains Rick Walker and Ken Theurer, the second by Major Sammy Samson and Captain Steve Williams) each delivered a single GBU-15 at supersonic speeds, while the third (flown by Captains Mike Russell and Brad Seipel) orbited about 50 miles (80 km) away, guiding the bombs to their targets.

During an LGB attack on 28 January, Captains Matt Young and Greg Chapman were flying the first of 20 F-111Fs attacking Tallil AB, in south-eastern Iraq. Their direct hit on an ammunition storage area resulted in the largest non-nuclear, man-made explosion ever detected by a Defence Support Program (DSP) missile warning satellite. After-

Above: Four F-111Fs loaded with GBU-24A/Bs prepare to follow an EF-111A to the Taif runway. The wait for the first mission had been a long one, the first 'Earth Pigs' arriving in Saudi Arabia on 25 August 1990. During the aerial onslaught which began on the night of 16/17 January 1991, the Lakenheath 'swingers' caused more damage to Iraq than any other weapon system.

Right: To simplify maintenance procedures, a sizeable force of 'Spark Varks' was also based at Taif, drawn from both Mountain Home (illustrated) and Upper Heyford. Much of the training during the Desert Shield phase involved low-level work over the featureless desert to acclimatise crews.

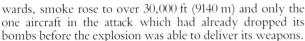

wards, smoke rose to over 30,000 ft (9140 m) and only the one aircraft in the attack which had already dropped its bombs before the explosion was able to deliver its weapons.

The campaign against bridges began on 29 January; it was soon discovered that the BLU-109 warheads which worked so well against HASs tended to go cleanly through a bridge and explode under it. Ordnance was switched to the older Mk 84 warheads, which proved more effective against this class of target. (Some GBU-15s were also tried on bridges, but LGBs were the primary weapon.)

Attacks on Iraqi tank and artillery concentrations began on 5 February, with F-111Fs dropping four GBU-12s per mission. This mission quickly became known as 'tank plinking' (much to the initial ire of General Schwarzkopf, but the term stuck). During one raid, on 13 February, 46 aircraft destroyed 132 tanks and armoured vehicles and, on another, 20 aircraft destroyed 77 tanks.

On 27 February, the final night of the war, two F-111Fs each delivered a single GBU-28/B 'Deep Throat' bomb against a deep command bunker at Al Taji AB, just north of Baghdad; one of three such bunkers where Saddam Hussein reportedly spent most of the war. (Developed and deployed in only 17 days, the first GBU-28 had been dropped only three days earlier by F-111F 74-0186 at the Nellis test ranges.) The GBU-28 dropped from the 495th TFS squadron commander's aircraft, 70-2391, hit where it was aimed, but missed the bunker. However, the one dropped from 70-2387 (a 493rd yellow-tail, flown by Lieutenant Colonel Dave White and Captain Tom Hines) scored a direct hit, killing several high-ranking Iraqis. Dropping the bombs from a much higher than normal altitude required climbing in afterburner across most of southern Iraq; the Mk 84 'ballast' was expended on Al Taqaddum AB, west of Baghdad, as the aircraft headed south for a much-needed inflight refuelling prior to returning to base. Plans to destroy the other two bunkers in downtown Baghdad were thwarted by the ceasefire, the second two bombs not arriving at Taif until two days later. 70-2387 originally belonged to the 494th TFS, but was maintained and flown by the 493rd TFS Freedom organisation during the war. While its red fin cap and main wheel hubs were overpainted yellow (it had no pin-stripes on the nose gear doors), it kept the 494th TFS patch on the right side of the fuselage, albeit with a very small block beneath it proclaiming the '493rd AMU' as its maintainers. After the war ended, it was due for programmed depot maintenance (PDM) in Sacramento and transferred to the 495th TFS, the first Lakenheath unit scheduled to disband. Before it was flown to America in early April 1991, its fin cap was painted green, but other markings were as during the war. After PDM, it was transferred to Cannon.

One of the most remarkable aspects of the F-111Fs' performance during Desert Storm is the fact that there was not a single unscheduled engine change during the entire war. It is also interesting that three of the four jets which flew the most sorties in Desert Storm also participated in the 1986 Libya raid, when aircraft performance was monitored for several months to determine which were the 'best flyers'. Aircraft with the most combat missions were 74-0181 from 492nd/Justice, which became the 492nd TFS/CC's aircraft after the war (this was the only one of the four not to participate in the Libya raid); 70-2396 from 493rd/Freedom; 74-0178 from 494th/Liberty, which became the 494th TFS/CC's aircraft after the war; and 70-2403 from 495th/Independence, which became the 493rd TFS/CC's aircraft after the war.

Operation Provide Comfort to defend the Kurdish population in northern Iraq began on 5 April 1991 and was supported by a rotating contingent of 11 Lakenheath aircraft and crews based at Incirlik from 25 September 1991 until 2 October 1992. At that time Provide Comfort operations were taken over by Cannon, which had begun to absorb Lakenheath's F-111Fs.

What the future holds

Production of F-111s ended in 1976 with the Fiscal Year 1974 purchase of 12 F-111Fs. In 1978, the Air Force leadership became seriously interested in the McDonnell Douglas 'Strike Eagle' proposal. An *ad hoc* group was formed, under the title of Tactical All-Weather Requirements Study (TAWRS), with the hidden agenda of justifying the 'Strike Eagle' programme. Told to 'look at everything', TAWRS did – and came back with an initial recommendation of buying more F-111s. However, they received further guidance and eventually generated the politically correct F-15 response. It was probably only a coincidence that shortly thereafter the

While the aircraft at Taif were bedded-down in superb shelters (above) in well-protected flow-through complexes, the troops had to make do with less effective accommodation. A 'tent city' sprung up within the shelter complex to house most of the personnel and ancillary offices (above left).

Below: F-111Fs dropped the majority of PGMs in Desert Storm, mostly laser-guided bombs such as the GBU-10Is shown here. The 493rd TFS crews revised their squadron badge to reflect the unit's speciality – the GBU-15 EO-guided bomb.

Below: Is the sun setting on the 'Earth Pig', or is it just time for another nocturnal foray? Although the immediate future of the 'Vark' seems assured, the fact that the force of expensive aircraft is now concentrated at one base makes it an extremely attractive and highly vulnerable target for axe-swinging politicians. Despite Desert Storm finally demonstrating beyond any doubt the awesome powers of the type, it remains perhaps the most misunderstood aircraft in the world's skies, even 25 years after its service entry.

F-111 production tooling was scrapped. (Beginning at about this time, the shortage of F-111s led to the rebuilding over several years of 13 aircraft that would have normally been written off.)

The proposed successor for the F-111, F-117 and F-15E was to have been a version of the Navy's highly-classified A-12 Avenger II, advanced tactical aircraft (ATA). Employing stealth technologies, it was being developed as a replacement for the carrier-based A-6 Intruder. However, the A-12 programme became bogged down with management and technical problems and was cancelled in January 1991, just before the beginning of Operation Desert Storm. It was replaced by the AX programme, which reduced the A-12's internal carriage requirement by two-thirds, to only 4,000 lb (1810 kg). Confronted with overwhelming budget constraints, and not scheduled to become operational with the Navy until well into the next century, AX requirements continued to fluctuate until, in late 1992, the programme became known as A/FX, reflecting the need for the next Navy aircraft to have multi-role capabilities. As this is written, it appears that the range capabilities of the A/FX will be de-emphasised to increase its manoeuvrability. While not surprising of a pro-

gramme which looks increasingly like a stealthy Tomcat, it will be interesting to see how well it stacks up against the considerable range/payload capabilities of the F-111.

How much longer the F-111 continues to serve will depend in great part on how much deeper the Clinton administration cuts the defence budget. With both the B-1B and B-2A having been freed from their strategic missions, the question of how important it is to have a 'tactical' aircraft that can 'reach out and touch someone' becomes very relevant, especially with all the F-111s now located in New Mexico. (It is interesting to note the shift in June 1992 of the 27th FW from 12th AF to 8th AF, putting all F-111s under control of what used to be SAC.) Under the original 'Base Force' plan, F-111s are scheduled to remain operational until about 2015, at which time the youngest surviving airframes will have seen front-line service for nearly 40 years – quite an accomplishment for an airplane often regarded as a failure.

The General Dynamics F-111 and EF-111 will be the subject of a future variant briefing in *World Air Power Journal*.

Above left: The most famous bomb of the Gulf War: the GBU-28 'Deep Throat' weapon is carried on its way to the command bunker at Al Taji by F-111F 70-2387 on the last night of the war. A 2,000-lb Mk 84 was carried on the starboard wing as ballast for the 4,800-lb weapon. Another GBU-28, dropped by 70-2391, did not penetrate the bunker. The F-15E had originally been earmarked for the GBU-28 drop.

Left: The future begins with 'F' – surviving as the main strike version for the USAF, the F models have left Europe behind for a new career at Cannon.

F-111 Operators

United States Air Force

Procurement of the F-111 for the USAF totalled 531 aircraft. Twenty-seven F-111As, including 17 pre-production (63-9766/82) and 10 'production' (65-5701/10) aircraft, were involved in the flight test programme (63-9776 was the only RF-111A). These were followed by 131 true production aircraft (66-0011/58, 67-0032/0114). The next aircraft to be delivered were 94 F-111Es (67-0115/24, 68-0001/84), between late 1969 and early 1971. Two YF-111As (67-0149/50) were completed as test aircraft using airframes from the RAF's cancelled F-111K programme. The 18th pre-production F-111A airframe (63-9783) was completed as the YFB-111A. The first two FB-111As (67-0159/60) were non-standard and only used as test aircraft. These were followed by 74 true FB-111As (67-0161/3, 67-7192/6, 68-0239/92, 69-6503/14) using many of the components already completed for the F-111Ks. FB-111A deliveries occurred during late 1971. Deliveries of the initial batches of 106 F-111Fs began at the end of June 1971, with the first 69 (70-2362/2419 and 71-0883/94) being delivered by the end of 1972 (70-2407 being lost prior to delivery). Meanwhile, the delivery of 96 F-111Ds (68-0085/0180) took place between November 1971 and March 1973. Deliveries of the final 36 F-111Fs (72-1441/52, 73-0707/18, 74-0177/88) were completed between 1973 and 1975.

Conversions include 42 F-111As to EF-111A Raven standard between November 1981 and December 1985 (aircraft involved being 66-0013/6, 0018/21, 0023, 0027/8, 0030/1, 0033, 0035/9, 0041, 0044, 0046/51, 0055/7, 67-0032/5, 0037/9, 0041/2, 0044, 0048, 0052) and 30 FB-111As to F-111G standard during 1990/91 (67-0162/3, 7193/4, 7196, 68-0240/1, 0244, 0252, 0255, 0257, 0260, 0264/5, 0272/3, 0276/7, 0281/2, 0284, 0289, 69-6503/4, 6506, 6508/10,

F-111Ds, Fs and Gs line the ramp at Cannon in mid-1992. In 1993 the entire 'Aardvark' force has been concentrated at this one base, the variant line-up now comprising F-111E, F-111F and EF-111A.

6512, 6514). Only 25 F-111Es received the extensive AMP changes during 1990/92 (68-0022, 0027, 0032, 0040/41, 0044, 0047/48, 0050, 0054, 0063, 0067/68, 0071/77, 0079/80, 0082/84). Other aircraft include nine GF-111As (63-9768, 9772, 9775, 66-0012, 67-0046/7, 0051, 0056/7) and one GF-111E (68-0027, an AMP aircraft) retired from flying duties to serve as ground instructional airframes.

20th Fighter Wing

Based at RAF Upper Heyford, USAFE's 20th Tactical Fighter Wing (motto: Victory by Valor) was assigned the F-111E from 12 September 1970. The first recipient squadron was the 79th Tactical Fighter Squadron ('Tigers'; yellow fin-band; 'UR' tailcode), joined by the 77th TFS ('Gamblers'; red fin-band; 'UT' tailcode) in December, and the 55th TFS ('Fightin' 55th'; blue fin-band; 'US' tailcode) in early 1971. In fact, the 55th did not get to adopt its first code, as these were changed in 1971 to 55th 'JS', 77th 'JT' and 79th 'JR'. In mid-1972 the 20th TFW changed from squadron to wing maintenance, and the tailcodes were further changed by mid-summer to 'UH', which was carried for the next 20 years. Other marking changes consisted of the 55th changing its fin markings to a blue/white check, and the 79th adopting a yellow/black tiger stripe to qualify for NATO Tiger Squadron status.

Eighty-nine F-111Es were eventually delivered to Upper Heyford, including 53 in late 1970 and 10 more in early 1971 (most

The 20th TFW has had three tailcoding systems since its switch to F-111Es. Shown above is a 79th TFS machine, wearing the 'JR' codes worn in 1971/72. At left is the wing's badge.

aircraft appear to have spent a few months at Cannon AFB, NM, before being sent). Virtually all F-111Es cycled through McClellan AFB, CA, during 1972/73 for a modification programme, the last returning to RAF Upper Heyford on 24 August 1973. Runway repairs at Heyford meant that the aircraft took up temporary residence at RAF Greenham Common for a time in the mid-1970s. F-111Es were dispatched to the 7440th Composite Wing at Incirlik for Operation Proven Force (the Turkey-based equivalent of Desert Storm), and following their return the unit was redesignated the 20th Fighter Wing on 2 October 1991, the three constituent squadrons also dropping the 'Tactical' designator. The 20th FW will be deactivated during 1993, the schedule calling

Left: EF-111As were assigned to the 20th TFW from early 1984, but were transferred to 66th ECW control the following year.

for the 79th FS to go in June, the 77th in September and the 55th in December. The non-AMP aircraft will go straight to AMARC for storage, including all those of the 55th FS. One 77th FS aircraft has gone to Sheppard AFB as a GF-111E ground instructional airframe. Twenty-four AMP aircraft will continue service with the 27th FW at Cannon.

For two periods in its career, the 20th also operated the EF-111A Raven. The 42nd Electronic Combat Squadron ('NATO Ravens'; tailcode 'UH') was assigned from 3 February 1984 until 30 June 1985, when control passed to the 66th ECW. The aircraft remained at Upper Heyford, and were reunited with the 20th TFW on 25th January 1991 during the Gulf War. During this conflict

Below: Examples from Upper Heyford's squadrons fly over Loch Ness. The 42nd ECS leads the 79th, 77th and 55th TFS.

Heyford 'Spark Varks' were detached to both Incirlik and Taif. In July 1992 the 42nd ECS was disbanded, and its aircraft transferred to the 366th Wing at Mountain Home.

Above: The 79th TFS was an important member of the NATO 'Tiger Squadron' club, and painted 68-0049 accordingly.

Above: 68-0050 was one of the 20th TFW's first F-111E AMP aircraft, and was the only such variant to fly in the Gulf War, complete with all-over grey scheme. Unusually, this aircraft also has a grey radome; on other repainted aircraft this is left black.

27th Fighter Wing

Cannon AFB, New Mexico, and its resident 27th Fighter Wing (motto: Intelligent Strength) is the unrivalled 'Home of the One-Eleven'. Its association with the type began in mid-1969 with the assignment of 10 F-111As loaned from Nellis prior to the delivery of F-111Es. First squadron assignments were to the 522nd TFS 'Fireballs' ('CC' tailcode; red fin-band) from 10 July 1969 and the 481st TFS 'Green Knights' ('CA' tailcode; green fin-band). The A models returned to Nellis by the end of the year, just before the imposition of a fleet-wide grounding.

The F-111Es arrived just prior to the grounding, and it is believed that only about 15 were supplied instead of the often-reported 29. The first F-111E for the 522nd TFS arrived on 30 September 1969, with the first for the 481st probably in November. Following the lifting of the grounding, most E models spent several months at Cannon before being passed on to the 20th TFW, between September 1970 and July 1971.

Ten F-111As were again loaned from Nellis (66-0027/8, 0030/1, 0034, 0036, 0038, 0052, 0054, and 0056), these serving with the 522nd TFS from September 1971 until August 1972 (except for 0038 which was assigned periodically until October). During this time the 481st TFS became temporarily non-operational.

The much-delayed conversion to the intended F-111D began with the delivery of

Cannon's first F-111s were 10 A models loaned from Nellis. The first squadron to get the 'Vark' was the 522nd TFS 'Fireballs', identified by a red fin-band.

four aircraft in 1971, starting on 12 November with the delivery of the first aircraft to the newly-created 4427th TFRS

Above: When the 27th received its intended D models, the first aircraft were delivered to a newly-formed squadron, the 4427th TFRS with 'CE' tailcode. This example carries AIM-9B Sidewinders.

Above right: Although F-111Es are again assigned to the 27th, they were indeed a rarity the first time around. This is one of the 15 or so E models which served at Cannon before being passed on to Upper Heyford. This machine was written off in 1979.

Right: The 27th TFW was the only operational unit to receive F-111Ds, and flew them for over 20 years. The yellow fin-band denoted the 524th TFS.

27th FW aircraft carry on the nose the 'Zia' emblem, often painted in low-vis dark grey.

Above: To centralise maintenance for the entire F-111 fleet, the Ravens are now based at Cannon, flying with the newly-formed 430th ECS.

training squadron ('CE' tailcode changing to 'CC' after the 27th TFW's conversion to wing maintenance in December 1971; purple fin-band). The 522nd TFS 'Fireballs' converted between May and November 1972, and the 524th TFS 'Hounds' (yellow fin-band) began converting from F-100D/Fs in August. Finally, the 481st TFS regained operational status in November 1972, concluding the conversion process, accepting the last F-111D delivered, on 28 February 1973. On 31 August 1973,

Below: The F-111E is used by the 428th FS for training purposes, having replaced the F-111G.

this unit renumbered as the 523rd TFS 'Crusaders' (dark blue fin-band). On 15 January 1976 the 4427th TFRS became the 481st TFTS, but continued the conversion role until 8 June 1980, when it disbanded for the final time, passing the training function to the redesignated 524th TFTS. (The 523rd TFS also had a training role.)

Radical changes affected the 27th Fighter Wing in the early 1990s. A fourth squadron, the 428th TFTS 'Buccaneers' (light blue fin-band) was established in June 1990 to operate the F-111Gs (ex-SAC FB-111As) in the training role. On 2 October 1991, the designations of the wing and the four squadrons (428th, 522nd, 523rd, 524th) deleted all references to 'Tactical' and 'Training'. In mid-1992, the 27th FW became a five-squadron wing with the establishment at Cannon of the 430th ECS 'Tigers'. The conversion of three squadrons with ex-48th FW F-111Fs was started by the 522nd FS in February 1992. The 524th FS received its first F-111F on 30 September, with the 523rd

FS completing the conversion at year's end; the F-111Ds all being retired to AMARC. Once equipped with F-111Fs, Operation Provide Comfort tasking in Turkey was transferred from the 48th FW to the 27th FW on 2 October 1992. The F-111Gs were retired by mid-1993 and replaced in the 428th FS by ex-20th FW AMP F-111Es. EF-IIIAs of the 429th ECS arrived from Mountain Home in mid-1993.

Above: The slight bulge forward of the cockpit identifies this 'Vark' as an F-111G, used only by the 428th TFS at Cannon.

Below: F-model 'Varks' from Lakenheath replaced the F-111Ds with Cannon's three operational strike squadrons.

46th Test Wing

Located at Eglin AFB, Florida, this wing took over from the 3246th TW and 3247th TS on 2 October 1992, and is primarily concerned with the testing and evaluation of aircraft ordnance, operating a variety of front-line USAF types. The fin-band for the unit is white with red diamonds and the tailcode is 'ET'. The 46th TW will assume an increasingly important role in the qualification test and evaluation (QT&E) of F-111 modifications. In the mid-1990s it will perform most of the functions previously associated with SM-ALC's Engineering Flight Test at McClellan. F-111E 68-0078 and F-111F 70-2400 will be assigned there at the completion of SMS/VCC testing.

48th Fighter Wing

The best-known operator of the 'Earth Pig', the 48th TFW 'Statue of Liberty Wing' was a USAFE stalwart, previously flying F-100s and F-4s from RAF Lakenheath, England. Its F-111F aircraft arrived in mid-1977 as part of Operation Creek Swing/Ready Switch. The first squadron to receive aircraft was the 494th TFS 'Panthers' (red fin-band) on 1 June, followed by the 493rd TFS (yellow fin-band) on 1 July, 492nd TFS 'Bowlers' (blue fin-band) on 11 July and the 495th TFS (green fin-band) on 13 July 1977. During the summer of 1983, the wing operated from RAF Sculthorpe, west of Fakenham, Norfolk, while the runway at Lakenheath was resurfaced. The 48th TFW represented the most potent strike force in the NATO inventory throughout its F-111 period, and was chosen as the USAF component of the Operation El Dorado Canyon, attacking targets around Tripoli, Libya, on the night of 14/15 April 1986. Eighteen aircraft took part, plus six spares, drawn from all four squadrons (70-2363, 2371, 2382/3, 2386/7, 2389/90, 2394, 2396, 2403/5, 2413, 2415/6, 71-0888/9, 0893, 72-1445, 1449, 73-0707, 74-0177/8).

In August 1990 the 48th TFW established a provisional wing as part of Desert Shield, and by the time Desert Storm began, on 17 January 1991, only a handful of aircraft remained at Lakenheath. The 48th TFW re-established at Lakenheath in mid-March 1991, but maintained a deployment at Incirlik in Turkey from 25 September 1991 as part of Operation Provide Comfort to protect Kurds in the northern part of Iraq. The 48th TFW changed to the 48th Fighter Wing on 2 October 1991. On 2 October 1992 the Provide Comfort tasking was passed to the 27th FW.

F-111 operations at Lakenheath began drawing down with the disbandment of the 495th TFS (which did not convert to an FS) on 15 December 1991. It was followed by the 492nd FS on 20 April 1992, the 494th FS on 13 August and the 493rd FS on 15

Below: An aircraft from the 493rd TFS over Turkey. This squadron specialised in GBU-15 delivery.

Above: Until the end of September 1992, the 48th FW manned the Provide Comfort F-111F detachment in Turkey.

December. After returning from Desert Storm, the 493rd reversed the yellow and black colours on its squadron patch and changed the colour of its fin caps to black with yellow pinstripes. All Lakenheath aircraft passed to the 27th FW at Cannon, but only the 492nd and 494th re-equipped with the F-15E.

Right: A 492nd TFS aircraft (with GBU-10) accompanies one from the 493rd. Only the 492nd and 494th Fighter Squadrons were retained when the wing adopted F-15Es.

For F-111s based in England, overhauls were performed by British Aerospace at Filton, where this 495th TFS 'green-tail' is seen.

F-111 Operators

48th Tactical Fighter Wing (Provisional)

Following the Iraqi invasion of Kuwait on 2 August 1990, the United States initiated Operation Desert Shield to protect Saudi Arabia. The first USAFE wing to deploy was from Lakenheath, with the initial contingent of 19 aircraft leaving for Taif on 25 August, composed of portions of both the 492nd TFS and 494th TFS. A second group of 14, which was essentially the 493rd TFS, followed on 2 September. Meanwhile, the elements of the 492nd TFS and 494th TFS remaining at Lakenheath had been reorganised as the 492nd TFS; this 'new' 492nd TFS was deployed with 12 aircraft on 29 November. A final contingent of 11 aircraft, with most of the 495th TFS instructors, was sent on 11 December. Another six aircraft were transferred piecemeal, bringing the total to 66 aircraft in place at the start of Operation Desert Storm on 17 January 1991 (70-2362/5, 2369/71, 2378/9, 2383/4, 2386/7, 2390/2, 2394, 2396, 2398/9, 2401/6, 2408/9, 2411/7,2419; 71-0883/92, 72-1442/6, 1448/52; 73-0708, 0710, 0712, 0715; 74-0177/8, 0180/2, 0184/5), with 70-2369 replacing 70-2384 (which was damaged in a collision with a KC-135 on the first night of the air war), and 74-0183 having been lost with its crew on 10 October during training at Askr bombing range, near Taif.

The 48th TFW(P) was established to control the aircraft at their new base. With the aircraft and personnel having been thoroughly mixed in the gradual deployment, the four maintenance squadrons were formed into 'teams', which situated themselves in the four shelter complexes at Taif and adopted the following names: 492nd, 'Justice'; 493rd, 'Freedom'; 494th, 'Liberty'; and 495th, 'Independence'. During the ensuing conflict, the F-111Fs proved to be the real workhorses of the aerial onslaught (dropping nearly 60 per cent of the war's LGBs), despite being outplayed by the F-117s in the glamour stakes. The figures speak for themselves: the 48th TFW(P) flew 2,417 sorties for 9,381.2 hours, during which they dropped 469 GBU-10, 389 GBU-10I, 2,542 GBU-12, 270 GBU-24, 924 GBU-24A and two GBU-28 laser-guided bombs; 62 IIR- and eight EO-guided GBU-15 bombs; and 530 CBU-87, 212 CBU-89, 12 Mk 82 and 146 Mk 84 cluster and iron bombs. Among the many notable achievements was the use of GBU-15s to staunch the flow of oil from a Kuwaiti oil refinery sabotaged by the Iraqis, the destruction of 245 of the 375 aircraft shelters (and the 141 aircraft in them) destroyed during the war, the use of GBU-12 LGBs on anti-armour 'tank-plinking' missions, and the dropping of two GBU-28 'Deep Throat' bunker-buster bombs on the final night of the war.

Also controlled by the 48th TFW(P) were 13 EF-111A Ravens drawn from the 390th ECS at Mountain Home (66-0014, 0027, 0030, 0033, 0037, 0044, 0046, 0057; 67-0037/41), dispatched in August 1990, and

Above: Towards the end of the campaign, the F-111Fs undertook 'tank-plinking' missions, armed with four 500-lb GBU-12 LGBs.

Many of the F-111Fs racked up impressive mission tallies (right), but there was little in the way of decoration. EF-111s picked up some nose art (below).

five from the 42nd ECS at Upper Heyford, which were transferred to the wing's control on the first day of the war (66-0016, 0023, 0038, 0050, 0056). The EF-111A flew 875 missions, lasting 4,401.4 hours. A 390th ECS machine, 66-0016, flown by Captains Jim Denton (AC) and Brent Brandon (WSO), scored an unofficial kill on the first night of the war when it decoyed a pursuing Mirage F1EQ into the ground. A 42nd ECS EF-111A (66-0023, a survivor of the F-111's first Combat Lancer deployment to Thailand) was lost with its crew on 14 February.

The 48th TFW(P) ceased to exist in March 1991, command reverting to Lakenheath (although elements of the 492nd TFS remained at Taif until 10 May 1991).

Right: A pair of Mountain Home 'Spark Varks' prepares to launch. Upper Heyford Ravens were also deployed.

Fully armed and ready to roll, an F-111F basks outside its shelter at Taif. In addition to the GBU-24A/B penetration bombs, it carries an AIM-9P-3 for self-defence.

57th Fighter Weapons Wing

Headquartered at Nellis AFB, Nevada, the 57th FWW is the USAF's main tactical evaluation and trials unit, tasked with assessing aircraft modifications (IOT&E) as well as developing and teaching new tactics to experienced fliers so they can pass them on to their squadrons. The 57th also evaluates the lessons of combat so they can continue to evolve better tactics. Therefore, small numbers of each tactical aircraft are assigned to the wing throughout the front-line careers of the type. In the case of F-111s, about six aircraft were assigned at any given time to each of the units.

The 57th FWW was created by the renumbering of the 4525th FWW on 15 October 1969. It was the 57th Tactical Training Wing (TTW) from April 1977 through

The badge of the 57th FWW reflects its work: development of tactical air power.

This was one of four F-111Es assigned to Det. 3, 57th FWW at McClellan AFB. This unit matured as the 431st TES soon after the aircraft was photographed in February 1980.

February 1980 before reverting to its original FWW designation. The yellow/black check fin-band has not altered throughout the unit's history.

The 57th FWW's F-111 unit at Nellis was the 422nd FWS; it took over from the 4539th CCTS on 15 October 1969, operating F-111As until 1973, gaining F-111Es in late 1969, and an F-111F in May 1972. Although the switch to wing level maintenance was made on 15 August 1971, the change from the squadron's old 'WF' to the new 'WA' tailcode took a few months; during 1972/73 there were five F-111Es assigned to testing duties (68-0099, 0101, 0174/6). Because of the unique complexities of F-111 maintenance, it was found to be more efficient to conduct the wing's testing and training functions where the aircraft could be most easily supported. As a result of this consideration, the operation at Nellis ceased on 15 August 1977, with its functions being taken over by 'detachments' using local maintenance, aircraft and tailcodes. Although several aircraft would usually bear the 57th FWW's black and yellow checkerboard, operationally the aircraft were used as necessary.

The first test and evaluation detachment was Det. 2, which existed without aircraft at Cannon from October 1970 through April 1972, when it moved to McClellan (although five aircraft for operational test duties were assigned to Cannon between March 1972 and December 1973), from May 1972 until August 1977. Det. 3 had existed at Mountain Home without aircraft (possibly borrowing F-111Fs from the 347th TFW), from August 1971 through April 1972, when it returned to Nellis. Det. 3 superseded Det. 2 at McClellan on 15 August 1977, moving from

Nellis with four F-111Es (67-0120, 0123/4 and 68-0033) and one F-111F (probably 70-2400) as part of Creek Swing/Ready Switch, while retaining Det. 2's F-111Ds (68-0085/6, and 0088) until becoming the 431st Test and Evaluation Squadron (TES) 'Red Devils' in March 1980. The 431st TES operated F-111Ds, F-111Es (until late 1991), and F-111Fs for the 57th FWW through June 1992, when it was disbanded. On occasion, F-111Cs were detached there for testing which could not be performed in Australia.

The F-111 Fighter Weapons School was formed as Det. 2/57th FWW, with F-111As, at Mountain Home, from July 1977 through December 1981. It was redesignated as Det. 1/USAF Fighter Weapons School in January 1982, and operated there through May 1988. From June 1988 through June 1992, it moved to Cannon and operated F-111Ds.

On 1 July 1992, Det. 3/57th FWW was reformed with F-111Fs at Cannon. It now performs all the functions which had belonged to both the 431st TES and the USAF Fighter Weapons School.

*Above: Based alongside the F-111 maintenance centre at McClellan, the 431st **TES** flew this F-111G.*

*Below: Det. 3 at Cannon is now the only 57th **FWW** sub-organisation remaining with F-111s. It only flies the F-111F.*

66th Electronic Combat Wing

On 1 July 1985, control of the 42nd Electronic Combat Squadron passed from the 20th TFW to the 66th ECW (motto: *Omnia Conspicimus*). Although the wing's headquarters were at Sembach AB, West

In the late 1980s, the 66th ECW provided electronic warfare coverage for the European theatre.

Germany (from where the wing's 43rd ECS flew EC-130H 'Compass Call' aircraft), the EF-111A Ravens remained at RAF Upper Heyford, England, and continued to wear the 'UH' tailcodes from their previous assignment.

The 42nd ECS was called into action twice, the first time on the night of 14/15 April 1986, for Operation El Dorado Canyon. Four aircraft participated, plus one air spare

which is believed to have tagged along for the entire mission, remaining with its tanker. Six aircraft were prepared for the mission, including a ground spare, which did not launch. These were 66-0030, 0033, 0057, as well as 68-0034, 0041, 0052.

For the 1991 Gulf War, aircraft from the 42nd ECS were assigned to the 7440th Wg (P) at Incirlik from late 1990, and others joined the 48th TFW(P) at Taif. 25 January marked the effective end of control for the 66th ECW, as aircraft returning from the war reverted to 20th TFW control.

*Although the Ravens switched wing control, the aircraft remained with the 42nd **ECS**, and also stayed at **U**pper Heyford.*

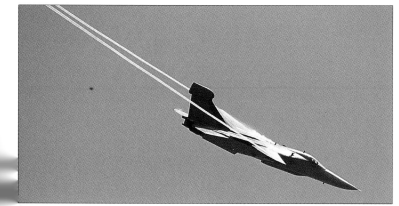

340th Bomb Group

Located at Carswell AFB, Texas, the 340th Bomb Group established the 4007th Combat Crew Training Squadron (CCTS) on 29 September 1969 to perform the training mission for the FB-111A force. This tasking ended on 9 September 1971 when the mission and squadron were transferred to the 380th Bomb Wing at Plattsburgh.

*Early FB-111As were delivered from the **GD** factory to the 4007th **CCTS**, co-located at Carswell **AFB**.*

F-111 Operators

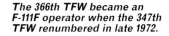

347th Tactical Fighter Wing

The 347th TFW was resurrected at Mountain Home AFB, Idaho, to receive the first F-111F aircraft and begin proficiency training. It was the 391st TFS 'Bold Tigers' ('MO' tailcode; blue fin-band) which received the first machine on 30 June 1971, followed by the 4589th TFS ('MP' tailcode; yellow fin-band) on 1 September 1971 and the 4590th TFS ('MQ' tailcode; red fin-band) on 1 January 1972. Squadron redesignations occurred on 15 October 1971 (4589th to 389th TFS 'Thunderbolts') and 1 July 1972

A 429th TFS F-111A, carrying ALQ-87 ECM pods, is seen on a mission from Takhli. The wing moved to Korat for the latter part of its existence.

(4590th to 390th TFS 'Boars'), both squadrons adopting the 'MO' tailcode (wing-level maintenance having been adopted on 15 December 1971). On 31 October 1972, the wing was redesignated as the 366th TFW while retaining the same squadrons.

The 347th was shortly to be reunited with the 'Earth Pig', but this time with the F-111A model. It had reformed at Takhli RTAFB, Thailand, and took control of the 474th TFW's Constant Guard V deployment on 30 July 1973. Two squadrons were assigned, the 428th TFS 'Buccaneers' (light blue fin-band) and the 429th TFS 'Black Falcons' (yellow fin-band), both wearing the 'HG' tailcode. Twelve aircraft returned to Nellis from Takhli on 11 September 1973 (this movement was probably six aircraft from each squadron: 429th TFS 67-0059, 0065,

0084/7 and 0090; 428th TFS 67-0058, 0067, 0100/1, 0104 and 0112). Aircraft 67-0060 was probably lost (non-combat) sometime after 12 September 1973. A move was made to Korat RTAFB on 13 June 1974, where the wing remained in South East Asia for contingency operations, on 13/14 May 1975 flying in support of the rescue of the SS *Mayaguez* from Cambodian forces. Fourteen aircraft from the 428th departed Korat for Nellis on 15 June 75 (Coronet Par), with the

Seen shortly after its return from South East Asia, this F-111A wears the 'HG' codes of the 347th TFW, although it returned to 474th control once back in the United States.

final 16 from the 429th leaving on 20 June 75 (Coronet Birdie), five others having returned earlier.

366th Wing

After a period under 347th TFW control at Mountain Home AFB, the 389th TFS 'Thunderbolts' (yellow fin-band), 390th TFS 'Boars' (red fin-band) and 391st TFS 'Bold Tigers' (blue fin-band) all transferred to the 366th TFW 'Gunslingers' (motto: *Audentes Fortuna* Juvat) at the same base, retaining the 'MO' tailcode on their F-111Fs. During the Mountain Home period, the F models were deployed to Taegu AB, South Korea, during the Korean Contingency of 16 August

to 19 September 1976.

As part of Operation Creek Swing/Ready Switch, the 366th dispatched its aircraft to Lakenheath on 3 June 1977 (from the 389th TFS), 1 July (from the 390th) and 11 July (from the 391st). With its F-111Fs gone, the 366th TFW resumed operations with F-111As and personnel transferred from the 474th TFW, and adopted a type conversion role in addition to providing combat aircraft. The 391st TFS was the first to get its new aircraft on 6 June 1977, followed by the 389th on 15 July. The 388th TFTS was established on 2 August, with no fin-band

The 366th TFW became an F-111F operator when the 347th TFW renumbered in late 1972.

Left: Mountain Home was the last bastion of the F-111A. Below are the the badges of the wing and the last two A model squadrons.

Above: The 366th TFW was the first operational wing to receive the 'Spark Vark'. EF-111s were assigned from 1981 to 1993.

colour. On 1 October 1979 the training role was augmented by the redesignation of the 389th as 389th TFTS.

The next major step for the 366th TFW was the establishment of an EF-111A 'Spark Vark' operation. The prelude to this was the disbandment of the 388th TFTS in early 1981, and its reformation as the 388th ECS 'Griffins' on 5 November. This was the first USAF EF-111A unit, and served until 28 March 1984. Three days later, on 1 April, it re-emerged as the 390th ECS 'Ravens'.

On 1 October 1991 the 366th became a Fighter Wing, and on 1 January 1992 became simply a Wing. That spring, the two F-111A squadrons disbanded and their aircraft dispatched to AMARC at Davis-Monthan AFB. The EF-111A squadron was redesignated the 429th ECS on 11 September 1992, and transferred to Cannon

in mid-1993, joining the 27th FW, to consolidate all F-111 operations at one base. Mountain Home, in the meantime, had been chosen as the base for the USAF's first 'super wing', the 366th now flying squadrons of F-15C, F-15E, F-16C, B-52G and KC-135R aircraft. EF-111As can be drawn from Cannon at any time to support this rapid reaction force.

Right: F-111As bowed out of service in the spring of 1992, after a career spanning 25 years.

380th Bombardment Wing (Medium)

Having previously flown the Boeing B-52, the 380th Bomb Wing (motto: Strength and Confidence) at Plattsburgh AFB, New York, was chosen as Strategic Air Command's second front-line FB-111A wing. The 4007th CCTS was assigned on 30 June 1971, assuming the training function from the 340th Bomb Group at Carswell, later being redesignated as the 530th CCTS.

The 528th Bombardment Squadron (Medium) (blue fin-band) was the first operational squadron to equip, achieving that status on 17 July 1971. The 529th BMS (red fin-band) followed suit on 1 October. Initially assigned to the 2nd Air Force, it transferred to the 'Mighty Eighth' on 1 January 1975.

During its early career, the wing won the SAC bombing and navigation contest, and the Fairchild Trophy in 1974, 1976 and 1977, with further Proud Shield victories in 1978

A blue fin-band was carried by the aircraft of the 528th BS (Medium).

and 1984. In July 1991 the FB-111A was retired from SAC service, some aircraft passing to the 27th FW as F-111Gs. This left the 380th as an Air Refueling Wing operating KC-135A/Qs.

Above: Proudly wearing the winged '2' of the 2nd Air Force, these FB-111As, seen in 1971, served with the 4007th CCTS.

Above: This 4007th CCTS aircraft carries badges commemorating the 380th Bombardment Group's wartime activities. The legend reads 'The Flying Circus'.

Below: This 528th BS 'Dark Vark' carries the 380th BW's apple insignia on the fin, reflecting the unit's basing in New York state.

F-111 Operators

474th Tactical Fighter Wing

Having spent some time without aircraft, the 474th TFW 'Roadrunners' moved to Nellis AFB, Nevada, to begin operations with the F-111A, taking over from the 4480th TFW. The first squadrons formed on 20 January 1968. These were the 428th TFS (which was a redesignation of the 4481st TFS) and the new 4527th CCTS. On the same date, the wing began to prepare for the Operation Combat Lancer deployment to South East Asia, which was installed as 428th TFS Det. 1 at Takhli RTAFB, Thailand, on 17 March 1968. The six Harvest Reaper aircraft initially sent to Takhli (66-0017/0018, and 0020/0023) all had a blue/yellow arrowhead marking on the fin. Aircraft 66-0017 was lost on 30 March 1968, and 0022 on 28 March 1968, with both crews. Two replacements (66-0024 and 0025) were sent by 5 April, with 66-0024 crashing on 22 April 1968, but the crew surviving. Despite this inauspicious start to the F-111's career, the deployment was not ended until 22 November, when the five survivors returned to Nellis after flying only 55 combat missions.

Back at home base, the 474th had begun the formation of operational squadrons, starting with the 429th TFS 'Black Falcons' on 15 May 1968. Tailcodes were assigned on 10 July, with the 428th getting 'NA' tailcode (light blue fin-band), the 429th 'NB' (yellow fin-band), and the 4527th 'ND' (green fin-band). The 430th TFS 'Tigers' ('NC' tailcode; red fin-band) was formed on 15 September 1968. On 15 October 1969, the 4527th CCTS was redesignated the 442nd TFTS. It received eight F-111Es in late 1969, shortly before a wing came off an F-111A, causing a fleet grounding which lasted from 22 December 1969 to 31 July 1970. One of the F-111Es (67-0117) was lost in April 1971, and the others were transferred to the 422nd FWS (67-0119, 68-0026, and 0058) or sent to SM-ALC (67-0121/2, and 68-0002/3) for modifications and eventual transfer to the 20th TFW by 21 September 1972. Wing-level maintenance was adopted by the 474th on 1 April 1972, with all aircraft adopting 'NA'. 474th TFW F-111As returned to South East

Below: On a training mission in 1976, this 428th TFS F-111A carries an ALQ-87 ECM pod and a practice bomb dispenser.

Asia with the Constant Guard V deployment to Takhli. The 430th TFS moved on 27 September 1972 with 24 aircraft (67-0059/61, 0063/6, 0068/72, 0074/6, 0078/80, 0083/4 and 0086/90). 67-0078 was lost on 28 September 1972 attempting to fly a combat sortie the same day it arrived in-

Above: Clutching 12 bombs on its pylons, this Harvest Reaper jet sets out from Takhli on the type's first mission.

Below: Eight F-111Es were briefly operated by the 474th TFW's 442nd TFTS. This aircaft was passed to the 57th FWW.

Below: Named 'Super Fly', this 429th TFS F-111A departs from Takhli on a Linebacker II mission on 27 December 1972.

theatre. The 429th TFS arrived with another 24 aircraft on 28 September (67-0073, 0077, 0085, 0091/107, 0110, 0112/4). Other losses and replacements were: 67-0066 was lost on 17 October, 67-0062 arrived on 23 October, 67-0067 arrived on 23 October, 67-0063 was lost on 8 November, 67-0058 arrived on 21 November, 67-0092 was lost

Above: The 4527th CCTS was the Nellis F-111A training unit, redesignated the 442nd TFTS in October 1969.

the same day, 67-0089 arrived on 25 November, 67-0109 arrived on 11 December, 67-0099 was lost on 18 December, 67-0068 was lost on 22 December, 67-0108 arrived on 9 January 1973, 67-0072 was lost (non-combat) on 20 February.

On 22 March 1973 the 428th took over the 430th's aircraft at Takhli. Aircraft 67-0081 and 0111 arrived on 8 May, but the latter was lost (non-combat) on 16 June 1973. The 428th and 429th were taken over by the 347th TFW on 30 July, and later moved to Korat RTAFB. Following service in Thailand, the two squadrons were returned to Nellis and 474th control on 15 June (428th) and 21 June 1975 (429th). In August 1977 the 474th ceased F-111 operations, sending its F-111As to the 366th TFW at Mountain Home, disbanding the training unit (442nd TFTS) and obtaining F-4D Phantoms from the 48th TFW at Lakenheath, all as part of Operation Creek Swing/Ready Switch.

An early 'swinger' of the 429th TFS cruises over the Nevada desert. The panels on the nose covered antennas for the warning suite, later painted over.

509th Bombardment Wing (Medium)

SAC's first FB-111A wing, the famous 509th, inherited its number from the 509th Composite Group which had been formed to deliver the two atomic weapons on Japan. The 509th BW (motto: *Defensor Vindex*) received FB-111As on 16 December 1970, the first aircraft being used for ground training. Two aircraft went on alert in July 1971 and the two squadrons, 393rd BMS 'Tigers' and 715th BMS 'Eagles', were declared fully operational at Pease AFB, New Hampshire, in January 1973. Like its sister 380th, the Pease wing switched from 2nd to 8th Air Force control on 1 January 1975.

The 509th BW was the first FB-111A wing to begin drawing down, the process initiated in June 1990. The deactivation date was 30 September, with many of its aircraft having undergone conversion to F-111G standard and transferring to the 27th FW at Cannon.

Right: A 509th BW FB-111A displays slats, vanes, flaps and spoilers.

Below: A 509th BW 'Dark Vark' heads for a conventional bombing mission with a load of Mk 82 AIRs. Some of the wing's aircraft sported a silhouette of New Hampshire state on the fin: all carried the wing badge, a winged mushroom cloud.

Right: Seen in August 1971, this FB-111A served with the 393rd BS at Pease. The wing had just assumed its nuclear alert function.

3246th Test Wing

Located at Eglin AFB, Florida, this wing was primarily concerned with the testing and evaluation of aircraft ordnance, and operated a variety of front-line USAF types. The fin-band for the unit was white with red diamonds.

A likely total of three F-111Es (67-0115/6, and 0118) was assigned from mid-1973 to the wing's 3247th Test Squadron (TS). 67-

The fourth F-111E was assigned to Eglin for armament tests. Seen here carrying orange-painted Mk 82 SEs, the aircraft has a ciné camera mounted under the wingtip to record bomb separation.

The same F-111E, seen some time later, wears the 'AD' tailcode worn during most of the 1980s, but does not have the red and white fin-band. Flying was conducted by the 3247th Test Squadron.

0116 was lost in October 1976, and replaced by 68-0058 from the 422nd FWS. 67-0115 was used in the Pave Mover synthetic aperture radar test programme in 1983. Other aircraft, including 67-0124, have been assigned from time to time. In late 1982, the 'AD' tailcode (for Armament Division) was added; this changed to 'ET' (for Eglin Test) on 30 September 1989. On 2 October 1992 the unit designations changed to 40th TS and 46th TW.

67-0015 was the first F-111E, and was used by the 3246th Test Wing to carry the Pave Mover synthetic aperture radar. This was an experimental programme to detect ground forces at long range, relay raw data to a ground module for analysis and provide guidance for either air or ground attack.

4404th Composite Wing

Following the end of the Gulf War, the United States maintained sizeable forces of tactical aircraft in Saudi Arabia as a deterrent to further Iraqi aggression in the Gulf region and to monitor the United Nations' 'No-Fly Zone' in the southern part of Iraq below the 32nd Parallel (Operation Southern Watch). Apart from Lockheed F-117s at Khamis Mushait, the tactical aircraft are based at Dhahran with the 4404th Composite Wing, composed of detachments from CONUS units of F-15Cs, F-15Es and F-16Cs. Also assigned are six EF-111A Ravens for radar jamming, initially drawn from the 366th Wing at Mountain Home but now from the 27th Fighter Wing at Cannon. During the attacks on Iraqi air defence systems on 13 and 18 January 1993, the strike forces were supported by 'MO'-coded EF-111As.

This 429th Electronic Combat Squadron, 366th Wing EF-111A was one of six Ravens deployed in December 1992 to Dhahran. They were soon in action over Iraq.

4480th Tactical Fighter Wing

The USAF's first operational F-111A unit was established at Nellis AFB, Nevada, on 15 July 1967, just before the arrival of its first aircraft on 18 July. Controlling only the 4481st TFS squadron, its primary purpose was to execute a programme called Combat Trident to prepare the Harvest Reaper aircraft (blue/yellow arrowhead on rudder) and their crews for deployment to South East Asia. The 4480th TFW became the 474th TFW on 20 January 1968, with the 4481st TFS becoming the 428th TFS.

4525th Fighter Weapons Wing

The 4525th FWW was activated on 1 September 1966 to control four combat crew training squadrons (CCTS) to conduct advanced testing and evaluation of the F-100 (4536th CCTS), F-105 (4537th CCTS), F-4 (4538th CCTS) and F-111 (4539th CCTS). The 4539th CCTS probably received its aircraft in mid-1968, at about the same time it was given the 'WF' tailcode (with yellow/black check fin-band). On 15 October 1968, the wing was renumbered as the 57th FWW, and the 4539th CCTS became the 422nd FWS.

The 4525th Fighter Weapons Wing was the forerunner of the 57th FWW, and its four squadrons undertook advanced tactical instruction. The 4539th Combat Crew Training Squadron was concerned with tactical development and instruction on the F-111. Both the black/yellow checkerboard and 'WF' codes were carried over to the 57th FWW.

6510th Test Wing

The 6510th TW conducted flying operations for the Air Force Flight Test Center (AFFTC) at Edwards AFB, California, the USAF's primary test facility for new aircraft, ongoing modification programmes, and many other operational and experimental trials. F-111s were assigned in small numbers to its 6512th TS from initial flight trials onwards. The first F-111A arrived on 2 May 1965 and was followed by most of the RDT&E and pre-production aircraft. When applied, wing markings consisted of a blue fin-band with white crosses and, from late 1982, the 'ED' tailcode.

The main version used was the F-111D, of which three (68-0085, 0086 and 0089) were assigned from delivery in late 1971; 68-0086 transferred to Cannon in October 1973, and 68-0085 went to the 431st TES for a time in the late 1980s. By March 1990 three F-111Ds were still assigned (68-0085, 0087 and 0089). F-111A 66-0053 was assigned from the 1980s until at least March 1990. FB-111A 68-0254 served during 1990/91 during the development of the F-111 digital flight control system (DFCS). Several other F-111s are believed to have been used for short periods by the 6510th TW, but all had been retired by 1 October 1992 when the wing was redesignated as the 412th TW (and the 6512th TS became the 445th TS).

Assigned to the 6512th Test Squadron for general trials duties was F-111A 66-0053.

Above: An excellent illustration of the three-tone green camouflage originally applied to FB-111As, this shot shows 68-0254, which was assigned to the 6510th TW for development work of a digital flight control system.

Right: 68-0085 was the first F-111D built, and spent all its life with test agencies. For most of its career it was assigned to Edwards, along with two other D models.

7440th Wing (Provisional)

Operation Proven Force was the codename by which operations from Turkey during the Gulf War were known. These missions were administered by the hastily-formed 7440th Wg (P) established at Incirlik, and the wing equipped almost exclusively with USAFE aircraft. Twenty-two F-111Es (67-0120/1; 68-0004/5, 0013, 0015/7, 0026, 0029, 0031, 0039/40, 0046, 0049/50, 0061, 0068/9, 0072, 0074 and 0076) were drawn from all squadrons of the 20th TFW from Upper Heyford and flown by the 79th TFS 'Tigers'.

The only AMP-modified aircraft to see combat was 68-0050, which was flown with an overall grey paint scheme. Five EF-111As (66-0047, 0055; 67-0034, 0041/2) also participated in Proven Force. They were from the 42nd ECS/66th ECW, which was returned to 20th TFW control on 28 February 1991.

Tiger nose art and Proven Force mission marks adorn the 79th TFS commander's F-111E.

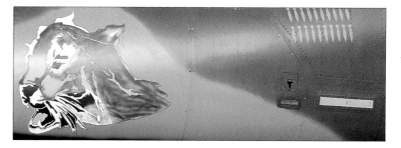

Left: F-111Es from Upper Heyford moved into Incirlik to bolster the attack force ranged against northern Iraq.

USAF Air Warfare Center

Two EF-111As (66-0013 and 67-0048) were allocated to the USAF's Tactical Air Warfare Center (TAWC) for trials and evaluation purposes. The flying squadron of this unit was the 4485th TS, based at Eglin, but the

The only Ravens to wear a fin-band were the pair assigned to the 4485th TS Det. 3 at Mountain Home, featuring a small black/white check stripe. The parent unit's 'OT' codes were also worn.

EF-111As flew with the 4485th TS Det. 3 at Mountain Home AFB, Idaho, while using the parent unit's 'OT' tailcode and black/white check fin-band. On 1 June 1992, the TAWC became officially the USAF Air Warfare Center (USAF AWC). Until disbanded, Det. 3 operations moved to Cannon in mid-1992. On 2 October 1992, the 4485th TS was redesignated as the 85th TS.

Sacramento Air Logistics Center

Based at McClellan AFB, California, the SM-ALC is the facility responsible for all F-111 maintenance and upgrade work. The Center's Engineering Flight Test (EFT) was the initial operating unit, redesignated the 2874th TS on 1 June 1992 and assigned the 'SM' tailcode. On 2 October it was again renumbered as the 337th TS. Although located at the same base as the 57th FWW's 431st TES (until its deactivation in 1992), EFT reports to Air Materiel Command, the modification developer, not Air Combat Command, the user. EFT performs two functions: test flight of all aircraft after they have undergone programmed depot maintenance (PDM), and performance of qualification testing (QT&E) on all new aircraft software and avionics modifications. After determining that modifications (software or hardware) work as the engineers think they should, the modification is turned over to the user (formerly the 431st TES, now Det. 3/57th FWW at Cannon) for operational testing (OT&E) to determine if it performs as desired. Only after that testing is the modification released to the operational units.

Permanently assigned aircraft have included FB-111A 67-0159 and F-111D 68-0175, the final D model retired to AMARC, on 28 December 1992. Other FB-111As loaned included 68-0247 and 0272 during

Below: While assigned to the SM-ALC, this FB-111A received a garish red/white scheme.

Assisting with the AMP programme in 1989 was FB-111A 68-0247. Here it is seen carrying a load of SUU-30 cluster bomb dispensers.

the late 1980s for the AMP programme. F-111D 68-0122 was also loaned for a time during the mid-1980s. F-111E 68-0040 was assigned for the A/E AMP programme during 1988/89. The sole AMP F-111A (67-0050) will be used for SMS/VCC flight tests during the summer of 1993, while an F-111F (74-0187) is on loan from the 27th FW for Pacer Strike tests, along with 70-2400. All flight test functions at Sacramento will be switched to Eglin by 1994/95.

Above: F-111D 68-0175 seen early in its career with Engineering Flight Test at SM-ALC. It was the last F-111D to be retired.

Below: This ex-20th FW F-111E was assigned to Sacramento ALC, seen here being prepared for its delivery flight.

NASA Dryden

Operating from its own site at Edwards AFB, NASA's Dryden Flight Research Facility's most important F-111 activity was the joint USAF/NASA research programme into advanced wing design during the 1980s. One of the F-111A RDT&E aircraft (63-9778) was extensively modified for the Transonic Aircraft Technology (TACT) programme. F-111E 67-0115 was also assigned during the mid-1980s to provide baseline aerodynamic data for comparison with TACT's supercritical Mission Adaptive Wing (MAW) configuration. The MAW had an unbroken wing surface made of flexible fibre-glass to investigate the benefits of this feature at variable camber and wing sweep angles.

Right: F-111E 67-0115 was used principally to provide baseline data for the TACT programme.

Below: The 13th F-111A was fitted with a supercritical aerofoil wing for the TACT (Transonic Aircraft Technology) programme.

Below right: The TACT aircraft was converted by Boeing with the MAW as part of the AFTI (Advanced Fighter Technology Integration) trials. The aircraft first flew with the MAW on 18 October 1985.

Royal Australian Air Force

Australia opted to buy the F-111 in October 1963 to replace its Canberra bombers, after evaluation of the F-111, F-4 Phantom, A-5 Vigilante, BAC TSR.Mk 2 and Mirage IV. Twenty-four aircraft were purchased (67-125/148 – RAAF A8-125/148) a year before the prototype first flew, originally comprising 18 F-111As and six RF-111As. The buy was subsequently altered to cover 24 of the F-111C version, which retained the TF30-P-3 engines and avionics of the F-111A, but incorporated the long-span wings and strengthened undercarriage of the FB-111A. Covered in the original agreement was the loan of Boeing B-47s pending the delivery of the F-111s, but this did not come to fruition, much to the relief of the RAAF, who continued using their Canberras.

First flight of an F-111C was in July 1968, and this aircraft was formally handed over to RAAF control on 4 September. However, the crash of an F-111A at Nellis (with an Australian crew member) caused a fleet grounding, and the RAAF did not accept its aircraft. Structural tests revealed further problems and the F-111Cs, which had all been built in 1968, were partially dissembled and stored at Fort Worth, pending a complete 'ironing-out' of the F-111's problems. Between September 1970 and June 1973, Nos 1 and 6 Sqns operated 24 F-4E Phantoms on loan (one was lost in Australian service), and crews were loath to give up their Phantoms when the F-111 arrived at Amberley.

In 1973, the aircraft were pulled out of storage, modified to meet the Australian standards and delivered. Throughout the 10-year acquisition process, controversy surrounded the Australian buy, and it became a national debating subject. Wags called the aircraft the 'Flying Opera House' (a reference to the cost and construction time of Sydney's best-known edifice) and said that it had been in 'more tests than Don Bradman!' (Australia's celebrated cricketer).

The F-111s were delivered in four batches of six, arriving on 1 June, 27 July, 28 September and 4 December respectively. To make up for attrition, four ex-USAF F-111As (serialled A8-108, 109, 112 and 114) were purchased, two arriving in May 1982, one in July and one in August. These were modified at Amberley with the long wings and other features of the F-111C. Known to Aussie maintenance troops as the 'Pig', the F-111C quickly proved its versatility, its great range being of particular significance to the Australians. Harpoon anti-ship missile capability was integrated in 1982, and in the mid-1980s all F-111Cs were reworked to accept the AVQ-26 Pave Tack pod, although only 10 pods were actually purchased. Modernisation and rework programmes covering both avionics and structure have extended the useful lives of the F-111Cs considerably, the current planned retirement date being 2010.

Following the USAF's cancellation of the RF-111A reconnaissance variant, the RAAF planned to modify some aircraft to carry out the maritime, strategic and tactical reconnaissance roles. It was not until May 1979 before the first such conversion (A8-126) took to the air at GD's plant with its new equipment. Fitting into the bomb-bay, the reconnaissance pallet mounts two TV cameras, two split vertical cameras, two low-altitude panoramic cameras, one high-altitude panoramic camera, an infra-red linescan and a high-altitude radar altimeter. Three further machines (A8-134, 143 and 146) were modified to RF-111C standard at Amberley in 1980.

Attrition of the Australian fleet amounted in 1993 to six aircraft (A8-126 lost April 1987, A8-133 lost September 1977, A8-136 lost April 1977, A8-137 lost August 1979, A8-139 lost January 1986 and A8-141 lost October 1978). In late 1992 the RAAF reportedly purchased 18 ex-USAF F-111s (probably FB-111As) to be stored for No. 82 Wing. These are intended to be upgraded for service as the existing F-111s reach the end of their fatigue lives, thereby extending the F-111's RAAF career well into the next century.

Above: RAAF 'Varks' on the prowl, graphically displaying the long-span wings adopted by this variant. The 82nd Wing has flown the type for 20 years.

Below: The 'Pig' from down under – a No. 6 Sqn F-111C demonstrates the approved method of terrain-following flight in the southern hemisphere!

Left: Four ex-USAF F-111As (67-0114 illustrated) were delivered in 1982. They were brought up to F-111C standard before delivery to the operational squadrons.

Below: Adoption of the Pave Tack pod has greatly expanded the F-111C's capabilities, although use of the GBU-15 is restricted to line-of-sight.

No. 82 Wing

Located at RAAF Amberley, Queensland, the wing has 21 aircraft and comprises two flying squadrons, No. 1 Squadron (yellow lightning flash or number '1') and No. 6 Squadron (blue lightning flash). No. 1 Squadron is the main operational unit, with a nominal strength of 12 F-111Cs for the overland and maritime strike roles. No. 6 Squadron nominally operates nine aircraft, and also undertakes the strike role, but is burdened with the taskings of type conversion/OCU duties and operating the RF-111C reconnaissance aircraft. With these aircraft it took part in the USAF's 1988 Reconnaissance Air Meet, taking many of the important prizes.

Basic maintenance is undertaken at squadron level, but intermediate maintenance is handled by No. 482 (Maintenance) Squadron on base. Also at Amberley is No. 3 Aircraft Depot, which is reponsible for deep maintenance, engine maintenance and modification programmes.

Left: No. 1 Squadron traditionally has a yellow lightning bolt as its unit markings.

Revised marks for No. 1 Sqn (left) feature a stylised numeral with a kookaburra superimposed, while No. 6 Sqn retains its lightning bolt.

Above: A No. 6 Sqn RF-111C in 1985 carries the formal squadron crest (consisting of a boomerang) forward of the RAAF kangaroo roundel.

Below: In addition to its type conversion duties, No. 6 Squadron also undertakes the reconnaissance mission with four RF-111Cs.

Aircraft Research and Development Unit

Based at RAAF Edinburgh, New South Wales, the ARDU undertakes various test and trials functions for the RAAF. One F-111C (A8-132) is permanently assigned and has been involved in various weapon integration programmes, notably that involving AGM-84 Harpoon and AGM-88 HARM.

Complete with white undersides and photo-documentation marks, A8-132 is the F-111C permanently assigned to the ARDU for test work. Depicted here in 1983, it carries test AGM-84 Harpoon rounds.

Royal Air Force

Following the catastrophic cancellation of the BAC TSR.Mk 2, the Royal Air Force opted for the marginally inferior F-111 in 1966, ordering 46 F-111Ks (67-153/8, 68-181/210, -229/238; RAF serials XV902/947) and four TF-111K operational trainers (67-149/152; RAF serials XV884/887). These too were cancelled in early 1968, but two virtually complete aircraft were finished for the USAF as non-operational YF-111As and the other components used in FB-111A manufacture. The RAF had to wait until the Tornado entered service in 1982 before it had an all-weather interdictor.

Armament
In the precision strike role, F-111Cs would use the Paveway II laser-guided bomb in conjunction with the Pave Tack designator pod. All F-111Cs can carry the pod, but only 10 such systems were purchased. Two LGBs are standard, the 500-lb GBU-12 and the 2,000-lb GBU-10 (illustrated). The latter features the regular Mk 84 warhead. AIM-9Ps are carried for self-defence.

Markings
The Australian 'Aardvarks' were delivered in the standard three-tone South East Asia camouflage of the USAF, with black undersides, and have retained this scheme throughout. However, the prototype AUP aircraft was repainted in all-over mid-grey, and this is likely to be adopted fleetwide. Standard markings consist of RAAF roundels forward of the intakes on either side, and on the wings. The fin is adorned with the squadron marking (in this case No. 6 Sqn), a fin-flash, Australian flag and the serial number in a reverse of the underlying camouflage.

General Dynamics F-111C

Eventually acquired in 1973 after a 10-year procurement nightmare, the F-111Cs have provided the RAAF with its prime strike capability ever since, while also branching out into other equally important roles such as reconnaissance and maritime attack. Currently undergoing the AUP upgrade, the F-111C fleet will serve for many years yet and, indeed, several FB-111s have been purchased to replace them when fatigue limits are reached.

Wing structure
The wings move between 16° and 72° 30'. They feature NACA 63 aerofoil section throughout, and are built around five spars. The skin is made from sculptured panels, each machined as one piece running from root to tip.

Engines
Although the wings and undercarriage of the FB-111 were specified for the RAAF F-111s, the original low-powered TF30-P-3 engines of the F-111A were retained, these providing 18,500 lb (82.32 kN) thrust each with augmentation. Triple Plow I intakes were fitted.

Long-span wings
Inheriting the wings of the FB-111A, the F-111C spans 70 ft 0 in (21.34 m) at minimum angle, compared to 63 ft 0 in (19.20 m) of USAF F-111s. At maximum sweep the span is 33 ft 11 in (10.34 m) for the F-111C and 31 ft 11.4 in (9.74 m) for USAF aircraft.

A8-145

Mosaero

Window on the World

The 1992 Moscow Aeroshow (Mosaero '92) marked the former Soviet Union's first full-scale international aviation trade show, in which the many design bureaux, factories and research and development institutes could market their products and services to a sceptical world. The result was an astonishing spectacle and an impressive confirmation of the strengths and weaknesses of the Russian and Ukrainian aircraft industry. A further, similar show is being organised for August 1993.

There have been annual air shows in Russia for decades. Usually held close to 16 August (Air Forces Day), they have habitually been closed to the public, witnessed only by the Soviet top brass and invited guests, sometimes including Western attachés. Often scarcely more than mass flypasts designed to show off the might of the Soviet air forces, the air shows have been little more than airborne May Day parades. Occasionally they have also been used to present new prototypes, although glimpses of such aircraft have normally been restricted to relatively fast, high flypasts.

Under the old order there was no need for a showcase for the Soviet aviation industry – it was not free to sell its wares wherever it chose, and most operators of Soviet-built aircraft received them as aid, and thus had no choice over what was procured. As the old USSR crumbled, Soviet aerospace companies began to look towards a world market for their products, and took the first steps towards integration into the world market by participating more fully at international trade shows like Paris (where civil types had been shown for many years) and Farnborough.

By the late 1980s, however, there was a clear need for a Russian aerospace show, not least to allow the plethora of components producers to exhibit their wares to a world audience. After a number of small shows at Frunze and other locations, a major show was organised at Zhukhovsky, familiar to generations of Western intelligence analysts as Ramenskoye (the name of a

Below: A Tu-22M-3 'Backfire-C' lumbers out for its display slot, past a row of Il-76 command posts and a Tu-142LL engine testbed. The heavily polluted sulphurous overcast was typical of Mosaero '92.

Left: Spectators on the public day were treated to the sight of an Il-78 'Midas' tanker refuelling a pair of Su-30s and the Su-27KU/IB prototype.

Above: Both of the Myasishchev VM-T Atlants were present at Zhukhovsky, one of them in the huge static line, seen here.

Right: The town of Zhukhovsky is proud of its aeronautical traditions, and this retired Mikoyan MiG-21F-13 is a civic monument.

nearby town) and the home of TSAGI (the Central Aerodynamics and Hydrodynamics Institute), the Gromov Flight Research Centre and a host of other test and research organisations.

Moscow Aeroshow '92 marked Russia's first full-scale aviation and aeronautical exhibition, and was regarded by its organisers, Glahe International KG of Cologne, as an unqualified success. Designed as a dedicated platform to allow

Right: Mosaero was full of spectacle, much of it bordering on the bizarre. On the public days the show was opened by a flag-towing Yakovlev Yak-38U 'Forger-B', seen here with a Zhukhovsky-based 'Hip'.

Below: Perhaps the biggest surprise of the show was the unveiling of the Ilyushin Il-102, derived from the Il-40 'Brawny' and developed as an unsuccessful competitor to the Su-25 'Frogfoot'. It first flew in 1978.

the Russian and former Soviet aerospace industry to ease itself into the international economy, the show ran for six days and attracted some 750,000 visitors. Its importance to Russia can be gauged by the fact that it was opened by Russian Federation Deputy President Alexander Rutskoi (a former Su-25 pilot) and was visited by a host of VIPs, including Ruslan Khasbulatov, the parliamentary leader, and Marshall Yevgeni Shaposhnikov (CIS armed forces commander-in-chief and former MiG-21 pilot).

While primarily an exhibition of the products of the Russian and former Soviet industry, the show also attracted some of the more visionary Western companies as exhibitors, and many others sent observers. USAF promises of participation by an F-15 and F-16 eventually came to

Another aerobatic team operates camouflaged DOSAAF Aero L-39 Albatros trainers, with the solo aircraft painted in a striking red and white scheme. This makes an impressive demonstration rarely seen in a jet aircraft.

nothing, however. The organisers built some 37 exhibition halls and chalets beside the runway, and planned to hold an even bigger, even better exhibition at the same site in 1993.

Named after Nikolai E. Zhukhovsky, father of Soviet aeronautics, designer of Moscow's sewage system and famous as a singer, the massive complex includes one of the world's largest airfields, with runways 5500 m and 3000 m (18,045 ft and 9,842 ft) long. The latter was used as parking for the incredible static display, which stretched for nearly 2 km (1.2 miles), and included more than 60 aircraft.

The sheer size of the establishment is hard to comprehend, since it is much larger (in terms of aircraft and personnel numbers) than Britain's Farnborough, Boscombe Down, Thurleigh and all the other RAE/DRA out-stations rolled into one, employing more than 30,000 scientists and engineers.

Besides its two magnificent runways, Zhukhovsky airfield also has huge parking areas and numerous hangars, and most of these, barriered off from the public areas, were crammed with a bewildering variety of often esoteric aircraft types, some active, some in storage and some derelict. Most of the development batch of Tu-160 'Blackjacks' (at least six complete airframes, plus a stripped forward fuselage shell) lay about in various states of disrepair, while older bomber types were represented by a couple of Tu-22M 'Backfires', and an impressive collection of 'Bears' including two 'Bear-F Mod. 4s', two 'Bear-Gs', a 'Bear-H', a 'Bear-C', and an engine

Right: A brand new Tu-142M (actually a 'Bear-F Mod. 4') dominated the static display, absolutely immaculate in an overall pale grey maritime camouflage. No picture, no words can adequately represent the 'Bear's' presence.

Above: Beriev's A-40 Albatross demonstrator gave its usual polished display. This remarkably versatile machine deserves success, and has attracted some interest from Western air forces.

*Above: This **S**u-27 'Flanker-B' is used by **NIIAKM** as a testbed for new cockpit displays and technology. It has a sidestick controller and an **S**u-35 multifunction **CRT** display screen.*

Right: One enterprise displaying its wares at Zhukhovsky specialises in trials of large-scale models prior to testing of full-size prototypes. These can be air-dropped or rocket launched, as shown here.

*Above: This **S**u-7U is used as an ejection seat test aircraft, with the test seat (and instrumented dummy) in the rear cockpit. It was lost within minutes of this photo being taken.*

Below: Camera pods are mounted on the wingtips of this An-12. These are used to film tests of upward- or downward-firing ejection seats mounted in the aircraft's modified tailcone.

testbed. There were also no less than five Tu-16 'Badgers' present, most, if not all, engine test-beds. A further Tu-22M lay with an Il-28 and another Tu-16 on the dump, alongside a real rarity, a Tu-126 'Moss' AWACS aircraft.

Other test aircraft included four Tu-144 'Chargers' (the Soviet 'Concordskii'), which some Russians averred were still in use as high-speed research platforms, with another cannibalised aircraft dumped on the far side of the airfield. There were huge numbers of more ordinary transport aircraft types, but most of these were heavily modified for research or experimental duties. There were Il-86s with huge dorsal canoe radomes (satellite trackers or 'Star Wars' test ships) and similarly configured Il-76 and Il-18 aircraft. Other interesting Il-76s included a handful of Il-78 'Midas' tankers and a number of aircraft equipped with rotodomes similar to those carried by the A-50 'Mainstay'. The latter wore Aeroflot colours and differed in many ways to the standard 'Mainstay' AWACS platform. There was some suggestion that they were dedicated missile trackers, perhaps designated Il-976.

All of these aircraft were clearly visible as the trade visitor drove into Zhukhovsky every morning, along with treasures like the record-breaking P-42 (a stripped-down Su-27 which shattered the records set by the F-15 'Streak Eagle'), and some very new prototypes which were still considered too secret to be displayed publicly. The latter included the MiG-31M, MiG-29M, Su-27KU/IB and the Su-35. Photography in these 'working areas' was not permitted, reportedly because the powers-that-be were concerned that the slightly down-at-heel buildings and working aircraft might give the wrong impression.

The flying display was impressive (especially on the last, public weekend) and was opened on the public days by a banner-towing Yakovlev Yak-38U. Individual trade days were dedicated to individual design bureaux, and the flying dis-

Above: This Tu-22M-3 'Backfire-C' is used by TSAGI to test wing leading edge sections and surfaces. It is available for hire, alongside MiG-25 flying laboratories, engine testbeds, icing spray aircraft and a host of other research aircraft. A yacht displayed next to the TSAGI Tu-22M attracted less attention.

Left: The Zhukhovsky-based test pilot's school provides pilots for the 'Test Pilots' display team. This has at least four colourfully decorated 'Flankers' and is sponsored by the Jupiter Insurance Company. This aircraft is an Su-27P, the others include at least two Su-30s (previously known as Su-27PUs) with inflight-refuelling probes and new avionics. The Su-30 can be used as an airborne command post or mini-AWACS, controlling other interceptors in the same manner as the MiG-31.

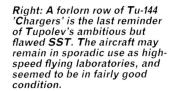

Right: A forlorn row of Tu-144 'Chargers' is the last reminder of Tupolev's ambitious but flawed SST. The aircraft may remain in sporadic use as high-speed flying laboratories, and seemed to be in fairly good condition.

Below: The VM-T lands, dragging behind it two enormous braking parachutes. In the background are some of the 37 exhibition halls, and behind them the second runway.

Above: Reportedly designated Il-976, this was one of about half a dozen rotodome-equipped Il-76s at Zhukhovsky which wore Aeroflot markings and differed from the production 'Mainstay' in several ways.

Below: A full standard production A-50 'Mainstay' was also shown. This differed from the Aeroflot aircraft in having a solid nose and refuelling probe, and in several other respects.

plays were weighted accordingly. The weekend display was more balanced, and included flights by the 'Russian Knights' Su-27s, the 'Swifts' MiG-29s, the unnamed DOSAAF L-39 team, and a team of specially painted Mil Mi-24s. Kamov and Mil both flew impressive mixed formations, while most manufacturers flew examples of their latest aircraft. Mikoyan, for example, flew a synchronised aerobatic display with a MiG-31 and two MiG-29s, while Sukhoi's participation included the two Ivanovs displaying the hitherto secret Su-27IB/KU.

The Zhukhovsky-based 'Test Pilots' team, sponsored by Jupiter Insurance which provided the Su-27s at Boscombe Down, Biggin Hill and Woodford, is based at Zhukhovsky with four Su-27Ps and PVs, though these are usually flown as a duo. These aircraft, and their pilots, were drawn from the test pilot's school based at Zhukhovsky. At Mosaero '92 they were flown by S. Tresvyatskii and A. Beschastnov. Gromov pilots also demonstrated a trio of MiG-29s on some days (led by Y. Sheffer), while V. Danilenko gave a superb solo MiG-29 display. The MiG-29s were not specially painted.

Other displays presented by the Gromov Flight Research Centre included a variety of live ejection demonstrations. A modified An-12 was used to demonstrate downward-firing seats installed in its extended tailcone, while an Su-7U demonstrated an ejection on take-off. The aircraft then got into difficulties after take-off, forcing its human pilot to emulate the dummy passenger and himself eject.

Left: The An-72P, a new coastal/maritime patrol version of 'Coaler', made its public debut at Zhukhovsky. The aircraft is armed with a scabbed-on 23-mm cannon pack on the starboard lower fuselage and underwing rocket pods.

Below: The Myasishchev M-55 Geophysica 'Mystic-B' gave a spirited display, resplendent in a new colour scheme and wearing new RF (Russian Federation) civil registrations. Myasishchev still hopes to obtain a military order for the type as a high-altitude reconnaissance platform.

For the record, the massive static display was lined up on Zhukhovsky's second runway, and included the new RB211-engined Tu-204, one of the two Myasishchev M-4 VM-T Atlant 'shuttle-carriers', the Myasishchev M-55 Geophysica prototype, the T-101 (a mock-up of a turbine-engined, float-equipped, monoplane derivative of the An-2), and the Buran Space Shuttle. Further along the static was the Ilyushin Il-96M and the new Ilyushin light aircraft, as well as the show's greatest surprise, the Il-102 'Jet Shturmovik'. This remarkable and old-fashioned looking aircraft was clearly a derivative of the 1953-vintage Il-40, and was apparently intended as a competitor to the Su-25 on the export market. Even more remarkably, Ilyushin actually had brochures on the aircraft, and professed to being serious about selling the anachronistic fighter-bomber. Other Ilyushins present included an air force 'Mainstay' and one of the similar 'Aeroflot' aircraft, and no less than three different Il-76s.

Tupolev was even more impressively represented, with the hydrogen-powered Tu-155 and a Tu-154 configured as a Buran shuttle simulator, beside a Tu-204 and three magnificent bombers. The Tu-160 'Blackjack' in the static display looked somewhat tatty, but the Tu-22M-3

'Backfire-C' (jointly operated by TSAGI, Gromov and the bureau as a high-speed research platform) was in rather better order and the Tu-142 'Bear-F Mod. 4' was clearly a brand-new aircraft. Next in the line-up were the fighters, comprising a MiG-31 with new wingtip ECM pods, an anti-shipping configured MiG-27, a MiG-25RB, a MiG-23MLD 'Flogger-K' and even a MiG-21. No less than three MiG-29s were shown, comprising the second prototype MiG-29K, an early production aircraft with ventral fins and a similar ventral-finned aircraft con-

Above: Russia's newest strategic bomber is the Tupolev Tu-160 'Blackjack'. Zhukhovsky houses several, mostly early development airframes, some stripped for spares and abandoned, but some, including this unpainted aircraft, still in use. Many of the production Tu-160s were taken over by the Ukraine when that republic gained its independence.

Below: This Tu-95MS 'Bear-H' was flown alongside a Tu-22M-3 and a Tu-160, in a unique display of current Soviet strategic bomber might. The silver and white colour scheme is strongly reminiscent of SAC's 1950s 'chrome dome' anti-flash bomber colour scheme.

Above: Among the 'Bears' littering the ramps at Zhukhovsky was this Tu-95MS 'Bear-H', reportedly awaiting repair and installation of new equipment. The mortal remains of an earlier-generation Tu-95 lie alongside, having served as a spares source. The operational areas at Zhukhovsky appeared run down, with many dumped airframes.

Above: This Tu-126 'Moss', equipped with non-standard wingtip pods, was dumped on the far side of the airfield alongside the hulks of a Tu-16 'Badger' and Tu-22M-2 'Backfire-B'. The scaffolding around the radome may indicate that the aircraft remains in use, at least as a ground test airframe.

*Above: 'Blue 18' is a **MiG-29KVP**, an early **MiG-29** (with ventral fins) modified for deck landing training with a carrier landing system and a heavy duty arrester hook. A picture of the same aircraft in Volume 2 showed it making a dummy approach on **T**bilisi.*

*Above: The second prototype **MiG-29K**, the definitive maritime 'Fulcrum'. Mikoyan was strangely reticent to let anyone photograph the cockpit, which is believed to incorporate multi-function **CRT**s controlled by **HOTAS** buttons.*

verted to MiG-29KVP configuration and equipped for training carrier pilots, with arrester hook and carrier landing systems, but without strengthened undercarriage or folding wings.

Sukhoi's products were displayed next to the MiGs, with a selection of Su-27 variants, including an Su-27K intended for operation from the *Kuznetsov*. These were backed up by the Su-25T and Su-24MR which were later to be displayed at Farnborough. Other design bureaux represented in the static line-up included Anto-nov, Mil and Kamov. Missile, weapons, engine and component manufacturers were impressively represented in the series of 37 exhibition halls, each being akin to a small hangar or very large Nissen hut.

All in all, the show was an impressive first attempt at an international trade exhibition, and the few Western companies which exhibited found it a valuable opportunity to meet their Russian competitors. Many reportedly began to set up joint ventures and the products of such liaisons will clearly begin to be seen over the forthcoming months and years. For the casual visitor it offered a remarkable opportunity to see at close quarters an astonishing array of Russian and Ukrainian aircraft, and to talk to Russian air-crew and engineers.

For numbers buffs the static display varied slightly from day to day, but included the following aircraft. The order given is approximately the order in which the aircraft were parked, but there may be some aircraft which are out of their strict order. It should be noted that the old USSR registration prefix 'CCCP', translated as SSSR, is falling into disuse, with many Russian aircraft carrying РФ (translated RF, for Russian Federation) or even РОССИА (translated ROSSIA, or 'Russia').

Above: One of the Sukhoi Su-27Ks shows off its folding wings and tailplane, as well as a full array of AA-10 'Alamo' and AA-11 'Archer' AAMs. The huge Mosquito anti-ship missile is carried under the centreline.

Below: The Yakovlev Yak-38U 'Forger-B' is an unusual sight even in Russia. Its participation at Mosaero was ensured by the loss of two single-seat Yak-38s before the show.

Tupolev Tu-204	SSSR-64004
(Tu-204 SSSR-64001 was also present, further down the line)	
Tupolev Tu-155	SSSR-85655
Myasishchev M-4 VM-T	RF-01502, c/n 9301502
Myasishchev M-55 Geophysica	RF-01552
Buran shuttle orbiter	
Myasishchev T-102 Yamal	Wing in ground-effect vehicle (mock-up)
Myasishchev M-101 Jakel	RF-70101 (unflown first prototype)
Rosk Aero	'T-101' (mock-up)
Beriev A-40	Red 378
Ilyushin Il-96	SSSR-96006
Ilyushin Il-103	(mock-up)
Ilyshin Il-102	10201
Ilyushin Il-114	SSSR-54001
Ilyushin Il-76	SSSR-76835, c/n 1013408244
Ilyushin A-50 'Mainstay'	Red 51, c/n 88634
Tupolev Tu-154	SSSR-85317
Sukhoi Su-27	Red 05, c/n 36911024205
Tupolev Tu-154	SSSR-85083
Ilyushin Il-976	SSSR-76453 (Civil 'Mainstay'?)
Ilyushin Il-76LL	SSSR-76492 (PS-90 engine testbed)
Mil Mi-17	SSSR-70880
Ilyushin Il-18	SSSR-75423, c/n 182005601
Antonov An-26P	SSSR-26542, c/n 2708
Tu-143A-3	SSSR-65917
Tu-142	No code, c/n 2605426
Tu-22M-3 'Backfire-C'	No code, c/n 4830156
Tu-160	Grey 63
MAI-90	
MiG-31	Red 79, c/n 69700115548
MiG-25RBK	Blue 701, c/n 02048127
MiG-29KVP	Blue 18
MiG-29K	Blue 312
MiG-29	Blue 25
MiG-27	No code, c/n 76802655535
MiG-23MLD	White 36, c/n 10919
MiG-21SM	Red 44
Sukhoi Su-27UB	Blue 03, c/n 49021002103
Sukhoi Su-27K	No code, c/n 49051002603
Sukhoi Su-27UB	Blue 09, c/n 96310424035
Sukhoi Su-24MR	Yellow 40, c/n 0941648
Sukhoi Su-25TK	Blue 10, c/n 181014
Sukhoi Su-26	Black 53

Antonov An-32B	48071, c/n 2909
Mil Mi-1	No markings
Mil Mi-2	900103
PZL Sokol/W-3	0411, c/n 390411
Mil Mi-4	No markings
Mil Mi-6	Yellow 12
Mil Mi-34	34
Mil Mi-38 mock-up	
Mil Mi-24V 'Hind-E'	White 60, c/n 03035
Mil Mi-26	RUSSIA-29101
Mil Mi-28	Yellow 042
Mil Mi-17	SSSR-70894, c/n 94053
Mil Mi-8TV-1	SSSR-25444, c/n 95583
Mil Mi-8	SSSR-22556, c/n 7795
Mil Mi-8	SSSR-10459
Kamov Ka-25	Yellow 19
Kamov Ka-26	c/n 7605318
Kamov Ka-27	Black 204
Kamov Ka-29TB	Yellow 20
Kamov Ka-126	SSSR-17500
Kamov Ka-62	'03' (mock-up?)
LET 410	OK-WDC
LET 410 UVP	OK-BYF
Aero L-59	0001

At least 176 aircraft were parked elsewhere on the field, including examples of the Aero L-39, Antonov An-2, An-12, An-26, An-32, Ilyushin Il-18, Il-62, Il-76, Il-78, A-50, Il-86, Il-96, Mikoyan MiG-21, MiG-25 (large numbers), MiG-29, MiG-29K, MiG-29M, MiG-31, MiG-31M, Myasishchev M-4, Mil Mi-8/17, Mil Mi-24, Mil Mi-10, Mil Mi-26, Sukhoi Su-15, Su-24, Su-25, Su-27, Su-27IB/KU, Tupolev Tu-104, Tu-126, Tu-16, Tu-95/142, Tu-22M, Tu-160, Tu-34, Tu-l44, Tu-154, Tu-204, Yak-40 and Yak-42. Many of the aircraft were one-off testbeds, differing significantly from the norm.

Above: Another two-seat trainer version of a front-line fighter displayed at Zhukhovsky was this MiG-25PU, used by the Gromov Flight Research Centre for test pilot training and miscellaneous test duties. MiG-25Us and Su-24s abounded at Zhukhovsky, littering several ramps.

Right: This MiG-21bis was shown in the static display carrying AA-10 'Alamo' and AA-11 'Archer' missiles, promoting Mikoyan's proposed MiG-21 upgrade, centred around the new Kuopio radar. Also of note is the unusual fairing below the starboard side of the cockpit.

Right: This camouflaged MiG-29 is bedecked with a Guards badge, but is believed to be a Zhukhovsky development workhorse, and was one of the two aircraft which visited Spain. The brown and green camouflage remains unusual on Soviet MiG-29s.

Below: Another Gromov-operated 'Fulcrum-C'. This aircraft has been used in support of the MiG-29M programme, and at one stage had its overwing air intakes blanked off. It was flown as part of a two-ship display by Test Pilot's School pilots.

Mirage III/5/50
Variant Briefing: Part 1

Dassault's Deltas

Dassault's concept of a lightweight, ultra-high-performance fighter resulted in a simpler and cheaper aircraft than its more sophisticated contemporaries. Many advances have been incorporated and the aircraft has spawned a myriad of sub-variants.

Unquestionably, the aircraft that restored the global reputation of France as a leader in aeronautical design was the Dassault Mirage III. Devastated by World War II, the local aircraft industry strove valiantly in the following decade to catch up with Britain and the United States and was gradually able to satisfy national pride with an increasing proportion of home-designed combat aircraft in the inventory of the Armée de l'Air. Some export successes were gained, but it was with the advent of the Mirage family that the world began to take serious notice of the French arms industry in general, and Générale Aéronautique Marcel Dassault in particular.

'Mirage' has become a generic name for almost all subsequent Dassault fighters and strategic bombers, the initial series (with which we are concerned here) being the III, 5 and 50. Adopted by a score of air forces, the remarkably tractable, combat-proven Mirage has enjoyed a production history in excess of three decades, and even now is being refurbished and modified for further service, guaranteeing that it will mark its 50th anniversary while still in harness. Few other aircraft can match the Mirage's diverse history of production, licensed production and pirate production, during which the aircraft has been de-sophisticated and re-sophisticated to meet diverse customer requirements. Mirage – also pronounced Milan, Nesher, Dagger, Kfir, Nammer, Pantera or Cheetah – has become a legend in its own service lifetime.

Delta development

Genesis of the Mirage may be traced back to early 1952 when Dassault received a study contract for a variant of its Mystère fighter series designated MD550 Mystère Delta. Some pre-

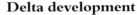
Left: Today the Mirage III is not confined to Third World air forces: many upgraded and modernised aircraft survive even in Western Europe, exemplified by this canard-equipped Swiss Mirage IIIS.

Above: Dassault's products line up before the 1977 Paris Air Salon. No less than four Mirage 5/50 sub-types share the ramp with Falcon biz-jets, Mirage F1s and a Mirage IV bomber.

Left: A South African Mirage IIIE lets rip with two full cans of unguided rockets. Rocket pods are commonly mounted in the nose of underwing fuel tanks on the Mirage III. Pilots seem to take with remarkable calmness the sight of searing rocket exhaust flames playing over fuel tanks.

Below left: An Armée de l'Air Mirage IIIE demonstrates its rarely fitted SEPR take-off/booster rocket engine.

paratory work had therefore been done when, on 28 January 1953, the Air Staff promulgated a requirement for a light fighter incorporating what it thought were the lessons being learned in the Korean War. Parameters included a 4-tonne maximum weight, top speed of Mach 1.3, carriage of a single 441-lb (200-kg) air-to-air missile and a landing speed less than 112 mph (180 km/h). Power choice was to be made from – if necessary in combination – the new SNECMA Atar afterburning turbojet, light turbojets, liquid-fuel rocket motors and even solid rockets.

Unmanned aircraft were permitted.

Responses included the Breguet 1002, Nord Harpon and Morane-Saulnier 1000, but it was the Sud-Est Durandal, Sud-Ouest Trident and Dassault Mystère Delta that received orders for two prototypes each. First flown on 25 June 1955, the rocket-boosted Mystère Delta – soon to be renamed Mirage I – was viewed by Dassault as being too small to carry radar plus effective armament. Also on the drawing boards were the twin-engined Mirage II; the Mirage III with a single Turboméca Atar turbojet and 'area ruled' fuselage later incorporating simple, but effective variable-geometry air intakes; and the Mirage IV.

The last-mentioned and most futuristic project impressed upon the Air Staff that the light fighter concept was a *cul de sac* in combat aircraft design and strategic defence. Accordingly, in 1956, the original specification was upgraded to 'Stage II', which called for a multi-role, radar-equipped fighter, which only Dassault was in a position to supply before the end of the decade.

Skipping the Mirage II stage, the firm de-

Below: Swiss Mirages are often fitted with a battery of external rocket-assisted take-off bottles under the rear fuselage to allow them to operate from small mountain airstrips.

Mirage III/5/50

Right: The diminutive Dassault MD550 Mystère Delta is grandfather of all the Mirage III, 5 and 50 family. Its compact size, twin engines and broad-chord tail make it immediately recognisable. The success of Britain's Fairey Delta 2 led to a major redesign.

veloped the III to the required standard, while the IV was scaled up into a strategic bomber. With incredible speed, Dassault produced a Mirage III fuselage within the year, permitting the aircraft to take to the air on 17 November 1956.

Turning a research machine into a service fighter was the task of 10 pre-production Mirage IIIAs, which gradually incorporated CSF Cyrano intercept radar and combat avionics during 1958-59. Considerable time was spent perfecting the SEPR 841 rocket installation in the lower rear fuselage, although it was little used in squadron service and aroused no interest in foreign customers. The rocket was to improve high-altitude performance, and was certainly not necessary lower down where, on 24 October 1958, IIIA No. 01 achieved twice the speed of sound with only the Atar operating. This was the first unassisted turbojet flight at that speed by a European aircraft, for the Mirage III beat the English Electric Lightning to Mach 2 by one month.

Into service

Deliveries of the definitive Mirage IIIC interceptor began to the first operational squadron in July 1961. Despite being an advanced aircraft, the Mirage required little in the way of specialised handling and was flown by pilots straight out of training with not much more than 300 hours in their logbooks. Only on the landing approach is special care required because of the narrow delta configuration and correspondingly nose-high attitude. At speeds below 240 kt (445 km/h; 276 mph) the Mirage is well on the back of the drag curve, where extra speed can only be achieved by a disproportionate boost in power. A marginal increase in angle of approach can greatly add to drag, while lowering the nose does not necessarily increase speed (as with conventional wings) but can result in sink. Provided that care is taken with attitude on landing, the Mirage III will approach at 183 kt (340 km/h; 210 mph) and touch down at 157 kt (290 km/h; 180 mph). From the outset, training included 'dead-stick' landings – something not attempted in contemporary deltas.

Compact, but well arranged, the Mirage cockpit contains a viewing scope for the Cyrano II air intercept radar as well as miniaturised controls for the navigation and weapons systems. Armed with a large MATRA R.511 (later R.530) radar-homing AAM under the fuselage as a complement to twin internal 30-mm cannon, the Mirage IIIC served two fighter wings (four squadrons) at its peak. Ground attack ordnance could also be fitted, and during the 1980s a pair of underwing MATRA Magics was added to replace the optional AIM-9 Sidewinders. In this guise Mirage IIICs provided the air defence of Djibouti, West Africa, until their last operational sortie on 12 August 1988.

The Mirage became truly multi-role on 5 April 1961 with the maiden flight of the first 'stretched' IIIE. While the IIIC shared the task of defending French skies, IIIEs were assigned to battlefield air superiority as well as surface attack with con-

ventional ordnance or the AN52 tactical nuclear weapon. A related variant, the IIIR, provided all the tactical reconnaissance for the French air force until phased out in 1988. By 1974, of 29 tactical jet squadrons in the Armée de l'Air, 17 were flying Mirages.

Export success

No lesser reliance was placed on the aircraft by other buyers. Australia adopted the Mirage III as its only single-seat fighter, and Israel made it the top combat machine in the IDF/AF. Significantly, it was with the internal cannon that the Mirage III scored its first victories when two Syrian MiG-17s were despatched by the IDF on 20 August 1963. The vaunted MiG-21 fared little better, the first encounter between four Syrians and only two Israelis ending in a 0:1 victory to the

latter. It was in the Six Day War that the Mirage III conclusively demonstrated its versatility. On 5 June 1967, wave after wave of Mirages and other IDF aircraft decimated the Egyptian, Jordanian and Syrian air forces on the ground. Working like men possessed, groundcrews refuelled and re-armed the aircraft in seven minutes, allowing each to mount 12 sorties in a single day.

The opposition, which prided itself on getting two flights out of a MiG in the same period, was convinced that the US and UK were lending other aircraft to Israel. Those MiGs that did get airborne to avenge the Mirage fighter-bomber raids found the same aircraft, reconfigured as interceptors, ready to meet them.

Some customers complained of high prices and slow delivery of spare parts, but Israel was

Above: Recognisably a Mirage, despite its short fuselage and rounded fin-tip, the Mirage III-001's Atar 101-G turbojet was augmented by a SEPR rocket under the rear fuselage, in the ventral fin.

Left: The first of the 10 pre-series Mirage IIIAs takes off from a grass strip. The missile under the centreline is a Nord 5103, designated AA20 in air force service. This primitive air-to-air missile was soon replaced by the slightly more effective R.511 and the more modern R.530.

Above: Mirage IIIs take shape on the line, with Mirage F1s on the adjacent assembly line.

Below: A Mirage 50 displays some of the weapons options available, including its internal cannon, unguided rockets, bombs and a Nord AS30 ASM.

well pleased with the Mirage and ordered a follow-on batch of a simplified variant, lacking radar. A fighter-bomber with fair-weather visual intercept capability, the resultant Mirage 5 opened new markets for Dassault by offering a low purchase price and reduced maintenance requirements. When a Starfighter required 35 maintenance hours for each flying hour – and a McDonnell F-4 Phantom 50 – the Mirage 5 needed only 15.

Also in the Mirage's favour was Dassault's ability to produce an aircraft to suit any financial status. Top of the range was the IIIE with radar and Doppler navigation, while the impecunious could have a basic Mirage 5 'bomb-truck' – although some air forces bought both for a financially and tactically effective high/low mix. Extra kit such as a radar-ranger or

Mirage III/5/50

inertial navigation system was installed in Mirage 5s, according to customers' requirements, with such success that the Mirage IIIE was re-invented and eventually surpassed.

Abu Dhabi, Egypt, Libya and Pakistan all received aircraft with 'Mirage 5' painted on the side, but which were IIIEs in all essential respects, including Cyrano radar. Perhaps this ploy was to obviate political and press criticism of high-technology exports, although it certainly has confused aviation historians since. Belgium declined radar, but its Mirage 5BAs were packed with American avionics that made them the most advanced of the non-Cyrano series.

Meanwhile, the Mirage 5 launch customer had been denied its aircraft when France correctly divined that there was more money to be made by selling arms to the neighbouring Arab nations. After the Mirage 5 was embargoed, Israel launched an ambitious programme to obtain by subterfuge the thousands of technical drawings necessary for building the aircraft and engine itself. The resultant IAI Nesher flew in 1971 and was available to take part in the 1973 Yom Kippur War, but a longer-term project concerned complete redesign of the aircraft with an American engine and Israeli avionics.

Delivered to squadrons from April 1975 onwards, the IAI Kfir remained unmistakably a member of the Mirage family. Though there have been difficulties in obtaining export permission for the General Electric J79 powerplant, Kfirs have been delivered to two foreign air forces and additionally leased by the US Navy and Marines for air combat training. Surplus

Above: A Mirage IIIBE of EC 13 on approach to Solenzara. The Mirage III's delta wing conferred unique handling characteristics, and a two-seat trainer was an early priority.

Below: Belgium was one of several customers for a tactical reconnaissance version of the Mirage delta. Belgium's aircraft are designated Mirage 5BR and are fitted with British cameras.

Mirage Colours – Anniversary Ships

In June 1987 *EC 1/13 'Artois'* painted up this *Mirage IIIE* to commemorate 20 years' service at *Colmar*.

Co-located *EC 3/13 'Auvergne'* painted one of its *Mirage 5Fs* in this attractive anniversary scheme to celebrate the same anniversary.

The other *EC 13* unit (*EC 2/13 'Alpes'*) applied this striking paint job to one aircraft to celebrate 20 years at *Colmar*.

Over the years, Belgian Mirages have worn a number of one-off paint schemes. This was from *No. 2 Wing's No. 1 Smaldeel/Escadrille*.

No. 2 Smaldeel at Florennes applied this gaudy paint job to one of its aircraft before converting to the *F-16*.

This *No. 8 Smaldeel* Mirage received a three-tone blue tailfin on 8 August 1988 for a *NATO '8 Squadron'* meet.

Twenty years of Mirage operation by *No. 8 Smaldeel* (of *No. 3 Wing*) was celebrated in eye-catching style.

No. 42 Smaldeel preferred to celebrate its 70th birthday, and went to town on one of its *Mirage 5BRs*.

Above: Many of Argentina's surviving Daggers (built as IAI Neshers) wear markings commemorating the brave part they played during the Falklands War, in which they attacked British ships and troops with great ferocity and élan, consequently falling in considerable numbers to SAMs and Sea Harriers. Surviving pilots also wear commemorative flying suit badges, as seen below, worn in conjunction with a representation of the Grupo 6 badge.

Neshers were sold to Argentina once the Kfir became available, and it was they who undertook many of the fighter-bomber raids against British forces during the 1982 Falklands War. Subsequently upgraded, they are partnered by an Argentine squadron operating survivors of the original Mirage IIICJs delivered to Israel in 1961-64.

In 1976, Israel revealed the canard-equipped Kfir-C2. A different form of canard (forward of the cockpit) had first been tried on the Mirage Milan from 1968 onwards in an attempt to interest Switzerland in more Mirages. The device improves manoeuvrability (for example, in close combat) and reduces some of the delta wing's shortcomings, of which long take-off runs are one. Several Mirage operators are currently equipping their aircraft with canards as part of mid-life improvement programmes featuring upgraded avionics and other changes. Once again, there is a programme for every pocket, the most advanced being the Mirage 3NG, which has the movable canards and fly-by-wire control system of the Mirage 2000.

No operator has yet specified this degree of updating, but a measure of extra performance has been obtained by installing a higher-powered version of the Atar to produce a Mirage 50. Only Chile and Venezuela have bought this variant off the production line, others following by retrospective modification. South Africa is remanufacturing some of its Mirages as Cheetahs using Israeli technology, and Chile is making slow progress with a similar-looking Pantera local modification. Of 1,422 Mirage III/5/50s built up to 1990, nearly 850 remain, together with 23 Daggers and 190 Kfirs, suggesting that the aircraft – at least in its updated form – will be flying for many years to come.

Most certainly the Mirage is a remarkable aeroplane, yet it is a paradox that this Gallic delta could never claim to be a wonder aircraft. Dassault showed no interest in pushing back the frontiers of aeronautical knowledge, being content to let others take the credit (and pick up the bills) for pioneering.

The key to the Mirage's ubiquity and longevity is to be found in careful blending of simplicity with adapted technology, such that the aircraft achieved its creditable performance despite being a 'minimum risk' programme relying on constructional materials and manufacturing techniques readily available in Europe during the mid-1950s. Likewise, the Atar turbojet lagged behind equivalent British and US engines in efficiency even when installed in the prototype Mirage III, yet has stood the test of time. One must be clever to make things look simple, and the genius of Dassault was to make an aircraft that was more than the sum of its component parts.

Above: The US Marine Corps has now retired the Kfirs it leased as adversary aircraft during the 1980s, under the designation F-21A.

Above: A pair of Pakistani Mirage 5PAs is seen in flight. These aircraft augment radar-nosed Mirage 5PA2s and 5PA3s. The latter carry the AM39 Exocet anti-ship missile. Pakistan also operates a handful of Mirage IIIEs, IIIRs and assorted two-seaters.

Right: The IAI Kfir (represented here by a trio of Ecuadorian aircraft) is an unlicensed derivative of the Mirage 5, with advanced Israeli avionics and powered by a General Electric J79 engine. Exports have been hampered by the need to gain US approval to export the engine. Later Kfirs have fixed canard foreplanes and other aerodynamic refinements.

Below: This Brazilian Mirage IIIDBR (designated F-103D in service) is typical of Mirages upgraded by Dassault, with new avionics, canard foreplanes and a host of other refinements. Some Brazilian Mirages are equipped with refuelling probes.

Dassault Mirage III/5/50 Variants

MD550/560 Mystère Delta, Mirage I and II

Preliminary company research into delta-wing configurations during 1950-51 was rewarded early in 1952 by an official study contract. Under the direction of Jean Cabrière, the Saint Cloud (Paris) experimental design offices of Dassault produced drawings later in the same year for a trials aircraft capable of forming the basis of an interceptor. Powered by an afterburning Rolls-Royce RA.7R Avon turbojet or the equally new but indigenous SNECMA Atar, the Mach 1.3 MD550 Mystère Delta was to possess a fuselage similar to the Mystère IV fighter, including a single air intake in the extreme nose, but without horizontal tail surfaces.

The three-spar wing, spanning 26 ft 10¾ in (8.2 m), was swept at 62° and had a thickness:chord ratio of 5.5 per cent, a further radical feature being a single skid undercarriage – although a proposed naval variant had conventional wheels. Grossing 10,362 lb (4700 kg), the aircraft would have been capable of reaching 39,370 ft (12000 m) in two minutes.

By 1953, a single-engined, Mach 1.8 MD560 Mystère Delta was under development, using a 9,259 lb st (41.19 kN) afterburning Atar 101G plus an SEPR liquid-fuelled rocket motor adding 1,323 lb st (5.88 kN) at high altitudes to compensate for reduced turbojet efficiency. Smaller, with a 22-ft 7¾-in (6.9-m) span but the same gross weight, the MD560 had both a radar above the

nose intake and tailfin resembling Vought's F8U Crusader, plus a tricycle, wheeled undercarriage.

Performance estimates included a climb to 49,213 ft (15000 m) in two minutes with a single air-to-air missile. Proposals submitted officially in June 1953 offered the Armée de l'Air (AA) a choice of three variants with a single Atar, two afterburning Armstrong-Siddeley Vipers or two Vipers plus a rocket. The third was Dassault's recommended choice, in anticipation of which the firm obtained a licence to build the Viper as the MD.30.

Two Mystère Delta prototypes were ordered, in the form suggested, early in 1954, together with a pair of competing designs: the Sud-Ouest Trident and Sud-Est Durandal. The first Mystère was initially without afterburning and rocket, while the second was to have two afterburning 3,306-lb st (14.7 kN) Turboméca Gabizo turbojets and two 1,653-lb st (7.35-kN) rockets, plus Dassault Aladin radar and other military equipment. The aircraft fabricated at Saint Cloud and assembled at the Melun-Villaroche test centre south of Paris had the designation MD550 painted on its rudder, but was different in several respects from earlier designs. A needle nose and twin cheek intakes replaced the single orifice, the whole being dominated by a fin of seemingly over-generous proportions.

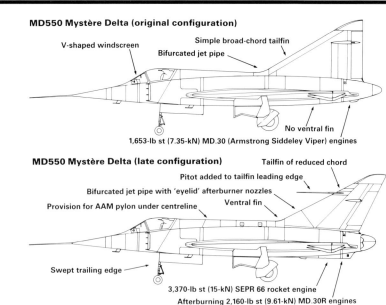

MD550 Mystère Delta (original configuration)
V-shaped windscreen · Bifurcated jet pipe · Simple broad-chord tailfin · No ventral fin · 1,653-lb st (7.35-kN) MD.30 (Armstrong Siddeley Viper) engines

MD550 Mystère Delta (late configuration)
Tailfin of reduced chord · Pitot added to tailfin leading edge · Bifurcated jet pipe with 'eyelid' afterburner nozzles · Provision for AAM pylon under centreline · Ventral fin · Swept trailing edge · 3,370-lb st (15-kN) SEPR 66 rocket engine · Afterburning 2,160-lb st (9.61-kN) MD.30R engines

Roland Glavany flew Mystère Delta No. 01 at Melun on 25 June 1955 at the start of a short initial trials programme. After receiving a new fin with backswept trailing edge and the addition of afterburning MD.30Rs rated at 2,160 lb st (9.61 kN) plus a 3,370-lb st (15.0-kN) SEPR 66 rocket in the lower rear fuselage, No. 01 flew again on 17 December 1956. It was later to demonstrate Mach 1.6 in level flight with rocket ignited, but equally significant was its change of name to

Mirage I. Spanning 23 ft 11½ in (7.30 m), the Mirage I had a gross weight of 11,023 lb (5000 kg), while its Gabizo-engined counterpart – now named Mirage II – would have grown to 24 ft 10½ in (10.48 m) and 12,535 lb (5686 kg) and achieved Mach 1.61. This second aircraft was cancelled early in 1956 when partly complete, while the historic Mirage I was broken up at the end of its trials programme.

Above: The diminutive Mystère Delta flies in its original configuration, with broad-chord fin and vertical rudder trailing edge. Fin area was later sharply reduced.

Above: In late configuration, the MD550 is pictured with an optically-guided MATRA R.510 air-to-air missile under the centreline. This later entered service as the R511 with semi-active radar homing.

Mirage III

Cancellation of the Mirage II was the result of changed AA requirements that now called for a better-equipped fighter able to take advantage of both the 9,920 lb st (44.12 kN) then offered by a single Atar 101G-1 turbojet and the rapid growth to 13,227 lb st (58.83 kN) promised by SNECMA. What was to become the standard Mirage powerplant had originated in the BMW-012 turbojet taken over from Germany in 1945 and developed in France by the Atelier Technique Aéronautique Reichenbach – hence ATAR (invariably rendered as Atar, which is a town in Mauretania). Wings of the part-completed Mirage II were used for the new aircraft, married to a redesigned fuselage, taking the span to 24 ft 10½ in (7.58 m). Height was 15 ft 4¼ in (4.68 m).

Re-engining was not the sole reason for changing the latter, for Dassault had been impressed with the advantages of 'area-ruling' observed at first hand when the company had offered its Istres test airfield to Britain's Fairey Aviation for trials of the very similar FD.2 during

work-up to its successful world airspeed attempt. Reconfigured under the direction of Jean-Jacques Samin and first flown on 17 November 1956, Mirage III No. 001 soon demonstrated a level speed of Mach 1.52, the limit with fixed-geometry intakes.

A most valuable thrust improvement of 20 per cent was then achieved with the addition of simple, manually adjustable half-cone centrebodies – nicknamed *souris* (mouse) – in the air intakes. These were moved forward as speed increased, so keeping the shock wave focused at the optimum point for air pressure recovery and so exclude unstable flow ('buzz') from the duct. With a 9,700-lb st (43.15-kN) Atar 101G-2 installed, No. 001 achieved Mach 1.65 on 17 April 1958, top speed with the SEPR 66 rocket also operating being Mach 1.8. Lightest of the Mirage IIIs – at 15,212 lb (6900 kg) fully laden – No. 001 had a theoretical ceiling of 59,055 ft (18000 m), although for safety reasons it was limited to 39,370 ft (12000 m).

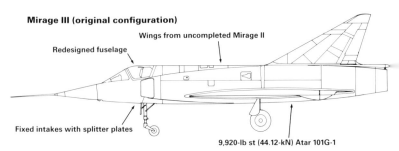

Mirage III (original configuration)
Wings from uncompleted Mirage II · Redesigned fuselage · Fixed intakes with splitter plates · 9,920-lb st (44.12-kN) Atar 101G-1

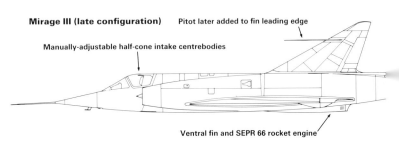

Mirage III (late configuration)
Pitot later added to fin leading edge · Manually-adjustable half-cone intake centrebodies · Ventral fin and SEPR 66 rocket engine

Above: The prototype Mirage III is seen in an interim configuration, before adoption of a fin-mounted pitot and ventral fin, retaining intake splitter plates, but with revised undercarriage doors.

The addition of shock-cones in the intakes dramatically improved performance, by focusing shock waves at the optimum point for air pressure recovery. The ventral 'fin' accommodated an SEPR rocket.

Mirage IIIA

In July 1957, two months before the Mirage III prototype was accepted for official tests, Dassault received a contract covering 10 pre-series aircraft that would take the Mirage from aerodynamic trials airframe to squadron interceptor. Designated Mirage IIIA, and redesigned by Phillipe Amblard, they differed externally in several respects from No. 001, notably in being further increased in size: the fuselage was stretched from 41 ft 6 in (12.65 m) to 46 ft 7 in (14.20 m), and wing area increased from 312.2 sq ft (29 m²) to 366.0 sq ft (34 m²). One reason for choosing a delta wing had been to obtain the low thickness:chord ratio necessary for supersonic flight without recourse to complex manufacturing techniques. At the root this was now 4.5 per cent once more (having risen to 5 per cent on No. 001), but still allowed traditional three-spar (two perpendicular; one oblique), all-metal wing construction with stressed skin covering. Tip ratio was 3.5 per cent.

Wings effectively formed two compartments, the forward section housing the inward-retracting undercarriage legs and single wheels and the rear being an integral tank for 115 Imp gal (525 litres) of fuel. This was increased in production aircraft to a combined total for both wings of 246 Imp gal (1120 litres). After trials on No. 001, conical camber was added to leading edges and chordwise slots inserted to perform the same functions as fences. Wing area consequently increased to 375 sq ft (34.85 m²) and the outer elevon sections assumed a prominent downward curve. Aspect ratio is 1.94; sweepback, 60° 34 seconds; and anhedral, 1°. Control surfaces occupy the entire trailing edge, the hydraulically-powered elevons featuring a Dassault-developed artificial feel system – as does the rudder.

The area-ruled *taille de guêpe* (wasp-waist) fuselage was built in five sections: nose, which was now intended to mount Dassault Super Aida radar; pressure cabin and rearward-retracting nosewheel; forward fuselage, containing electrical equipment and including air intakes; centre fuselage, with engine mountings and four tanks for a total of 224 Imp gal (1020 litres) of fuel; and rear fuselage, complete with drag-parachute compartment and fitments for an optional SEPR 84 rocket motor. The rocket operated on aviation fuel mixed with nitric acid, 69 Imp gal (315 litres) of which replaced the ammunition bays (125 shells per gun) when high-altitude flight was required.

Thrust of the rocket was 3,000 lb st

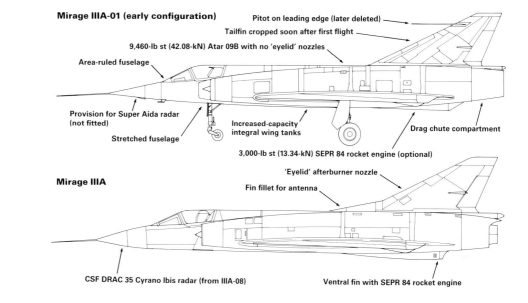

Mirage IIIA-01 (early configuration)

- Pitot on leading edge (later deleted)
- Tailfin cropped soon after first flight
- 9,460-lb st (42.08-kN) Atar 09B with no 'eyelid' nozzles
- Area-ruled fuselage
- Provision for Super Aida radar (not fitted)
- Stretched fuselage
- Increased-capacity integral wing tanks
- Drag chute compartment
- 3,000-lb st (13.34-kN) SEPR 84 rocket engine (optional)

Mirage IIIA

- 'Eyelid' afterburner nozzle
- Fin fillet for antenna
- CSF DRAC 35 Cyrano Ibis radar (from IIIA-08)
- Ventral fin with SEPR 84 rocket engine

Above and below: The Mirage IIIA quickly picked up the 'Mach 2' label. It is seen here with the original tall fin, and with test pilot Roland Glavany.

Above: The first of the Mirage IIIAs on finals, with the cropped fin associated with all subsequent sub-types.

Below: Mirage IIIA 07 is very similar in appearance to a production Mirage IIIC, with the production standard rear fuselage.

(13.34 kN) for 80 seconds at sea level, or half that for twice the time, high altitude performance being 3,360 lb st (14.95 kN). If the rocket were deleted, the Mirage could use its guns and carry a tank of 121 Imp gal (550 litres) of aviation fuel in the rocket compartment, increasing total internal capacity to 592 Imp gal (2690 litres) in production aircraft. Loss of cannon was not as operationally serious as might at first appear, for it was unlikely that any aircraft would be sufficiently stable to engage in a manoeuvring gunfight at high altitude. This was an environment for missiles.

An Atar 09B specified for early production aircraft developed 9,460 lb st (42.08 kN) dry and 13,228 lb st (58.84 kN) with afterburning, as the result of additional turbine and compressor stages. The fin, swept at 63°, was also built on three spars and in later aircraft was fitted with a fillet to accommodate one of the seven antennas required in production machines. Almost every aspect of the IIIA was redesigned to some degree, only the undercarriage being a direct transfer from III-001.

Equipment standards varied among the Mirage IIIAs as 12 items of avionics were progressively installed, but a typical gross weight was 17,582 lb (7975 kg). IIIA-01 first flew on 12 May 1958 with Glavany in command, later achieving Mach 2.0 on Atar alone and 2.2 with rocket assistance. Following trials elsewhere, the CSF (Compagnie générale de télégraphie Sans Fil) DRAC 35 Cyrano air intercept radar was specified by the AA in place of Super Aida. IIIA-05 was the first aircraft to production standard, and thus had the nose radome, although not until No. 08 was the Cyrano Ibis unit fitted. The last IIIA flew on 15 December 1959, the series undertaking numerous development tasks with Dassault, SNECMA, the Centre d'Essais en Vol (CEV) and Centre d'Expériences Aériennes Militaires (CEAM) until 28 February 1975, when Nos 04 and 08 were retired.

Right: One of the later Mirage IIIAs augments its turbojet with the optional SEPR rocket.

Mirage IIIB (Prototype)

With commendable foresight, the AA formulated a requirement for a dual-control Mirage III in July 1957, specifying tandem seats and the ability to carry drop tanks and ordnance externally. Fitted with a nose radome, the aircraft was not required to mount Cyrano, however. The prototype, B01, flew on 20 October 1959 (i.e., before A07 and A10), although production IIIBs were not delivered to the AA until after the service entry of single-seat Mirage fighters. Installation of the second cockpit was made at the expense of internal cannon and some fuel accommodation, despite fuselage length increasing to 50 ft 2¾ in (15.31 m). Empty weight rose 1,808 lb (820 kg) to 13,779 lb (6250 kg) compared with the IIIA –

although that was a mere 331 lb (150 kg) more than that of the definitive IIIC single-seater. Grossing up to 26,015 lb (11800 kg), the IIIB could, at a normal operating weight of up to 19,552 lb (9050 kg), reach Mach 2.15 or climb to 59,055 ft (18000 m) in nine minutes, despite having no rocket motor. Its service ceiling was slightly lower, at 58,070 ft (17700 m). Power was provided by an Atar 9B-3 production version of the 101 with equal output and with 'eyelid' afterburner nozzle.

Right: The Mirage IIIB prototype was based on the airframe of the Mirage IIIA, preceding the Mirage IIIC.

Mirage IIIC

In September 1957, Dassault received two Mirage production contracts, of which the first (5567/57) concerned 10 pre-series IIIAs. The other (5569/57) was for 100 production IIIAs, manufacture of which was due to begin in October of the following year, after its confirmation on 5 August 1958. Adoption of Cyrano and other detail changes resulted in the new designation, IIIC being bestowed on these machines, the first of which, No. 1, flew at Bordeaux-Mérignac on 9 October 1960, piloted by Jean Coreau. All Dassault's series-built aircraft are completed at Bordeaux, only the prototypes flying from elsewhere. While fuselages came from the company's Argenteuil plant in Paris, wings were sub-contracted to Nord (later Aérospatiale) at Meaulte, and several other assemblies were allocated elsewhere in offset agreements. Despite having gained

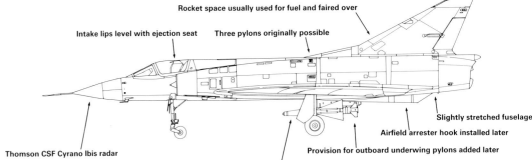

Mirage IIIC

Rocket space usually used for fuel and faired over

Intake lips level with ejection seat

Three pylons originally possible

Slightly stretched fuselage

Airfield arrester hook installed later

Thomson CSF Cyrano Ibis radar

Provision for outboard underwing pylons added later

Centreline pylon for MATRA R.511, Nord 5103 AAM or MATRA 530 (shown here)

additional floorspace on its take-over of Breguet Aviation in December 1971, Dassault was manufacturing only 14 per cent by value of a Mirage III by the late 1970s.

In all important respects, the IIIC was a productionised IIIA with identical span, wing area and height (13 ft 11¼ in/4.25 m), the fuselage having been extended to 48 ft 4 in (14.73 m). Maximum weight

was 26,015 lb (11800 kg), and the normal range between 17,548 lb (7960 kg) and 21,451 lb (9730 kg). When the Atar 09B turbojet was aided by an SEPR 841 rocket, it was possible to achieve

Left: The first Mirage IIIC is prepared for flight. Interestingly, there seems to be no SEPR rocket. Above: An EC 1/2 Mirage IIIC carries an R511 on the centreline.

Above: For ground attack this aircraft carries JL-100 rocket pod/fuel tanks and free-fall bombs.

9,055 ft (18000 m) in 6 minutes 10 seconds yet, as with the IIIB, practical ceiling was 984 ft (300 m) lower.

Entering service just as bombers began to resort to the security of low-level penetration, the Mirage III had little need of its rocket and preferred to use that space for further fuel. A small ventral fin replaced the protruding portion of the rocket and was itself later supplanted by the housing for an airfield arrester hook.

Cyrano Ibis radar fitted to the IIIC was a simple monopulse unit optimised for interception, duties including illumination of the target for a MATRA R511 'twist-and-steer' semi-active radar homing (SARH) AAM. Also available were the Nord 5103 (later AA20) – Europe's first operational AAM – which was a tailless cruciform weapon steered by radio command; and the American AIM-9B Sidewinder heat-seeker. Initially, three weapon pylons could be fitted to the IIIC: one under the fuselage and two beneath the inner wing, all of them rated at 1,102 lb (500 kg). For air combat, standard [fit]tment was an R511 on the centreline, plus two 110-Imp gal (500-litre) supersonic drop tanks, a Sidewinder replacing each tank on short-range missions. Later, MATRA's R530 was adopted, this 11 mile (18 km) weapon being available in IR-homing and SARH forms. For attack, one 1,000-lb (454-kg) bomb and/or underwing JL100 fuel/rocket pods were specified. Subsequently, [h]ardpoints for Sidewinders were installed [u]nder the wings, outboard of the original pylons. For training sorties and ferrying, the AA fits RP62 (Réservoir Pendulaire) 264-Imp gal (1200-litre) drop tanks under the wing.

Production of the IIIC for France ended [l]ate in 1962 at the 95th aircraft, original recipients being the 2ᵉ and 13ᵉ Escadres de Chasse (two squadrons each) at Dijon and Colmar. These later passed their aircraft on to the 5th and 10th Wings (Orange and Creil), the last-mentioned being the sole operator from 1975, by which time some aircraft had replaced natural metal for a light bluish-grey overall camouflage. The usual partner to their Sidewinders was an IR R530E, not the SARH version, as might be expected. A tactical, low-level scheme of 'sand and chestnut' was applied to a half-squadron deployed to defend Djibouti in 1979. By August 1984, the last of the 11 deployed had received minor updating with new VHF/UHF radios, air conditioning, re-wiring and provision for MATRA R550 Magics (range 6.2 miles/10 km) in place of the ageing Sidewinder. The final IIIC operational sortie was flown in Djibouti on 12 August 1988.

Export customers accounted for a further 89 aircraft, including 72 IIICJs delivered to Israel between July 1961 and July 1964 and used in combat. At least two gained camera noses in later service. Nineteen survivors were sold to Argentina in 1982. South Africa received 16 IIICZs (still in service, but not considered worth conversion to Cheetah standard), while a single IIICS was supplied to Switzerland in December 1962 for weapon trials.

Right: The last Armée de l'Air Mirage IIICs were retired from Djibouti-based EC 10 during August 1988.

Below: South Africa's No. 2 Squadron, the 'Flying Cheetahs', demonstrate their Mirage IIICZs.

Below: Below: This Mirage IIICZ carries an indigenous V3 Kukri missile, identifiable by its four forward control fins and two fixed canards ahead of these.

Right: Four Israeli Mirage IIICJs on patrol. Israeli Mirage IIICJs saw combat service in 1967 and 1973, gaining a large number of kills.

Right: Israel sold 19 surviving Mirage IIICJs to Argentina in 1982, and these continue to give sterling service.

Above: A Mirage IIIC of EC 1/10 'Valois' bears clear evidence of previous ownership by EC 13, whose chevron is still just visible on the fin.

Below: For most of its career, the Mirage IIIC used the disappointing R530 as its long-range missile, seen here on an EC 2 aircraft.

Mirage IIIC2

In the sometimes perverse system of Dassault designations, the sole IIIC2 was not a Mirage IIIC at all, but the 'stretched'-fuselage IIIE No. 406 fitted for trials purposes with an Atar 09K-6 turbojet. First flown on 10 May 1965, IIIC2 No. 01 lacked the underfuselage Doppler of the IIIE, but was reconverted to production standard for issue to the AA at the end of its test programme. As the first of what would later be known as the Mirage 50, the aircraft was described as having improved high-level performance, although the increased power of the 09K was later stressed in the context of better load-carrying and shorter take-off.

Mirage IIIC2

Optimised for high-altitude interception

Based on Mirage IIIE (not IIIC) airframe

No fin fillet

No Doppler bulge

Intake lips behind cockpit, like IIIE

Lengthened fuselage with extra volume avionics bay

SNECMA Atar 09K-6 engine

Above: The Mirage IIIC2 was a one-off high-altitude interceptor prototype, with an Atar 09K-6 engine in a modified Mirage IIIE airframe. As such, the aircraft was effectively the Mirage 50 prototype, and served in that aircraft's development programme. It is seen here with 250-kg bombs mounted on its underwing fuel tanks.

Mirage IIIB (Production)

Despite having ordered a prototype trainer Mirage III at the time of the first contract award, the AA took no further steps towards acquisition until August 1960, when 26 more were purchased. The first, serialled 201, flew on 19 July 1962, deliveries proceeding to squadrons operating the IIIC, IIIE, IIIR and larger Mirage IVA strategic bomber. In 1966, all two-seat training for the tactical units was concentrated within an OCU squadron of EC 2 at Dijon, this moving to EC 13 at Colmar in 1986. One further IIIB was built for CEV, while exports comprised four IIIBJs to Israel, four IIIBSs to Switzerland (the last assembled locally from French parts) and three IIIBZs to South Africa.

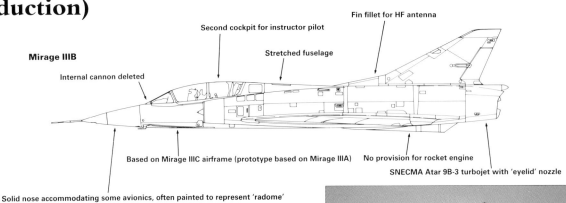

Mirage IIIB

Second cockpit for instructor pilot

Fin fillet for HF antenna

Stretched fuselage

Internal cannon deleted

Based on Mirage IIIC airframe (prototype based on Mirage IIIA)

No provision for rocket engine

SNECMA Atar 9B-3 turbojet with 'eyelid' nozzle

Solid nose accommodating some avionics, often painted to represent 'radome'

Above: The production Mirage IIIB was based on the airframe of the Mirage IIIC. The first example is seen here.

Right: Switzerland received four Mirage IIIB trainers under the designation IIIBS. Two remain in service today.

Above: Most Mirage IIIBs had black-painted noses, although no radar (and thus no radome) was fitted.

Mirage IIIB-1

Five Mirage IIIBs (Nos 231-235) were ordered specifically as testbeds for the Centre d'Essais en Vol (CEV) trials establishment at Cazaux, Brétigny-sur-Orge and Istres, and the Ecole du Personnel Navigant d'Essais et de Réception test pilots' school at Istres.

Right: Mirage IIIB-1s typically wear a silver or grey overall finish, with large patches of Dayglo to enhance conspicuity. The five aircraft were delivered specifically for test and test pilot training duties.

Mirage IIIB-SV

No. 225, a former AA aircraft, was passed to the CEV for modification to a variable-stability testbed (Stabilitié Variable). Reflown on 17 February 1975, it made the first fully fly-by-wire sortie of a French aircraft on 8 September, and by 17 October 1975 had completed 94 useful flights. Results of the trials, originally for the abortive ACF, were incorporated in the Mirage 2000.

Mirage IIIB-2(RV)

Between July 1967 and October 1968, the strategic air forces OCU at Bordeaux (CIFAS 328) took delivery of 10 Mirage IIIBs (Nos 241-250) fitted with dummy refuelling probes in the extreme nose. Designated IIIB-2(RV) to indicate Ravitaillement en Vol (inflight refuelling), the aircraft are flown by future Mirage IV pilots in exercises with the AA's Boeing C-135FR tankers.

Mirage IIIB-2(RV)

Dummy refuelling probe in extreme nose for inflight refuelling practice

Above: This Mirage IIIB-2(RV) served with EC 13 after retirement by CIFAS 328.

Above: The Mirage IIIB-2(RV) has a non-functional refuelling probe in the nose and is used for training Mirage IV pilots in inflight refuelling techniques.

Above: A Mirage IIIB-2(RV) wears the fin badge of CIFAS 328, the Mirage IV conversion unit.

Mirage IIIBE

The second series of Mirage III two-seat trainers was compatible with the IIIE multi-role aircraft. In addition to some alterations in cockpit layout to reflect the newer single-seat variant, the revised trainer dispensed with the radome (which was not entirely empty, as it housed repositioned avionics) in favour of a 'solid' nose with the pitot probe slightly above a camera/gun port in the extremity. In common with the Mirage IIIE, the fillet (incorporating an HF aerial) at the base of the fin was deleted, but an additional feature was the pair of strakes beneath the forward fuselage. The latter were fairings for cables connecting the nose avionics bay to the centre fuselage without passing through the pressurised cockpit. In export aircraft, these modifications resulted in redesignation as Mirage IIID or 5D, according to the single-seat version used by the customer. Those with Mirage IIIs received trainers with black nosecones that appeared to be radomes until closely inspected.

The opportunity was taken to adopt an Atar 09C-3 turbojet, brought in with the Mirage IIIE and externally recognisable by its 'petal' type of afterburner nozzle, replacing the 09B's two 'eyelids'. Compared with the earlier 09B-3 fitted to Mirage IIIBs and IIICs, this powerplant featured a new, nine-stage compressor (five steel and four light alloy stages), self-contained starter and an improved

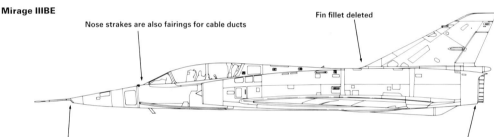

Mirage IIIBE

Nose strakes are also fairings for cable ducts

Fin fillet deleted

Solid nose with pitot probe above forward-facing (gun) camera port

SNECMA Atar 09C-3 engine with 'petal'-type afterburner nozzle

overspeed that engages at Mach 1.4 and 36,089 ft (11000 m), giving power equivalent to a sea-level thrust of 14,109 lb st (62.76 kN). Mass flow and pressure ratio are the same as for the 09B – 150 lb (68 kg) per second and 5.5:1 – and weight is increased from 2,976 lb (1350 kg) to 3,131 lb (1420 kg). Compensation comes in the form of extra dry thrust (reheat rating is the same) and reduced fuel consumption, the 09C-3 generating 9,436 lb st (41.97 kN) for an SFC of 1.01, compared with 9,369 lb st (41.68 kN) and 1.03 for the 09B. In afterburner, the thirsty 09B's SFC is 2.2, against the 09C's 2.03.

French orders for Mirage IIIBEs totalled 20 aircraft (Nos 257-276) delivered from February 1971 to EC 2 at Dijon, the survivors now based with EC 13 at Colmar. Two IIIBLs were supplied to Lebanon in 1968-69, but saw little use.

Above: The Mirage IIIBE had a recontoured nose with a relocated pitot probe and a camera gun. This one wears the markings of EC 2, the Mirage III training unit.

Left: Twenty Mirage IIIBEs were delivered to the Armée de l'Air, serving with EC 2 and then being passed to EC 13 or exported.

Right: The Mirage IIIBE was the first two-seater to feature prominent strakes/cable ducts on the lower part of the forward fuselage. Rails in the top of the front canopy allowed an instrument training hood to be slid forward.

Mirage IIID and two-seat 5D

The basic configuration of the second-generation trainer Mirage is explained previously. Most export aircraft received the designation IIID or 5Dx (plain '5D' was a single-seat version) in accordance with the single-seat version flown by the operator, Switzerland being a partial exception. There were minor variations in equipment standard between customers, but the IIIBE, IIID and 5Dx are virtually indistinguishable, apart from the black-painted noses of some Mirage III users. Surplus French IIIBEs were exported, whereupon they became IIIDBR for Brazil (two) and 5SDD for Egypt (three). Three trainers delivered to Chile in 1982-87 were described as model 50DC, but fitted with Atar 09C-3 turbojets and not

the 09K-50 version suggested by their designation. South African IIID2Z aircraft also had the 09C.

New two-seat Mirage were: 5DAD for Abu Dhabi (three), IIIDA for Argentina (four), IIID Australia (16 assembled by CAC), 5BD Belgium (16, all but one assembled locally), IIIDBR Brazil (two locally designated F-103D), 50DC Chile (three), 5COD Colombia (two), 5SDD Egypt (three), 5DG Gabon (four), 5DD Libya (15), IIIDP/5DPA2 Pakistan (five and two), 5DP/5DP3/5DP4 Peru (four, one and one), IIIDZ/IIID2Z South Africa (three and 11), IIIDE Spain (six locally designated CE.11), 5DS Switzerland (two), IIIDV/50DV Venezuela (three and one) and 5DM Zaire (three).

Above: The Mirage IIID was externally indistinguishable from the Mirage IIIBE. This aircraft is a Spanish Mirage IIIDE.

Below: Argentina's Mirage fleet includes a handful of Mirage IIIDAs and similar looking two-seat Daggers.

Above: Many Mirage IIIC and IIIE operators painted the noses of their two-seaters black, to simulate a radome, as on this Australian IIID.

Below: Gabon's four two-seaters were designated Mirage 5DG. The survivors remain in use alongside six Mirage 5s at Libreville.

Right: A Pakistani Mirage IIIDP on approach, instrument flying hood pulled over the rear cockpit.

Below: Chilean two-seaters are designated Mirage 50DC, although they retain Atar 09C-3 engines, and not the 09K-50 of the Mirage 50.

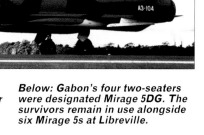

Mirage IIIE

Transformation of the Mirage IIIC interceptor into a dual-role combat aircraft was achieved in the IIIE, which served the AA in both air defence and tactical strike/attack squadrons. Principal among the changes introduced was a fuselage stretch of 11¾ in (30 cm) to extend the avionics bay to the rear of the cockpit, resulting in a new length of 49 ft 3¾ in (15.03 m) and wheelbase of 16 ft 0 in (4.87 m). Wheel track was unaltered (at 10 ft 4 in/3.15 m), although the main legs were raked slightly forward to give clearance for larger underfuselage stores – notably the AN52 free-fall nuclear bomb. Whereas the IIIC's air intakes were below the ejection seat, those of the IIIE were effectively moved back to the level of the canopy's rear hinge. Power was provided by an Atar 09C-3, described under the Mirage IIIBE heading, and as on the latter aircraft the fin fillet was omitted.

To accommodate surface attack, radar installed in the IIIE was a Thomson-CSF Cyrano II operating in the I/J-bands – formerly known as X/Ku(Q)-bands – housed in a pressurised radome.

Mirage IIIE

CSF97 pilot's sight
Thomson-CSF Cyrano II radar
Fairing for Marconi Doppler antenna on most sub-variants
1300-litre RP62 fuel tank with hardpoints for weapons carriage
Main undercarriage legs raked forward slightly to give greater clearance for stores

Fuselage stretch for increased volume avionics bay
Intake lips appear further aft because of stretch
No fin fillet (except Argentinian aircraft)
Forward-facing RWR (not always fitted)
Rearward-facing RWRs immediately above rudder
SEPR 844 rocket engine not normally fitted
SNECMA Atar 09C-3 engine with 'petal'-type afterburner nozzle

Transmitting a peak of 200 kW, this monopulse equipment has search, track, air-to-air interception, air-to-ground and ground mapping modes in its IIbis form. Oblique range between aircraft and a designated ground point can be displayed on the complementary CSF 97 pilot's sight, this latter also including air-to-air displays for missile or cannon attack; air-to-ground displays for dive-bombing or LABS; and a navigational facility to indicate heading and horizon. For

interception in radio silence, the radar/gunsight can be controlled from the ground, the pilot merely following the steering data presented in the sight.

A sophisticated navigation suite – at least, for pre-microcomputer days – gives constant heading and distance to target and included a rotating magazine holding up to 12 plastic punch-cards, each representing the co-ordinates of a position. Navigational data is given to the pilot to take appropriate manual action as

he flies a pre-selected path derived from the cards, flexibility being provided by the ability to nominate unplanned waypoints in flight. Bearings and distances to TACAN beacons are displayed on the instrument panel, and groundspeed and drift information for navigation is provided by a Marconi Doppler radar housed in a blister fairing beneath the forward fuselage, ahead of the nosewheel.

Four underwing pylons and one on the centreline allow the Mirage IIIE to carry

up to 8,818 lb (4000 kg) of stores in between its empty weight of 15,543 lb (7050 kg) and maximum take-off weight of 30,203 lb (13700 kg). RP30 drop tanks of 374 Imp gal (1700 litres) may be fitted to inboard wing pylons as an alternative to smaller RP62 and 110-Imp gal (500-litre) Supersonique tanks first used by the IIIC. From No. 519 onwards, aircraft are stressed to carry 374-Imp gal (1500-litre) RP30 drop tanks beneath the wings and fitted with an extra 27.5 Imp gal (125 litres) of capacity in each wing, increasing total internal volume (without rocket pack) to 647 Imp gal (2940 litres). With this and two RP30s, the IIIE has a nuclear strike radius of 764 miles (1230 km) lo-lo-lo. Even with the SEPR 844 fitted and developing 3,307 lb st (14.71 kN), the heavier IIIE lagged behind the IIIC in climb performance, arriving at 49,212 ft (15000 m) in 6 minutes 50 seconds, flying at Mach 1.8. Service ceiling is 55,774 ft (17000 m) or 75,459 ft (23000 m) with rocket assistance, maximum speed reducing to Mach 2.0.

Seldom did French squadron aircraft attain those heights and speeds. In the tactical nuclear strike role a single AN52 15-kT bomb was fitted to the centreline pylon of EC 4's aircraft at Luxeuil, these also having Cyrano IIB radar, lacking air-to-air modes. Also under the fuselage may be installed a MATRA AS30 or HSD/MATRA AS37 Martel missile for precision attack or a MATRA R530E in air defence. Wing positions mount bombs, rocket pods and tanks inboard; MATRA R550 Magic AAMs and/or Philips-MATRA Phimat chaff/flare pods outboard.

Three prototype IIIEs were produced, of which No. 01 flew on 5 April 1961. Production began with No. 401, flown 14 January 1964 and ended nine years later at No. 625, although diversions to meet priority foreign orders meant that only 183 aircraft between those numbers were delivered to the AA, CEV and CEAM. Operating wings were the 2nd at Dijon (battlefield air superiority and attack), 3rd at Nancy (defence

suppression), 4th at Luxeuil (tactical nuclear) and 13th at Colmar (battlefield air superiority and attack). The IIIE's radar warning receivers by Thomson-CSF are fin-mounted and combine a forward-facing 'bullet' and two rear antennas immediately above the rudder for aircraft of EC 3 and EC 4, but only the rear component for EC 2 and EC 13 machines.

Most customers obtained the aircraft in its more-or-less standard IIIE form, variations including horizontal VOR aerials high on each side of the fin (e.g. Argentina and Brazil); a radar-warning system (e.g. Egypt and Spain); and fin-base fillet for an HF aerial (Argentina and Egypt). Adapted variants were the IIIO and IIIS, described separately, while some 'Mirage 5s' were IIIEs in all but name, and therefore qualify for inclusion here. Exports were: Mirage 5EAD, Abu Dhabi (14 with Cyrano and Doppler); IIIEA, Argentina (17); IIIEBR, Brazil (16, locally designated F-103E); 5SDE, Egypt (54); IIIEL, Lebanon (10 without Doppler); 5DE, Libya (32 with Cyrano and Doppler); IIIEP, Pakistan (18); 5PA2/5PA3, Pakistan (18 and 12); IIIEZ, South Africa (17); IIIEE, Spain (24, locally designated C.11); and IIIEV, Venezuela (seven). Pakistan's Mirage 5PA2s have track-while-scan Thomson-CSF Cyrano IVM radar, as installed in later Mirage F1s, its modes being air-to-air search, automatic tracking, interception/fire computations, dog-fight, home-on-jam, ground mapping, contour mapping, terrain-avoidance, blind let-down, air-to-ground ranging and air-to-sea search and tracking. The Mirage 5PA3, however, is equipped to carry an Aérospatiale AM39 Exocet sea-skimming anti-ship missile on the centreline and has compatible Thomson-CSF Agave I/J-band monopulse radar in the nose. Agave is optimised for naval applications including designation of targets for Exocet, but also has search, tracking and ranging facilities for both air and surface targets. Weight of equipment in the radome is 106 lb (48 kg), compared with 414 lb (188 kg) for Cyrano II.

Above: A Mirage IIIE wears the 118 code of CEAM at Mont-de-Marsan (Base Aérienne 118) and carries an AS30 test round.

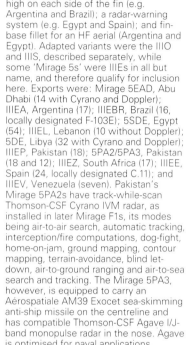

Mirage IIIEs of EC 4, EC 13 and EC 3 carry an AN52 nuclear bomb, an R530 AAM and a Martel ASM respectively.

Below: Mirage as target tug. A IIIE of EC2/3 'Champagne' has an underfuselage target winch for gunnery practise.

Above: The first Mirage IIIE reveals the undernose Doppler fairing and lengthened fuselage.

Below: Spain has just retired its Mirage IIIEEs, having cancelled an extensive upgrade for the aircraft.

Above: The Mirage IIIEs of EC 2/3 served until replaced by the Mirage 2000N in December 1990. This one carries a Martel on the centreline.

Below: The Mirage IIIEA/R530/R550 Magic combination seen here proved no match for the BAe Sea Harrier/AIM-9L in the Falklands.

Above: A Brazilian Mirage IIIEBR (designated F-103) shows off its clean lines. These aircraft are presently undergoing major modifications, with canard foreplanes and new avionics.

For political reasons (the recent war with Israel being one) the first batch of Egyptian Mirage 5SDEs was delivered in Saudi markings.

Above right: Although designated Mirage 5PA3, Pakistan's Agave-equipped Mirages are effectively Exocet-capable Mirage IIIEs in all but name.

Dassault Mirage IIIE

1. Glass-fibre tip aerial fairing
2. VHF aerial
3. Tail navigation and anti-collision lights
4. Tail radar warning antenna
5. Rudder construction
6. Fin main spar
7. Passive radar antenna
8. UHF aerial
9. Rudder hydraulic actuator
10. Magnetic detector
11. Parachute release link
12. Brake parachute housing
13. Parachute fairing
14. Exhaust nozzle shroud
15. Variable-area exhaust nozzle flaps
16. Nozzle jacks
17. Cooling air louvres
18. Jet pipe
19. Rear fuselage frame and stringer construction
20. Wingroot trailing-edge fillet
21. Fin attachment main frame
22. Fin spar attachment joint
23. Control cable runs
24. Engine bay/jet pipe thermal lining
25. Afterburner duct
26. Elevon compensator hydraulic jack
27. Ventral fuel tank
28. Main engine mounting
29. Wing spar/fuselage main frame
30. Main spar joint
31. Engine gearbox driven generator
32. Engine accessory compartment
33. SNECMA Atar 9C afterburning turbojet
34. Cooling system air intakes
35. Heat exchanger
36. Engine oil tank
37. IFF aerial
38. Port wing integral fuel tank, total internal capacity 3330 litres (733 Imp gal)
39. Inboard elevon
40. Outboard elevon
41. Port navigation light
42. Cambered leading-edge ribs
43. Port wing pylon fixing
44. Leading-edge notch
45. Port leading-edge fuel tank
46. Main undercarriage pivot fixing
47. Fuselage dorsal systems ducting
48. Air system piping
49. Turbojet intake
50. Engine starter housing
51. Fuselage fuel tanks
52. Equipment cooling system air filter
53. Computer system voltage regulator
54. Oxygen bottles
55. Inverted flight fuel system accumulator
56. Intake ducting
57. MATRA 530 missile computer
58. VHF radio transmitter/receiver
59. Gyro platform multiplier
60. Doppler transceiver
61. Navigation system computer
62. Air data computer
63. Nord missile encoding supply
64. Radio altimeter transceiver
65. Heading and inertial correction computer
66. Armament junction box
67. Radar programme controller
68. Canopy external release
69. Canopy hinge
70. Radio and electronics bay access fairing
71. Fuel tank stabilising fins
72. 1300-litre (286-Imp gal) auxiliary fuel tank (1700 litres/374 Imp gal alternative)
73. 600-litre (132-Imp gal) drop tank
74. Cockpit canopy cover
75. Canopy hydraulic jack
76. Ejection seat headrest
77. Face blind firing handle
78. Martin-Baker (Hispano licence) RM.4 ejection seat
79. Port side console panel
80. Canopy framing
81. Pilot's head-up display
82. Windscreen panels
83. Instrument panel shroud
84. Instrument pressure
85. Thomson CSF Cyrano II fire control radar
86. Radar scanner dish
87. Glass-fibre radome
88. Pitot tube
89. MATRA 530 air-to-air missile
90. Doppler radar fairing
91. Thomson CSF Doppler navigation radar antenna
92. Cockpit front pressure bulkhead
93. Rudder pedals
94. Radar scope (head-down display)
95. Control column
96. Cockpit floor level
97. Starboard side console panel
98. Nosewheel leg doors
99. Nose undercarriage leg strut
100. Landing/taxiing lamps
101. Levered suspension axle unit
102. Nosewheel
103. Shimmy damper
104. Hydraulic retraction strut
105. Cockpit rear pressure bulkhead
106. Air conditioning ram air intake
107. Moveable intake half-cone centre-body
108. Starboard air intake
109. Nosewheel well door (open position)
110. Intake centre-body screw jack
111. Air conditioning plant
112. Boundary layer bleed air duct
113. Centre fuselage bomb rack
114. 400-kg (882-lb) HE bombs
115. Cannon barrels
116. 30-mm DEFA cannon (2) 250 rounds per gun
117. Ventral gun pack
118. Auxiliary air intake door
119. Electrical system servicing panel
120. Starboard 30-mm DEFA cannon
121. Front spar attachment joint
122. Fuel system piping
123. Airbrake hydraulic jack
124. Starboard airbrake, upper and lower surfaces (open position)
125. Airbrake housing
126. Starboard leading edge fuel tank
127. AS37 Martel, radar-guided air-to-ground missile
128. Nord AS30 air-to-air missile
129. Starboard mainwheel
130. Mainwheel leg door
131. Torque scissor links
132. Shock absorber leg strut
133. Starboard main undercarriage pivot fixing
134. Hydraulic retraction jack
135. Main undercarriage hydraulic accumulator
136. Wing main spar
137. Fuel system piping
138. Inboard pylon fixing
139. Leading edge notch
140. Starboard inner stores pylon
141. Control rod runs
142. Missile launch rail
143. AIM-9 Sidewinder air-to-air missile
144. JL-100 fuel and rocket pack, 250 litres (66 Imp gal) of fuel plus 18/68-mm unguided rockets
145. Outboard wing pylon
146. Outboard pylon fixing
147. Front spar
148. Starboard navigation light
149. Outboard elevon hydraulic jack
150. Starboard wing integral fuel tank
151. Inboard elevon hydraulic actuator
152. Wing multi-spar and rib construction
153. Rear spar
154. Outboard elevon construction
155. Inboard elevon construction
156. Elevon compensator
157. 500-litre (110-Imp gal) auxiliary ventral fuel tank

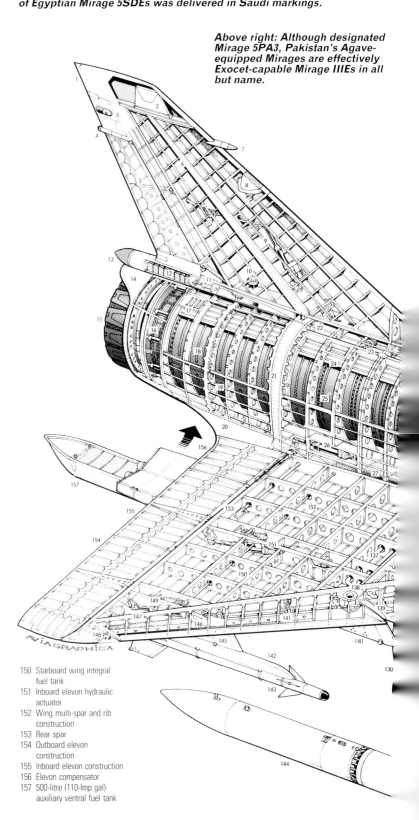

AVIAGRAPHICA

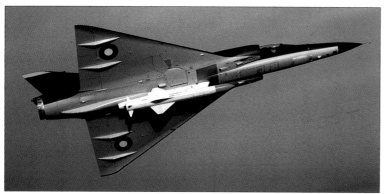

Above: A Mirage F1CG destined for Greece escorts an Egyptian Mirage 5SDE.

Above: The cockpit of a Mirage IIIEE, typical of a late 1950s/early 1960s fast jet.

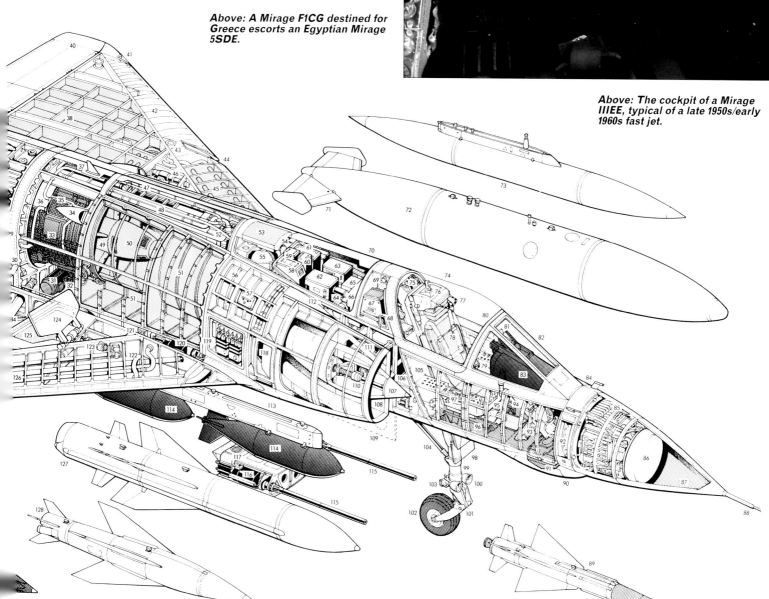

Mirage IIIF

Under this designation, Dassault investigated versions of Mirage with conventional swept wings located high on the fuselage, the move being possible because of advances in constructional technique that made low thickness:chord ratios attainable without complex manufacturing procedures. The resulting aircraft possessed better short take-off and landing characteristics and were easier to handle at low speeds because, unlike a delta, swept wings can benefit from high-lift devices.

The IIIF1 was a private-venture single-seat fighter that had begun life in the drawing office during mid-1964 as the IIIE2. It was scaled up by Jean-Jacques Samin as the two-seat IIIF2, which received an official order for one aircraft, flown on 12 June 1966, to meet a 1963 AA specification (in which Israel was also interested) calling for a supersonic attack aircraft with an approach speed less than 162 mph (259 km/h) and capable of operating from semi-prepared airstrips. Power was provided by a Pratt & Whitney TF30. The F2 and a proposed single-seat air-superiority version, designated IIIF3, were abandoned in 1967 when the AA became interested in the

variable-geometry Mirage G. The IIIF1, meanwhile, was finalised by François Cordié and Pierre Atlan and built with an Atar 09K, flying for the first time on 23 December 1966 with the abbreviated name of Mirage F1. Ordered by the AA in quantity, it became the second-generation Mirage fighter and thus properly deserves separate consideration at a later time.

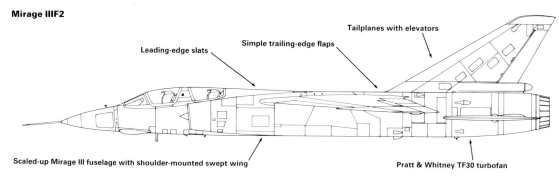

Mirage IIIF2

Leading-edge slats — Simple trailing-edge flaps — Tailplanes with elevators

Scaled-up Mirage III fuselage with shoulder-mounted swept wing — Pratt & Whitney TF30 turbofan

Right: The Dassault Mirage IIIF2 was a scaled-up Mirage III with a shoulder-mounted wing and conventional tail.

Mirage IIIG

Dassault first proposed a swing-wing Mirage in May 1964, drawing up a twin RB153-powered strike fighter in Project Daphne. A pivot was designed and built and subjected to 2,500 simulated flights. This eventually led to the single-engined Mirage G technology demonstrator, which made its maiden flight on 18 October 1967, in the hands of Jean Coureau, powered by a TF-306 turbofan. By the seventh flight, the wings had been swung to 70°. The aircraft was flown over a speed range from 98 kt to Mach 2.15, and demonstrated take-off and landing distances of less than 450 m. The aircraft was lost on 13 January 1971 at Istres.

It had always been intended to build a twin-engined derivative for production, and two Mirage G4s were therefore ordered, powered by a pair of Atar 09K-50s, but costs resulted in cancellation in favour of the G8, which would have eventually progressed to SNECMA M53 powerplants. A production version, the G8A was intended to fulfil the AA's 'Avion de Combat Futur' programme but was cancelled in December 1975. A G2 carrier-based fighter and scaled-up G4 two-seat bomber fared no better.

Below and below right: The Mirage G tailfin was first cropped and then restored to its original profile, while ventral fins were added after the aircraft lost its fin tip. These were retained.

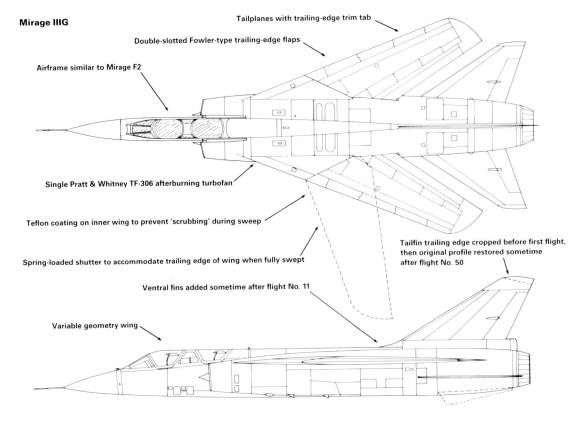

Mirage IIIG

Tailplanes with trailing-edge trim tab
Double-slotted Fowler-type trailing-edge flaps
Airframe similar to Mirage F2
Single Pratt & Whitney TF-306 afterburning turbofan
Teflon coating on inner wing to prevent 'scrubbing' during sweep
Tailfin trailing edge cropped before first flight, then original profile restored sometime after flight No. 50
Spring-loaded shutter to accommodate trailing edge of wing when fully swept
Ventral fins added sometime after flight No. 11
Variable geometry wing

Mirage IIIG8

Proposed collaboration on a VG Mirage with Britain centred around a single-engined aircraft for the Armée de l'Air and Aéronavale and a twin-engined version for the RAF. In fact, the planned single-engined Mirage IIIG2 never progressed beyond the drawing board, and the AFVG (Anglo-French Variable-Geometry) aircraft was cancelled, the French assuring Britain that they would not develop a VG strike aircraft based on the Mirage G. Inevitably two prototypes of the twin SNECMA Atar 9K-50-engined Mirage G4 were ordered within months, with the expectation that these would form the basis of a purely French production aircraft, with two M53 turbofans. The G4 itself proved too expensive, and was replaced by the lighter, simpler G8. The two G4s were completed as G8s, the second as a single-seater. The G8-01 made its maiden flight on 8 May 1971, and was followed by the G8-02 on 13 July 1973. In a further bid to save money Dassault eventually proposed the F8 or G8A ACF, which abandoned the VG wing, and which was itself abandoned in favour of the Mirage 4000.

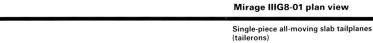

Mirage IIIG8-01 plan view

Single-piece all-moving slab tailplanes (tailerons)

F1-type cropped tailfin and fillet later fitted

Variable geometry wing

Cyrano II-type radome (radar not fitted)

No glazing between canopies

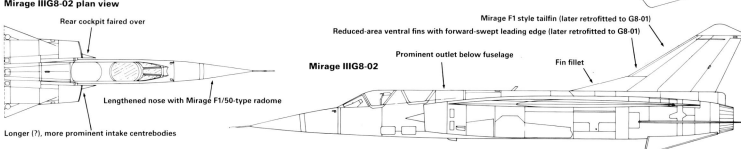

Mirage G tailfin shape (later replaced by F1 type fin)

Ventral fins later reduced in area with forward-swept leading edge

Mirage G-type ventral fins

Mirage IIIG8-01

Twin SNECMA Atar 9K-50 turbojets

Mirage IIIG8-02 plan view

Rear cockpit faired over

Lengthened nose with Mirage F1/50-type radome

Longer (?), more prominent intake centrebodies

Mirage F1 style tailfin (later retrofitted to G8-01)

Reduced-area ventral fins with forward-swept leading edge (later retrofitted to G8-01)

Prominent outlet below fuselage

Fin fillet

Mirage IIIG8-02

Below: The first Mirage IIIG8 was a two-seater, and initially flew with an original Mirage G-type tailfin.

Above: The second Mirage IIIG8 was a single-seater with a revised fin shape, ventral fins, new radome and enlarged intake centrebodies.

Below: The two Mirage G8s fly in formation, after the G8-01 had received a new fin and cropped ventral fins.

Mirage IIIK

The Royal Air Force was offered a version of the Mirage III powered by an afterburning Rolls-Royce Spey turbofan, but did not pursue the suggestion.

Mirage IIIM

A naval Mirage was proposed for operations from French aircraft-carriers, featuring catapult spools and an arrester hook. It was not adopted.

Mirage IIIO

Australian Mirages were based on the IIIE airframe, embodying 178 (mostly minor) engineering changes. Initially the RAAF considered the radical alternative of fitting a Rolls-Royce RB.146 Avon Mk 67 turbojet, rated at 12,000 lb (53.38 kN) dry and 16,000 lb (71.17 kN) with afterburning. A prototype, the Mirage IIIO, flew on 13 February 1961, and although requiring no drastic engineering changes, was passed over for the Atar version in the interests of simplicity. Two standards were received: the Mirage IIIO(F) interceptor with Cyrano IIA, MATRA R530 and AIM-9B Sidewinder AAMs; and Mirage IIIO(A) attack aircraft featuring Cyrano IIB, internal Doppler (no blister), radio altimeter and revised cockpit lighting. Of 100 built – all but two of them in Australia by CAC (which assigned the designation CA.29) – 49 of the first 50 were fighters, although all but one of the survivors from this batch were converted to IIIO(A) configuration in 1967-70, the whole fleet gaining the designation IIIO(F/A).

CAC's first Mirage (assembled from

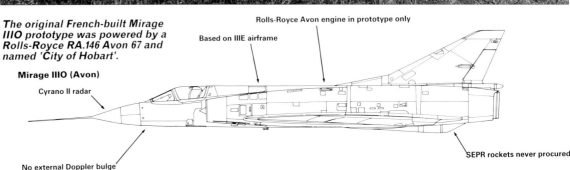

The original French-built Mirage IIIO prototype was powered by a Rolls-Royce RA.146 Avon 67 and named 'City of Hobart'.

Rolls-Royce Avon engine in prototype only

Based on IIIE airframe

Mirage IIIO (Avon)

Cyrano II radar

No external Doppler bulge

SEPR rockets never procured

French components) flew on 16 November 1963. Attack weapons included Mk 83 1,000-lb bombs, Mk 82 500-lb bombs, 68-mm rocket pods and Aérospatiale AS30 (formerly Nord 540) ASMs. Later in its career (1982-83), the aircraft discarded AIM-9Bs for R550

Magics and had the Martin-Baker Mk 84 zero-altitude ejection seats upgraded to 'zero-zero' Mk 4B standard. Drop tanks were mainly 'supersonic' and RP62 types. Of 192 engines obtained for the IIIO and IIID, 140 were built by CAC, all to Atar 09C-5/03Z standard. These became

09C-4/03Y when actuator feed pipe bleed-valves were installed, and 09C-5/03Y with an emergency oil system and other changes. SEPR rockets were not obtained. The RAAF's last operational Mirage sortie was flown on 26 September 1988.

Left: Mirage IIIOs from all four of Australia's Mirage squadrons. The production IIIO was basically an Australian-assembled IIIE.

Below: This colourful Mirage IIIO served with ARDU as a test aircraft. None remains in use, survivors having gone to Pakistan.

Mirage IIIR

The 'R' designation was allocated out of sequence to cover a reconnaissance derivative of the Mirage III, based on the IIIE airframe but with largely IIIC avionics and air-ground weapons capability. As a result, the IIIR became operational prior to the aircraft from which it was derived. Changes included the obvious camera nose, replacing radar, producing an overall length which was increased to 50 ft 10¼ in (15.5 m) and a reduced empty weight of 14,550 lb (6600 kg). Maximum weight remained unaltered from the IIIE at 29,762 lb (13500 kg), later 30,203 lb (13700 kg). A secondary attack role was envisaged for the IIIR, to which end it retained the standard Mirage III armament of two 30-mm DEFA 552 cannon with 125 rounds each, firing through the lower section of the air intakes. The DEFA weapon was developed by Direction des Etudes et Fabrication d'Armament from the World

Mirage IIIR

Basic Mirage IIIE airframe with IIIC avionics

French OMERA cameras in five positions in reconfigured nose

DEFA cannon retained

No Doppler

Camera station 1 (forward oblique)

Chisel window (prism for panoramic camera) in station 2 on some aircraft only

Camera stations 2-5 (vertical and side/oblique) numbered from front to rear

War II German revolver-principle Mauser MG213C (which also formed the basis of the British ADEN) and fires 1,300 rounds per minute. Five weapon hardpoints are available, the inboard-wing positions often accommodating two RP30 fuel tanks of 374 Imp gal (1700 litres), while outboard wing positions mounted Phimat chaff/flare dispensers. Alternatively, a

single 286-Imp gal (1300-litre) RP62 went on the centreline and the twin Phimats were moved inboard.

Up to five cameras are fitted to the IIIR, No. 1 looking forwards and slightly downwards in the extreme nose (below the pitot probe) and Nos 2-5 (numbered front to rear) in a detachable crate immediately behind. These look

sidewards/downwards through rectangular glass flats and may be slightly changed in inclination. General-purpose camera is the OMERA 33 (originally 31), taking 12×12 cm negatives at up to five per second at shutter speeds between 1/200 and 1/3,200 sec. A 148-ft (45-m) magazine is sufficient for 360 photographs. For high altitude missions

Above: The first prototype Mirage IIIR was basically a Mirage IIIE with IIIC avionics and a new camera nose.

Above: The Mirage IIIR was supplied to ER 3/33, who passed their aircraft on to ER 1/33 and ER 2/33 on receipt of the Mirage IIIRD.

Right: The camera bay of the Mirage IIIR had a single window offset to starboard at station 2. This was sometimes replaced by a larger chisel window for the prism of a panoramic camera.

Below: The Mirage IIIRS (17 of which were built under licence in Switzerland, following delivery of a French pattern aircraft) was essentially similar to the French IIIR, as was the Mirage IIIRZ exported to South Africa.

between 11,500 and 49,000 ft (3505 and 14935 m), cameras in Nos 3, 4 and 5 positions are fitted with 600-mm lenses and adjusted to give a 30° downward field of view. At medium altitudes from 2,300 ft (701 m) upwards, 200-mm lenses are fitted and the field increased to 85°.

Low-level missions down to 500 ft (152 m) are flown with four cameras: Nos 2 and 3 with 100-mm lenses, their cones of view overlapping directly underneath the aircraft, and Nos 4 and 5 with 200-mm lenses directed at the distance, giving a 167° horizon-to-horizon view. No. 1 camera may be fitted as desired, often as a long-range OMERA 53.

When plan views are required at low level, a vertical OMERA 60 is fitted, backed by a pair of 150-mm OMERA 33s directed at the horizon from Nos 4 and 5 positions. Taking 57×57 mm negatives through a 37.5-mm lens at up to 10 per second, OMERA 60 has a 74° cone of vision, which means a slight gap in coverage in the middle distance between it and the two OMERA 33s. This may be overcome by fitment of a single OMERA 40 panoramic camera in the No. 2 position, the equipment producing a 180° view (i.e. including both horizons) on each negative. The distortions inherent in using a 'fish-eye' lens are obviated by reflecting light through a rotating prism to produce the picture. Mapping at higher altitudes is accomplished by fitting lenses of up to 450 mm to the OMERA 60.

Two prototype IIIRs were built, No. 01 flying on 31 October 1961. Production

aircraft Nos 301-350 followed from 1 February 1963 onwards, and all had been supplied to the 33ᵉ Escadre de Reconnaissance at Strasbourg by mid-1965. Exports comprised four IIIRZs to South Africa and one IIIRS to Switzerland, where 17 more were built under licence and are now being upgraded with canards. Swiss airframes were strengthened and fitted with the Hughes TARAN 1S navigation system, similar to TARAN 18 in the Mirage IIIS. One IIIR was modified at CEV Brétigny in 1983 as an elementary fly-by-voice aircraft, having non-critical systems such as radio operated by the pilot's verbal command.

Mirage IIIRD and 5R

Accurate positioning is as important to reconnaissance as to attack, for which reason the AA obtained 20 Mirage IIIRDs with the IIIE's navigation system, including Doppler radar in the underfuselage blister, gyro gunsight, automatic camera control and Thomson-CSF radar warning receiver antennas on the leading and trailing edges of the fin, as retrofitted to some Mirage IIIEs. Two air data probes were positioned immediately ahead of the windscreen. Variables for export aircraft included VOR aerials on the fin (Abu Dhabi, Colombia, South Africa), radar-warning receivers (Abu Dhabi, Egypt, South Africa) and fin-base fillets (Egypt, Libya).

French IIIRDs had the IIIR's camera system but were additionally wired to carry two supplementary sensors. First of these was the SAT Cyclope infra-red linescan sensor mounted in an RP62 fuel tank on the centreline – distinguishable from a normal kerosene carrier by the viewing window in the lower side immediately behind the nose (giving the pod a shark-like appearance). Alternatively in the same position is an SLR1 side-looking airborne radar pod, readily identifiable by an extremely flattened, oval intake in the nose. French IIIRDs had the full fin-mounted radar warning receiver fitment of forward 'bullet' and twin rear-sector antennas above the rudder, while IIIRs had only the latter.

Deliveries of the IIIRD (Nos 351-370) to ER 33 took place in 1967-69, the type being the last reconnaissance Mirage III to serve the AA when it was finally

replaced by Mirage F1CRs early in 1988. A further 65 similar aircraft were exported (including 26 built in Belgium), some classified as Mirage 5s. All are believed to have Doppler, although this was installed internally. Belgian aircraft were fitted with a high proportion of US-produced avionics, but had British-made Vinten 626/636 cameras in place of the OMERAs, including an optional panoramic unit in the No. 2 position. Exports were Mirage 5RAD for Abu Dhabi (three), 5BR Belgium (27, all but one built locally), 5COR Colombia (two), 5SDR Egypt (six), 5DR Libya (10 with

external Doppler), IIIRP Pakistan (13 with external Doppler), and IIIR2Z South Africa (four). The last-mentioned were of note in being the first Mirage III/5s exported with an Atar 09K-50 turbojet, and consequently had the curved intake splitter plate described in the Mirage 50 entry.

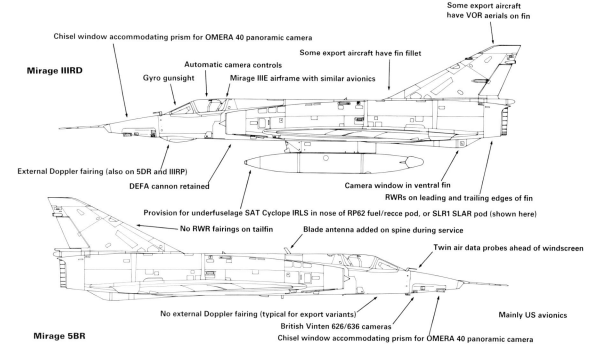

Mirage IIIRD

Chisel window accommodating prism for OMERA 40 panoramic camera

Gyro gunsight

Automatic camera controls

Mirage IIIE airframe with similar avionics

Some export aircraft have fin fillet

Some export aircraft have VOR aerials on fin

External Doppler fairing (also on 5DR and IIIRP)

DEFA cannon retained

Camera window in ventral fin

RWRs on leading and trailing edges of fin

Provision for underfuselage SAT Cyclope IRLS in nose of RP62 fuel/recce pod, or SLR1 SLAR pod (shown here)

No RWR fairings on tailfin

Blade antenna added on spine during service

Twin air data probes ahead of windscreen

Mainly US avionics

Mirage 5BR

No external Doppler fairing (typical for export variants)

British Vinten 626/636 cameras

Chisel window accommodating prism for OMERA 40 panoramic camera

Above: This colourfully marked Mirage IIIRD was specially painted to commemorate a unit anniversary.

Above left: This Mirage IIIRD carries a sharkmouthed centreline SLR1 sideways-looking radar pod. Alternatively, an IRLS could be carried in the same position.

Left: Belgium's Mirage 5BRs have no external Doppler bulge and are equipped with British-made cameras and mainly US avionics.

Above: The camera pack of the Mirage 5BR (or IIIRD) can be hinged down for access. The forward-most camera here is a panoramic camera. A forward oblique camera is fixed in the tip of the nose cone, still further forward.

Left: This is one of Abu Dhabi's three Mirage 5RADs. These aircraft are essentially similar to the French Mirage IIIRD.

Below: The Mirage IIIR2Z was an export version of the IIIRD for South Africa and was powered by an Atar 09K-50. The IIIR2Z has an external Doppler bulge and no fin fillet.

Status
No. 8 Smaldeel disbanded in September 1991, leaving only No. 42 Smaldeel with a mixture of Mirage 5BRs, 5BAs and 5BDs. This will disband in December 1993, following delivery of the last upgraded aircraft in November. This ludicrous situation was caused by clauses which made cancellation of the upgrade more expensive than completion.

Local participation
Belgium procured 27 Mirage 5BRs between 1970 and 1973, all but the first example being built under licence by SABCA (Société Anonyme Belge de Constructions Aéronautiques) at Gosselies. It also manufactured 63 Mirage 5BA attack aircraft and 16 Mirage 5BD two-seat trainers. As well as assembling all but the first examples of all Belgian aircraft, SABCA manufactured rear fuselages for all three variants and nosecones for the single-seaters. SABCA's electronics division at Cobelda manufactured the aircraft's IFF equipment. The company also assembled and tested Atar 09 turbojets for these aircraft. A proposed upgrade by local industry fell victim to cuts, becoming progressively less ambitious.

Above: *The open camera bay door of a Belgian Mirage 5BR shows off the widened 'chisel-shaped' window for the panoramic camera, closest to the ground.*

Operational equipment
For the reconnaissance role, the Mirage 5BR is equipped with five British-made Vinten-type 360° cameras, although one of these can be replaced by a panoramic Vinten in station 2. Loral Rapport II ECM pods were fitted from mid-1978.

Guns
The Mirage 5BR, like the Mirage IIIR and IIIRD, retains twin DEFA 552 30-mm cannon, each with up to 125 rounds.

Dassault Mirage 5BR

This Mirage 5BR wears the striking colours applied to celebrate No. 42 Smaldeel/Escadrille's 70th anniversary. Red and gold flames were applied to the leading edges, and the squadron's traditional 'Mephisto' was painted below the centre-section. The squadron is part of No. 3 Wing, based at Bierset (at first alongside No. 8 Smaldeel/Escadrille), moving when No. 2 Smaldeel, and the previously Bierset-based No. 1 Smaldeel, converted to the F-16 at Florennes.

Powerplant
The Mirage 5BR is based on the airframe and engine combination of the Mirage IIIE, and thus has the same stretched forward fuselage (with intake behind the rear edge of the canopy) and the same variable-area petal-type afterburner nozzle associated with the 58.8-kN (13,228-lb st) Atar 09C-3 turbojet. Engines for Belgian Mirages were locally assembled and tested.

Fuel tanks
The Mirage 5 has two integral tanks in each wing, with a combined capacity of 685 litres (150 Imp gal) per side. Total internal fuel capacity is 3330 litres (733 Imp gal), and can be augmented by underwing fuel tanks totalling up to 1000 litres (220 Imp gal).

Dassault Mirage III/5/50 Variants

Mirage IIIS

Swiss Mirage interceptors were based on the IIIE airframe, but with avionics changes sufficient to warrant a new designation. In deference to the 'firm' landings required when operating from short, valley-floor air bases, fuselage, wing and undercarriage were strengthened. All except the first two of 36 built were constructed locally by Fabrique Fédérale d'Avions with Atar 09C-3 powerplants from Sulzer AG. The Hughes TARAN 18 (Tactical Attack Radar And Navigation) suite replaced Cyrano and French nav/attack equipment, giving the interceptor compatibility with the Hughes HM-55 (AIM-26B) Falcon 6-mile (9.7-km) range, semi-active radar homing AAM. Also carried were AIM-9B

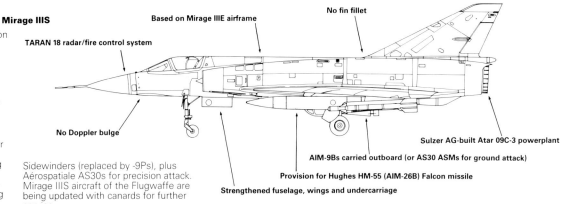

Mirage IIIS

TARAN 18 radar/fire control system
Based on Mirage IIIE airframe
No fin fillet
No Doppler bulge
Sulzer AG-built Atar 09C-3 powerplant
AIM-9Bs carried outboard (or AS30 ASMs for ground attack)
Provision for Hughes HM-55 (AIM-26B) Falcon missile
Strengthened fuselage, wings and undercarriage

Sidewinders (replaced by -9Ps), plus Aérospatiale AS30s for precision attack. Mirage IIIS aircraft of the Flugwaffe are being updated with canards for further service.

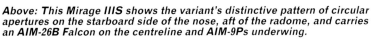

Above: This Mirage IIIS shows the variant's distinctive pattern of circular apertures on the starboard side of the nose, aft of the radome, and carries an AIM-26B Falcon on the centreline and AIM-9Ps underwing.

Above: The Mirage IIIS is essentially a Swiss-assembled Mirage IIIE with a new Hughes TARAN 18 fire control system replacing the French Cyrano. A two-tone air superiority camouflage has been adopted.

Mirage IIIT

To test the forward propulsion unit for the Mirage IIIV Dassault built a Mirage IIIT trials aircraft, which first flew on 4 June 1964 with a single, non-afterburning SNECMA TF104B turbofan of 10,417 lb st (46.33 kN) in a bulged rear fuselage. The TF104 was a modified version of the Pratt & Whitney JTF10 (military TF30), but the production version, designated TF106 and rated at 19842 lb (88.27 kN), did not fly in the IIIT until 25 January 1965. Trials continued until 1970, but a proposed IIIT2 twin-seat equipment testbed was not built.

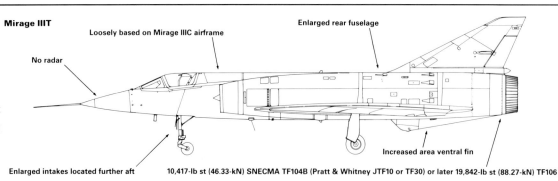

Mirage IIIT

Loosely based on Mirage IIIC airframe
Enlarged rear fuselage
No radar
Enlarged intakes located further aft
10,417-lb st (46.33-kN) SNECMA TF104B (Pratt & Whitney JTF10 or TF30) or later 19,842-lb st (88.27-kN) TF106
Increased area ventral fin

Below: The Mirage IIIT was a scaled-up trials aircraft designed to test the TF104 turbofan intended for the IIIV.

Right: The Mirage IIIT ended its days as a gate guardian, mounted on a plinth. Its swollen rear fuselage contours are apparent.

Balzac V and Mirage IIIV

NATO-sponsored interest in VTOL aircraft during the 1960s prompted Dassault to modify the Mirage III in the hope of securing large production contracts from other European nations. As a first step, the unique Mirage III-001 was redesigned by Jacques Alberto and rebuilt (by Sud Aviation under sub-contract, employing a new fuselage) with four pairs of Rolls-Royce RB.108 Stage 1a lifting engines and a single Bristol Siddeley Orpheus BOr.3 for forward flight. The RB.108s each weighed 274 lb (124 kg) and produced 2,210 lb (9.83 kN) – comfortably overcoming the aircraft's 14,330 lb (6500 kg) gross weight – while the Orpheus was rated at 5,000 lb (22.24 kN). The aircraft had earlier gained the nickname 'Balzac' (a Paris telephone exchange) from the self-publicity trailer of the Jean Mineur cinema advertising agency, 'Call Balzac 0001'. Marked 'Balzac V', the aircraft made its first tethered hop at

Melun on 12 October 1962, a conventional flight on 1 March 1963 and the first transition on 28 March. The Balzac was involved in two serious accidents, gaining the rare and unhappy distinction of killing pilots on both occasions.

Twice the size and weight, the definitive Mirage IIIV, designed by a team under François Cordié, made its first free vertical flight at Melun on 12 February 1965, supported by eight RB.162s of 4,409 lb st (19.61 kN) and with a TF104B for forward flight (see Mirage IIIT). The world's heaviest VTOL aircraft, No. 01, weighed 26,455 lb (12000 kg) gross and spanned 28 ft 7¼ in (8.72 m). No. 02, which had several changes, including revised air intakes and a Pratt & Whitney JTF10, followed it into the air on 22 June 1966 and demonstrated Mach 2.04 three months later. By now, the lifting-engine

concept was viewed by all as impractical, and the IIIV programme was shelved after the crash of 02 on 28 November 1966.

Above: The Dassault Balzac in flight displays its later configuration.

Above: The Balzac in its original configuration shows the unpainted nose, early telemetry antennas and undercarriage fixed in the extended position.

Balzac V
- Tandem side-by-side pairs of pop-up intakes for lift engines
- Brake chute fairing added during test programme
- Based on Mirage III-001 with new fuselage
- Eight 2,210-lb st (9.83-kN) RB.108 lift jets
- Sensitive pitch and yaw vanes on nose
- Undercarriage originally fixed and braced
- Retractable deflector plates ahead of lift jet outlets
- Lift jet exhausts covered by fore-and-aft doors
- Ventral fin added during development programme
- 5,000-lb st (22.24-kN) Bristol Siddeley Orpheus BOr.3

Mirage IIIV
- Tandem side-by-side pairs of pop-up intakes for lift engines
- Eight 4,409-lb st (19.61-kN) RB.162 lift jets
- Enlarged, scaled-up Mirage III airframe and wing
- Retractable deflector plates ahead of lift jet outlets
- Sensitive pitch and yaw vanes on nose
- SNECMA TF104B (modified Pratt & Whitney JTF10 or TF30) turbofan (JTF10 in the IIIV-02)

Below: The second Mirage IIIV differed from the first only in detail, notably in the design of the intakes for the lift jets.

Right: The first of the two Mirage IIIV prototypes tethers unhovered. The lift jet concept proved impractical.

Mirage IIIW

Returning almost to the Mirage I concept, the IIIW was a lightweight fighter offered in competition to Northrop's F-5A, when the US government began supplying that aircraft in large numbers to allied nations. Had it been adopted as a military aid aircraft, the Mirage IIIW would have been built by Boeing in the USA.

Mirage IV

Realisation by the AA in 1956 that its lightweight fighter concept was not the best way forward was prompted by two advanced versions of the design: Mirage III with a 9,920-lb st (44.13-kN) Atar 101G-1 plus SEPR rocket; and Mirage IV mounting an Atar 9 developing 13,228 lb st (58.84 kN). In the event, the larger engine was installed in the Mirage III together with the rocket, but for a while the IV appeared likely to be a successor. With a 312-sq ft (29-m²) wing, the IVA and IVB variants were similarly sized to the III prototype, the first-mentioned

being slightly lighter, at 14,110-lb (6400-kg) gross weight, and the IVB heavier, at 16,270 lb (7380 lb).

Projected maximum speeds were Mach 2.0-2.5, and times to 49,212 ft (15000 m) estimated as 3 minutes 25 seconds and 6 minutes respectively. A scaled-up aircraft, the Mirage IVC, was also offered to the AA with two Atar 9s, 463 sq ft (43 m²) of wing, 24,251-lb (11000-kg) gross weight, top speed of Mach 2.9 and a time of 3 minutes 20 seconds to the aforementioned height. Subsequently, the IVB was supplanted by a similarly-designated aircraft with a 538-sq ft (50 m²) wing and a single de Havilland PS.26-3 Gyron generating

27,000 lb st (120.10 kN) with reheat.

By November 1956, the IVA had been given an SEPR rocket to become the Mirage IVF, which would have been capable of Mach 2.5 and a ceiling of 78,740 ft (24000 m). The navy expressed an interest in a carrier-based IVC, which would have become the Mirage IVM if adopted. It transpired that the Mirage III was ordered into production and received the benefit of further development, but effort on the IV was not wasted. The IVC interested the AA as a potential strategic, supersonic bomber, so Dassault began again with the Mirage IV designation for this larger machine, which eventually entered production.

PACAF Power

Photographed by Randy Jolly

Having swelled to an enormous size at the height of the Vietnam War, Pacific Air Forces contracted rapidly after the end of the conflict, returning to peacetime levels. Although PACAF gained control of Alaskan units (under 11th Air Force control) in 1990, it was forced to leave the Philippines by local demand. In the event, this withdrawal was hastened by the 1991 eruption of Mount Pinatubo, which effectively closed Clark Air Base. Today the force is concentrated in Japan, Korea and Alaska, and in this feature we look at the 5th Air Force in Japan and the 7th Air Force in Korea.

Kadena is the cornerstone of PACAF, housing the largest concentration of firepower in the region. Here the base illustrates its 'superwing' status, with a KC-135R from the 909th Air Refueling Squadron leading an E-3 from the 961st Air Control Squadron, watched by the wing commander's F-15C, which in turn leads squadron commanders' Eagles from the 44th and 67th Fighter Squadrons.

Left: In northern Japan, the F-16s of the 432nd Fighter Wing form a powerful counter to the nearby Russian forces.

Below: Any conflict in Korea would be a 'dirty' war, highly dependent on the abilities of ground forces. Aiding attack aircraft in supporting the troops are Fairchild OA-10s.

Above: From their base at Kadena Air Base, on the souther Japanese island of Okinawa, the F-15C Eagles of the 18th Wing are well placed to command the entire Pacific Rim region, especially in facing China and Korea. The northern area of the region can be covered by 3rd Wing Eagles from Elmendorf in Alaska. North Korea is seen as the principal threat to stability in the Far East, and 18th Wing aircraft periodically deploy to Osan to stand alert. Depot level maintenance for the wing is handled by Korean Air Lines a Pusan. PACAF Eagles were the first to adopt the darker 'Mod Eagle' camouflage with low-visibility markings. This the wing commander's aircraft, the fin-stripe reflecting the numerous squadrons now assigned to his control.

Above: Based at Yokota AB in Japan, the 20th Air Ambulance Squadron operates the McDonnell Douglas C-9A Nightingale on aeromedical evacuation duties throughout the Pacific region. The 20th AAS is part of the 374th Airlift Wing, which also controls the 345th and 1403rd Airlift Squadrons with C-130s and C-21s respectively.

Right: The cutting edge of the 18th Wing is its three Eagle squadrons, comprising the 12th Fighter Squadron (yellow fin-band), 44th FS (blue) and the 67th FS (red). The first F-15 was delivered to the wing on 26 September 1979, and the original machines are still in service. This is one of the two-seat F-15Ds assigned to the unit (marked for the 67th FS), seen carrying an AGAT towed target.

Left: Liaison and staff transport support is provided for the 18th Wing by the 13th Airlift Squadron's Beech C-12Fs. These aircraft previously reported to the 603rd Airlift Support Group but are now directly controlled by the wing.

Below: An important support role is combat rescue, performed at Kadena in late 1992 by the ancient Sikorsky HH-3Es of the 33rd Rescue Squadron. These were due for imminent replacement by the smaller HH-60G Pave Hawk.

Kadena Air Base

...dena is located on the island of ...inawa, and has been a US ...tallation for many years. It ...ved as a major strategic base ...d deployment stopover during ...e Vietnam War, and continued to ...use detachments of Strategic Air ...mmand aircraft (KC-135, RC-135, ...71) long after. RC-135s still fly ...ssions from here, but the SR-71 ...tired and the resident tankers ...e been absorbed by the 18th ...ng. That unit began its ...ociation with the base in 1954, ...g consecutively the F-86, F-100, ...5, F-4 and F-15. RF-4Cs were ...gned alongside F-15s in the ...0s. Today the 18th is the single ...ager at the base, although ...ena also houses the 353rd ...cial Operations Group after its ...nature departure for Clark. This ...g operates the MC-130E (1st ...), HC-130N/P (17th SOS) and ...53J (31st SOS) for Special ...es Command.

Above: Transient Air Mobility Command Hercules and a single Navy Orion are visible in the background as a 67th FS F-15C lifts off the Kadena runway.

Below: Kadena experiences the full range of tropical weather conditions, from balmy sunsets to raging monsoons. Whatever the weather, the F-15s are ready.

Right: Much in keeping with the traditions of the host nation, the F-15s of the 18th Wing wear this Shogun character on the inside of the fins.

Below: Misawa houses a rescue detachment in the shape of the 39th Rescue Squadron, recently established with Sikorsky HH-60Gs. In addition to their primary combat rescue role, the Pave Hawks also undertake peacetime rescue work.

Above: A mixture of Mk 82s and Mk 84s is carried by these F-16s, seen during a pre-strike tanking from a 19th Air Refueling Wing KC-135R. The aircraft nearest the camera is armed with wingtip AIM-120 AMRAAM missiles, an increasingly common sight on F-16 squadrons.

Misawa Air Base

Located at the northern end of the principal Japanese island of Honshu, Misawa guards against aggression from the north, and also keeps watch on vital sea lanes around the nation. US association with the base dates from occupation in September 1945 under various host units, but it was not until April 1985 that the 432nd TFW began flying the F-16 from the base. This wing had earlier been associated with the Far East as a Thailand-based reconnaissance/fighter unit at Udorn. F-16A/Bs were operated for a short while prior to upgrading to F-16C/D model in 1986. The wing now flies two squadrons, the 13th FS (red fin-band) and 14th FS (yellow fin-band). The base also houses 3 and 8 Hikotai of the JASDF flying Mitsubishi F-1s, and 601 Hikotai flying E-2 Hawkeyes.

ove: Out on the ranges, a h Fighter Squadron F-16C s fly with four Mk 84 '00-lb bombs. The aircraft carrying an ALQ-184 ECM d, the standard self- otection aid for PACAF 6s and A-10s. The 432nd ' Fighting Falcons have a al role, regularly ctising air-to-air fighting l ground attack.

Left: Low-visibility representation of the 432nd FW badge.

Right: The Misawa wing set up for business with the F-16A Block 15, but traded these for F-16C/D Block 30s. These are 'hot-rod' aircraft with the General Electric F110 engine and 'big-lips' intakes.

Cleaning up, the 80th FS commander's F-16C sets off on a training mission. Such missions are undertaken with great dedication, for Korea is still regarded as one of the most politically delicate regions in the world.

Above: The 'Wolf Pack' has kept the peace in Korea since 1974. The presence of US F-16s, and the supply of such aircraft to the Republic of Korea air force, has helped to deter the North from any aggression. The F-16 force is more than a match for North Korea's ragged air force, despite the delivery of a handful of MiG-29s.

Above: Kunsan F-16s proudly wear the 'WP' tailcode, reminding current pilots of the Vietnam War years, when the 8th TFW 'Wolf Pack' was the most successful air-to-air unit.

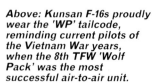

Right: Entrance to the 'Panther's' lair: the sign outside the 35th Fighter Squadron's complex depicts the squadron badge. The aircraft wear blue fin-bands.

Kunsan Air Base

Kunsan was built by the Japanese in 1938, and occupied by US forces in 19[...]. It is located in the central west coast region of South Korea, and has played host to several USAF units over the years. During the *Pueblo* crisis of 1968 activated Air National Guard F-100 squadrons were based here. It currently provides a base for the 8th Fighter Wing, which moved to Korea in Septem[...] 1974 with F-4Ds. On 15 September 1981 the F-16A arrived, making the 8th [...] first overseas wing to fly the type. October 1987 saw the arrival of F-16C/D [...] Block 30s.

Above: The 'Headhunters'
of the 80th Fighter
Squadron (their sign
having lost its 'Tac'
designator at the end of
1991) fly yellow-tailed
F-16Cs.

Right: Kunsan's F-16s are
Block 30s with the F110
engine, and also feature
the large intake. This
production standard is
much lighter and more
powerful than most other
F-16s, and is consequently
tasked with more air
defence work than the
attack-dedicated Block 40/
42/50/52 machines.

Left: *Osan's* **F-16s** *are dedicated to the attack role, and operate with the* **LANTIRN** *targeting and navigation pods for night/ adverse weather capability.* **The LANTIRN** *also provides the ability to launch laser-guided bombs for greater accuracy.*

Above and right: *Supportir the attack* **F-16s** *by supplyir a forward air control functi are the Fairchild* **OA-10s** *of the 51st Fighter Wing's 19th Tactical Air Support Squadron.*

Above: Pararescuemen from the 37th Rescue Squadron practise fast-roping technique in front of the tower at Osan. The squadron is assigned to the 51st Wing, providing combat rescue and some peacetime coverage for the Korean peninsula.

Left: Osan supports only one F-16 squadron, the 36th Fighter Squadron flying F-16C/D Block 42s.

Osan Air Base

Also on the western side of South Korea, Osan is further north than Kunsan, just south of the capital Seoul. When the runway was opened in December 1952 to support the war, the airfield was known simply as K-55, receiving its present name in 1956. The 51st ABW began flying from the base in November 1971 with transports, but changed to the 51st Composite Wing with F-4Es and OV-10As. F-16s and OA-10s are the current equipment, with an accent on CAS/BAI missions. Osan also hosts a detachment from the 9th Reconnaissance Wing with Lockheed U-2Rs.

Hungary

The end of the Cold War and the dissolution of the Warsaw Treaty Organisation have opened up Eastern Europe to more detailed scrutiny, allowing the compilation of an accurate and detailed Air Power Analysis featuring the Hungarian air force, previously covered in Volume 3.

Magyar Honvédség Repülő Csapatai (Hungarian Air Defence Group)

The break-up of the Warsaw Pact and Hungary's transition to democracy destroyed the old Magyar Légierö (Hungarian air force) and its role, and has led to budgetary constraints which threaten to undermine the operational readiness of its successor, the Magyar Honvédség Repülő Csapatai (Hungarian Air Defence Group). Such difficulties are serious, but the Hungarian air arm has had to deal with equally difficult problems during its turbulent past.

Ignominious defeat during World War II (Hungary bound itself to the TriPartite Pact in November 1940) led to Soviet occupation. Wartime agreements, notably in the 3rd Moscow Conference of October 1944, that Hungary would be an area of equal Soviet and Western influence were not honoured. With a pro-Soviet Communist government installed, Hungary rapidly became a Soviet ally and Warsaw Treaty signatory.

1956 rebellion

By January 1956 the Hungarian air force included four MiG-15-equipped regiments (with 240 aircraft), six independent fighter groups (two equipped with all-weather MiG-17Ps), two Il-10 attack regiments and two Tu-2 bomber regiments, one of which was converting to the Il-28. Despite playing virtually no part in the October 1956 rebellion, Hungary's air force was purged and had much of its front-line equipment taken away in the aftermath of the insurrection, and was completely grounded until 25 March 1957. Many training aircraft were transferred to civilian clubs, and the transport arm was transferred en masse to Malev.

On 15 April 1957 the first unit was officially reconstituted at Kecskemét, this being the RKK – Repülő Kikepzo Kozpont (Air Instruction Centre). This was somewhat misleadingly named, since it consisted of two full squadrons of MiG-15s and a mixed squadron of Li-2s and Tu-2s for transport and reconnaissance. By the Day of Liberation Parade on 4 April 1958, the RKK had gained a squadron of MiG-17s and another of Yak-18s, while a separate transport squadron operated Mi-4 helicopters and the Li-2s returned from Malev. Two squadrons of MiG-17PFs equipped a regiment at Szentkirálylyszabadja, while the reconnaissance flight at Kiskunlachaza had received two Il-28Rs.

The fact that the air arm has never regained its pre-1956 numerical strength, and remained the second smallest WarPac air force (after Bulgaria), disguises the fact that rehabilitation of the army and air force was very rapid, and that Hungary rapidly rose to become one of the most reliable of the USSR's Warsaw Pact allies. Within four years of 1956, for example, Hungary had three squadrons of MiG-19PMs to replace the MiG-17PFs and was receiving its first MiG-21F-13s (the first WarPac nation to do so) to equip a fighter regiment at Taszar. A similarly momentous step was the creation of a three-squadron ground attack regiment equipped with MiG-17Fs at Kalocsa, with another similar unit reforming at Borgond in 1961, and an Il-28 bomber regiment forming at Kunmadaras at the same time. The RKK by now had one squadron each of MiG-17PFs, MiG-19PMs and MiG-21s, and was functioning as an operational training regiment. Sup-

Above: A handful of MiG-15s remain extant, like this pylon-mounted example.

Below: A retired MiG-17PF in the Hungarian air force museum collection.

Above: The MiG-19PM once provided all-weather fighter cover for Hungary.

Below: A retired MiG-21PF, many of which remain in use as instructional airframes.

Left: This camouflaged MiG-15 'Fagot' wears an unusual brown/green camouflage similar to that worn by today's Su-22s. Before 1956 Hungary had four MiG-15 squadrons, and the type was important after the air force was reformed following the abortive rebellion, many surviving as trainers into the 1970s.

Right: This Aero L-29 Delfin in the museum collection at Szolnok is a reminder of the time when Hungary conducted its own pilot training, recently carried out in Czechoslovakia. There have recently been reports that such training is to begin once more, with an order for PZL-130 Turbo Orliks being strongly rumoured.

Above: Hungary's Cold War-era national marking, a red star and white/green centre.

Above: The last Il-28s were retired from service in 1973 but this example lingers.

Right: The Ka-26 was retired from air force service during the early 1980s.

Above: Pre-war unit badges are back, this one denoting the Boszorkany squadron.

Above: The second MiG-21bis unit at Taszar is the Turul squadron.

Above: Some of Taszar's MiG-21bis fighters, armed with AA-2 'Atoll' and AA-8 'Aphid' AAMs. Alert has been maintained since the start of the troubles in Yugoslavia.

Above: MiG-21UM 'Mongols' serve with all of the MiG-21 squadrons for standardisation, continuation and conversion training.

Above: Taszar-based MiG-21bis fighters are refuelled between sorties.

Right: Only a handful of aircraft wear the newly-resurrected Turul insignia.

Above: This dummy cruise missile, a 'target' for teaching Taszar's MiG-21 pilots during the Cold War, has now been dismantled.

port came from a Mi-1/Mi-4-equipped regiment, a 14-aircraft Li-2 squadron and a second transport squadron equipped with Il-14s.

The Air Academy at Szolnok reopened in September 1961 with Yak-18s and MiG-15s, gaining L-29s during 1964. With its own training and transport assets, and five three-squadron combat-capable regiments, the Hungarian air force had been restored to a genuinely operational force, although Soviet observers were attached to every unit, approving every flight plan, and operations were closely monitored by the Soviets. Defections were discouraged by the presence of Soviet fighters at several bases, which were held at constant readiness.

Modernisation began in 1966, when MiG-21PFs and Su-7Bs were taken on charge to replace larger numbers of Il-28s, MiG-15s and MiG-17s. On 7 September 1967 a new military co-operation agreement was signed between Hungary and the USSR. 1968 marked a turning point for the Légierö, which participated in the largest WarPac exercises ever held, and then in the intervention in Czechoslovakia. Hungary's loyalty was rewarded by the transfer of 40 Czechoslovakian-built MiG-19SFs, allowing the MiG-17s to be transferred to Vietnam as aid. The USSR supplied Mil Mi-8s to replace the elderly Mi-4s, and MiG-21PFMs were also taken on charge.

Re-equipment

The air force was split into two in October 1971, with the formation of the Csapatrepülö Parancsnokság (Troop Air Command or, perhaps more accurately, Air Support Command) to control all aircraft not assigned to the intercept role, which remained under the command of the Orszagos Légvédelmi Parancsnokság (National Air Defence Command). In 1972 and 1973 the last of the Il-28s, Li-2s and MiG-19s were retired, and MiG-21MFs and An-26s were introduced.

During the rest of the 1970s, the MiG-21bis was introduced, and by 1977 the air force had two three-squadron (40 aircraft) MiG-21MF/MiG-21bis regiments, and one three squadron regiment with Su-7BMKs. These were backed up by an An-26-equipped transport squadron, two three-squadron (40 aircraft) helicopter regiments, one with Ka-26s and one with Mi-8s, together with a training group and the three-squadron OCU with L-29s and elderly MiG-21Fs, PFs and PFMs.

The first of the MiG-23MFs arrived in 1979, and Mil Mi-24s began to arrive a couple of years later. Twelve Su-22M-3s were taken on charge in 1981. The Ka-26s were reassigned to civil duties and to the Danube River Guard, and the liaison role was taken over by a handful of Mil Mi-2 'Hoplites' (25 were delivered). Other types introduced during the late 1970s and 1980s included two LET 410s (probably for calibration), a pair of An-24Vs and a VIP-configured, civil-registered Yak-40. Two Tu-134As were transferred to the civil register in 1976, and then later to Malev. Various government bodies and ministries operated four Pilatus PC-6 Turbo Porters, three Mil Mi-2s and, with the paramilitary Security Police, about a dozen assorted helicopters and light aircraft, including examples of the Aero 45, L-200 Morava, PZL-104 Wilga and Mil Mi-2.

Above: This red, white and green 'arrow head' chevron, similar to the pre-war national insignia, was formally adopted on 31 March 1991.

Above: One of three Su-22UM-3s in service, two of which are assigned to the Furkeszdarazs squadron at any one time.

Above: This MiG-23MF carries a full operational load of two AA-7 'Apex' and four AA-8 'Aphid' air-to-air missiles.

Above: Hungary's 12th MiG-23MF spits shock cones as it makes a full afterburner take-off from Pápa, home to the Saman squadron.

Above: Hungarian air force fighters wear red nose codes, outlined in white. These can be of two, three or four digits.

Above: This bumble bee insignia is now being applied to the fins of the Su-22s of the Furkeszdarazs squadron at Taszar.

Above: At Pápa, this MiG-19PM is one of two gate guardians. It retains old-style national insignia and a silver finish.

Above: Nine single-seat MiG-23MFs survive in Hungarian service, of 12 delivered. They wear camouflage, having been delivered in grey.

Above: The MiG-23 has greater range and combat persistence than the MiG-21, and has genuine BVR and look-down/shoot-down capability.

Above: The MiG-21bis serves alongside the MiG-2. at Pápa, with the Griffon squadron. The unit's aircraft do not carry a unit badge.

Above: The variable-geometry Su-22 replaced the earlier Su-7 in Hungary.

Below: This MiG-21F-13 is the second of Pápa's gate guardians.

Tyres stream smoke as a Taszar-based Su-22M-3 lands heavily at its home base. Variable-geometry wings allow this popular heavyweight high-performance fighter-bomber to land relatively slowly, and when swept forward confer greater manoeuvrability.

Above: The Stromfeld Aurel wing badge incorporates the Saman and Griffon badges.

Above: This insignia of the Saman squadron is worn by the unit's MiG-23s.

Above: Three of four MiG-23UBs delivered remain active. These were transferred directly from Frontal Aviation, and not all have been repainted in the scheme shown here.

Above: This MiG-23MF wears the Saman insignia on the intakes and the wing badge on the tailfin.

Below: The MiG-21's handling and performance make it a pilot's favourite, but it lacks capability.

Above: A MiG-21bis returns to base with an underwing A-2. Such stores remain uncommon on Hungarian air force aircraft, despite their usefulness for realistic training.

In a bizarre rumour that has never been confirmed, it has also been suggested that Hungary started to receive Su-25s during 1985. One was supposedly written off in a crash landing at Budapest-Matyasfold during preparations for an entry-into-service flypast, while the other allegedly hit a train. This reportedly led to the withdrawal of the type. This story was probably caused by the presence of Soviet Su-25s in Hungary.

Force reductions

1990 saw a 40 per cent reduction in armed forces manpower and equipment, prompted by the CFE Treaty, economic constraints, and a desire, in the changing world, to present a less threatening military posture. Plans were announced to reduce the number of interceptors from 99 to 61, and the number of battlefield helicopters from 79 to 66, while retaining 11 specialist strike aircraft.

The primary role of the air force was the support of the Warsaw Pact ground forces in the Southwestern TVD (Theatre of Military Operations), and this role virtually disappeared overnight when the Soviets withdrew their forces from Hungary. The air defence of Hungarian airspace was a secondary role, and was also shared with Soviet units. The Soviet air power assets withdrew between March 1990 and June 1991, consisting of two Mil Mi-8/Mi-24 regiments at Csakvar and Kalocsa, three MiG-29 regiments from Kiskunlachaza, Sarmellek and Tokol, a MiG-23M squadron and a MiG-27D regiment from Debrecen, and an Su-17/Su-24 recce regiment and a MiG-27 regiment from Kunmadaras.

The withdrawal of the Soviet forces left a vacuum in the shape of a national air traffic control system. Previously closely integrated with the Warsaw Pact system, and relying in part on Soviet officers, Hungary had very restricted airspace, with large areas set aside for military training (almost two per cent of the total land area was set aside for military training, for example) and with international airways only half the usual width. Hungary's new system was produced by the air force working in association with the Ministry of Transport, and has been presented to ICAO, NATO and Eurocontrol. The system was first put to the test during the Gulf War, when many coalition aircraft transited through Hungarian air space. Russian military activity was limited to lower altitudes, and was sometimes stopped entirely to clear the skies for these movements.

New rules, new problems

Although the air force has lost its WarPac support role, it is now solely responsible for the air defence of Hungary, and control of Hungarian air space. Since it is equipped with elderly and largely ineffective aircraft (Soviet MiG-29s were previously the primary air defence aircraft), this has led to an urgent need for new fighter aircraft. The Minister of Defence has been quoted as saying, "I have been told by my advisors that the F-16 would best suit our needs. The question is, when will the country have enough money to buy the Fighting Falcon?" Hungary already has the smallest and weakest air force in the region, and the obsolescence of its equipment is of increasing concern as tension

in the region and 'none-too-friendly' meetings with Yugoslav fighters become more common.

Although it has maintained a painstaking neutrality with regard to Yugoslavia, Hungary has been unable to prevent itself being drawn into the conflict to some extent. Pairs of Mil Mi-8s and Mil Mi-24s have been forward deployed from Szentkirályszabadja and used for border patrols, and Hungarian fighters have had to react to intrusions by Yugoslav aircraft (which even accidentally strafed a Hungarian village in October 1991), and have made more scrambles in the last two years than in the whole of the previous 15 years. This has given Hungarian fighter pilots welcome extra flying hours, which otherwise stand at only 80 hours per year. In the wake of the October incident a 10-km (6.2 mile) buffer zone (or ADIZ) was established on each side of the border, and direct 'hotline' links were established between the Yugoslav and Hungarian operations centres.

RAF and NATO Boeing E-3 Sentry AWACS platforms monitoring the UN-applied air exclusion zone and watching out for sanctions-busting flights have been operated inside Hungarian air space, where they would be protected, if necessary, by the alert fighters at Kécskemet and Taszár. Intrusions have reduced during recent months, since fighting shifted from the north to Bosnia, although the alert commitment has not been scaled down.

Hungary has reportedly considered a number of aircraft in its search for a new fighter, including the F-16, the Mirage 2000, the Panavia Tornado and the Saab JAS 39 Gripen. Politically, the country is keener to establish links with the USA than with Western Europe, although loose plans exist for joining the EEC and some in Hungary even harbour ambitions of joining NATO. Funding of any Western fighter would be extremely difficult, however, and a more likely solution could be the MiG-29, which is believed to have been evaluated (and perhaps even selected) during 1989/1990. Some reports suggest that a handful of Hungarian air force pilots actually underwent conversion to the aircraft in Russia. One report suggested that some MiG-29s were delivered to Hungary, but before they could be introduced into service were sold on to another customer, possibly Iraq, to solve a short-term cash crisis.

Russia apparently owes Hungary some $2 billion and President Yeltsin has offered to pay $800 million of this in the form of advanced weapons, including 26 MiG-29s. Since the Hungarian air force is already set up to operate Soviet aircraft, with much appropriate ground support equipment and with pilots and ground crew used to operating MiG fighters, this would represent a cost-effective solution to Hungary's fighter requirement. Such a purchase would enjoy strong support among many Hungarian air force pilots, who prize the MiG-29's excellent handling and BVR capability. As an interim measure $14 million has been allocated from the 1992 defence budget to provide Western radar, avionics and IFF systems for 20 of the lowest-houred MiG-21bis fighters.

The break-up of the Warsaw Pact has also revealed deficiencies in the training system. In previous years, Hungary has 'screened' its own

Above: Kecskemet's MiG-21F-13 gate guardian has gained new chevron-type national insignia, although its plinth retains a Communist-era winged star.

Above: Hungary's MiG-21UMs wear a variety of colour schemes. About 10 are in service, two with each squadron. Code numbers vary, being of two, three or four digits.

Left: One of Kecskemet's MiG-21MF units has adopted the insignia of the pre-war Puma squadron, but this has not yet been applied to any aircraft.

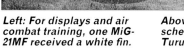

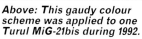

Left: For displays and air combat training, one MiG-21MF received a white fin.

Above: This gaudy colour scheme was applied to one Turul MiG-21bis during 1992.

Below: A Kecskemét MiG-21MF and MiG-21UM show two colour schemes.

Above: A slightly smaller spine differentiates the MiG-21MF (here) from the later MiG-21bis. The MiG-21MF equips the two-squadron wing at Kecskemet, while MiG-21bis squadrons are at Taszar and Pápa.

Right: A Kecskemet MiG-21MF takes off past a battery of SAM-3 'Goa' anti-aircraft missiles, used for airfield point defence.

Below: This MiG-21UM is seen here taxiing in from a post-major overhaul test flight. A visit to the paint shop will precede its return to service.

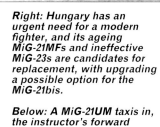

Right: Hungary has an urgent need for a modern fighter, and its ageing MiG-21MFs and ineffective MiG-23s are candidates for replacement, with upgrading a possible option for the MiG-21bis.

Below: A MiG-21UM taxis in, the instructor's forward vision periscope still deployed.

Above: This Ilyushin Il-28 'Beagle' lies dumped on the field at Kecskemet, a plaything for the base fire section and battle damage repair teams.

153

pilot trainees using civilian flying clubs and the paramilitary Magyar Honvedelmi Szovetseg at Bekescsaba, which have then received basic, advanced and conversion training in Czechoslovakia (on L-29s and L-39s at Kosice) and in the USSR. There is some doubt as to whether Hungary ever had its own L-29s.

Priorities after the Soviet withdrawal were the training of air traffic controllers and the provision of English language courses, but *ab initio* pilot training was halted while different options were studied. Overseas training in Austria, Belgium, France, Germany, Holland and Switzerland was studied, but rejected on cost grounds, and it is now hoped to establish a jet training school at Szolnok beside the existing helicopter training unit. The BAe Hawk is understood to be the air force's choice, although procurement of such an expensive type would seem unlikely. RAF Hawks have visited Hungary for air show appearances, and made a very favourable impression. A more realistic option could be the purchase of 24 L-39 Albatros trainers rendered surplus by German reunification.

Traditions revived

The air force was reorganised, and renamed the Magyar Honvédség Repülő Csapatai (Hungarian Air Defence Group), on 31 March 1991, adopting at the same time a new national insignia. This was applied to all active aircraft, including gate guardians and ground instructional airframes, but excluding museum aircraft. The old-style Communist star was replaced by a forward-facing 'arrow head' chevron in the national colours. This was introduced after consideration of two designs, the unsuccessful design being a chevron superimposed on a roundel. Variations of this were painted onto a VIP Mil Mi-8 (for the Pope's visit in October 1989) and on at least one MiG-21. This process has been accompanied by a revival of traditions from the pre-Communist era, including the adoption of squadron badges and unit identities in place of the old numerical unit designations.

Organisationally, the air defence group is split into two commands, the Légvédelmi és Repülőparancsnokság (Air Defence and Aviation Command) headquartered at Veszprém, and the Csapatrepülő Parancsnokság (Troop Air Command) at Székesfehérvár. Regiments now report directly to these organisations, a previous divisional sub-structure having vanished.

The Légvédelmi és Repülőparancsnokság controls three fighter regiments, based at Taszár, Pápa and Kecskemét. The Taszár wing is equipped with two squadrons with the MiG-21bis and one with the Su-22M-3 and is classed as a multi-role tactical fighter wing, and is named after the Kapos region. The small number of Su-22M-3s on charge (only 10 single-seaters) are useful, but are scarcely viable. Numbers could not easily be topped up, since most other former WarPac nations (who might have surplus 'Fitters' for sale) operated the Su-22M-4 'Fitter-K' whose different powerplant would make its use by Hungary difficult.

The other two regiments are fighter interceptor wings and are named after wartime Hungarian fighter aces. Pápa's 'Stromfeld

Aurel' fighter wing uses a mix of nine MiG-23MFs and 10 MiG-21bis 'Fishbed-Ns'. These are backed up by two MiG-21UMs and two MiG-23Bs. The MiG-23MF is now showing its age, and its lack of agility makes it unpopular, though its BVR capability is unique among Hungarian fighter types. Interestingly, Hungary seems determined to upgrade its MiG-21bis with new radar and BVR missiles, rather than improving its MiG-23s.

The Kecskemét wing has 20 MiG-21MFs (and some four two-seat trainers), and these, like the MiG-23s, are ripe for replacement.

The Csapatrepülő Parancsnokság controls two regiments, one of battlefield helicopters, and one (actually designated as a division) of transport aircraft and helicopters. Both are named after the local regions in which they are located. One of the assault helicopter squadrons operates a mix of eight Mil Mi-24D 'Hind-Ds' and eight Mil Mi-24V 'Hind-Es', while the other has 16 modified 'Hind-Ds', these having some 'Hind-E' avionics and systems, but retaining AT-2 'Swatter' ATMs rather than the tube-launched AT-6 'Spiral' used by the Mi-24V.

The battlefield helicopter wing also includes a Mil Mi-8 squadron, and a mixed squadron with Mi-8s and Mi-17s, including some EW/ECM/command post sub-variants. Most of these aircraft can be armed with rocket pods for use in the assault role. The transport regiment at Szolnok includes an An-26 squadron, two Mi-8 squadrons and two liaison/light transport squadrons equipped with the Mi-2. The organisation also parents a liaison unit named after a wartime hero, and based between two airfields. This operates a mix of two An-24s, three LET 410s and four Zlin 43s.

If Hungary recommences its own pilot training, a new organisation will probably be formed. This is now beginning to seem more likely, although the expense of providing a training system, with aircraft, simulators, staff, etc. has tempted Hungary to look at collaborative schemes with other countries in the region, as described above. While procurement of an advanced jet trainer remains as far away as ever, Hungary may have decided to institute its own primary/basic flying training school. Such a conclusion is not unreasonable, since in February 1993 reports began to circulate that Hungary was about to order 12 PZL-130TB Turbo Orliks and a simulator.

Above: The badge of the Bakony wing includes an Mi-24, an eagle, and the national colours.

Above: The Badger's head badge of the Mi-8 equipped Borz squadron.

Above: The Bakony wing's Mil Mi-8 'Hips' can be armed with rocket pods, which are suspended from braced pylons on the cabin sides. The pods are seldom carried.

Below: Mil Mi-8s of the Bakony wing's Borz squadron, with a Mil Mi-24 in the background. The Bakony wing is dedicated to the assault role.

Above: The Phoenix badge of the Mi-24D- and Mi-24V-equipped squadron.

Above: The Phoenix squadron operates eight 'Hind-Es' and 'Hind-Ds'.

Right: Most unmodified 'Hind-Ds' wear this brown and green camouflage.

Above: Hungary's unmodified 'Hind-Ds' serve with the Bakony Wing's Phoenix squadron.

The Mil Mi-24 equipped Kerecsen squadron uses this Falcon badge.

Above: The Kerecsen squadron Mil Mi-24Ds are modified with some Mi-24V systems, and wear a similar camouflage scheme, while retaining AT-2 missiles.

Above: The 'Hind-D' Mod has prominent antenna fairings on each side of the forward fuselage, like those fitted to the Mi-24V 'Hind-E'.

Above: This pair of Mil Mi-24V 'Hind-Es' wears the old-style Hungarian national insignia, but carry modern 80-mm rocket pods underwing. They are painted in the same stone and grey-green colour scheme as the modified Mi-24Ds.

Above: Two Mi-17Ps serve with the Vegyes (mixed) squadron of the Bakony wing. These have huge antenna arrays mounted on the tailboom/cabin intersection.

is badge is worn by the crew of the Vegyes (mixed) helicopter unit.

Left: A single Mil Mi-9 'Hip-G' airborne command post is in service.

Above: A handful of Mil Mi-17s are in service, all painted green and brown.

Air Power Analysis

Légvédelmi és Repülőparancsnokság (Air Defence and Aviation Command); headquarters Veszprém

SQUADRON	EQUIPMENT
'Kapos' Harcászati Repülő Ezred ('Kapos' Tactical Fighter Flying Wing), Taszár	
1 Vadász Repülő Század 'Boszorkány' (1 Fighter Flying Squadron 'Witch')	MiG-21bis (10), MiG-21UM (2)
2 Vadász Repülő Század 'Turul' (2 Fighter Flying Squadron 'Eagle')	MiG-21bis (10), MiG-21UM (2)
3 Felderítő Repülő Század 'Fürkészdarázs' (3 Reconnaissance Aircraft Flying Squadron 'Bumble Bee')	Su-22M-3 (10), Su-22UM-3 (2)
'Stromfeld Aurel' Vadaszrepulo Ezred ('Stromfeld Aurel' Fighter Flying Wing), Pápa	
1 Vadász Repülő Század 'Sámán' (1 Fighter Flying Squadron 'Shaman')	MiG-23MF (9), MiG-23UB (2)
2 Vadász Repülő Század 'Griff' (2 Fighter Flying Squadron 'Griffon')	MiG-21bis (10), MiG-21UM (2)
'Vitéz Szenfgyörgyi Deszó' Vadaszrepulo Ezred ('Vitéz Szenfgyörgyi Deszó' Fighter Flying Wing), Kecskemét	
1 Vadász Repülő Század 'Puma' (1 Fighter Flying Squadron 'Puma')	MiG-21MF (10), MiG-21UM (2)
2 Vadász Repülő Század 'Dongo' (2 Fighter Flying Squadron 'Wasp')	MiG-21MF (10), MiG-21UM (2)

Above: Some of Hungary's seven An-26s wear a smart grey and white colour scheme, with a broad red cheat line.

Above: Other Hungarian An-26s wear an overall light grey colour scheme. The An-26 is the air force's only fixed-wing military freighter.

Above: The Szolnok mixed transport brigade operates some 20 Mil Mi-8s of various types, including Mi-8T 'Hip-Cs' like this one.

Above: The Szolnok-based 'Hips' wear the same camouflage as their tactical cousins at Szentkiralyszabadja.

Csapatrepülő Parancsnokság (Troop Air Command); headquarters Székesfehérvár

Left: The flying suit badge of the Szolnok-based mixed transport aircraft brigade.

Above: The Mi-8S features distinctive enlarged and squared-off windows.

Below: The Mi-8S has a VIP interior, with large airline-type seats.

SQUADRON	EQUIPMENT
'Bakony' Harcihelikopter Ezred ('Bakony' Combat Helicopter Wing), Szentkirályszabadja	
1 Harcihelikopter Század 'Fönix' (1 Combat helicopter Squadron 'Phoenix')	Mil Mi-24D (8), Mil Mi-24V (8)
2 Harcihelikopter Század 'Kerecsen' (2 Combat Helicopter Squadron 'Falcon')	Mil Mi-24D(Mod) (16)
3 Szállító Helikopter Század 'Borz' (3 Transport Helicopter Squadron 'Badger')	Mil Mi-8TB (12)
4 Szállító Helikopter Század Vegyes (4 Transport helicopter Squadron Mixed)	Mil Mi-8TB (8), Mil Mi-17 (6), Mil Mi-17P (2), Mil Mi-9 (1)
'Szolnok' Vegyes Szállítórepülő Dandár ('Szolnok' Mixed Transport Aircraft Brigade), Szolnok	
1 Szállító Repülő Század 'Teve' (1 Transport Aircraft Squadron 'Dromadery')	An-26 (7)
2 Szállító Helikopter Század (2 Transport Helicopter Squadron)	Mil Mi-8T/S (10)
3 Szállító Helikopter Század (3 Transport Helicopter Squadron)	Mil Mi-8T/S (10)
4 Futárrepülő Helikopter Század (4 Liaison Aircraft Helicopter Squadron)	Mil Mi-2 (16)
5 Futárrepülő Helikopter Század (5 Liaison Aircraft Helicopter Squadron)	Mil Mi-2 (15)
'Vitéz Háry Laszló' Vegyes Repülő Osztály ('Vitéz Háry László' Mixed Aircraft Unit), Tokol and Budaors	
1 Szállító Repülő Század 'Sárkány' (1 Transport Aircraft Squadron 'Dragon')	An-24V (2), LET 410 (3)
2 Futárrepülő Raj (2 Liaison Aircraft Flight)	Zlin 43 (4)

Above: The PZL-built Mil Mi-2 'Hoplite' serves with two squadrons in the liaison role. The fleet totals 31 aircraft.

Above: Hungary's Mil Mi-2s are unarmed and do r have a front-line role. They were procured to replace Ka-26 'Hoodlums'.

Left: The flying suit badge of the Hary Laszlo transport unit at Tokol and Budaors.

Right: Four Zlin 43s are used for liaison and communications work. They could also be used for screening potential pilot trainees in an indigenous training system.

Above: A pair of An-24Vs is used for VIP transport and liaison work by the Dragon transport aircraft squadron at Tokol.

Above: Despite having been relegated to instructional duties at Szolnok, this MiG-21MF was repainted with the new national insignia.

Above: This MiG-21MF at Csepel retains the old communist-era star national insignia, and is used for engineer training.

Above: The LET 410 is in use for liaison and calibration duties, and one aircraft is also equipped for the survey role.

Below: Hungary's 'flying squad' now operates the MD-500, a far cry from the Mi-2s previously used by the police.

Above: The Rendorseg's (police) air wing used to rely on Mil Mi-2s, like the aircraft shown here, fitted with an auxiliary fuel tank.

INDEX

Picture acknowledgments

Front cover: Jim Rotramel. **4:** GEC Ferranti via Paul Jackson, Peter R. Foster. **5:** Bruno Cowet, Paul Jackson, Raffaele Mancini. **6:** Hermann Buttigieg (two), Carmine de Napoli, Salvador Mafé Huertas. **7:** Ian Black, Paul Jackson. **8:** Paul Jackson, Sergei Popsuevich/Avia Data (two). **9:** Václav Šimeček (two). **10:** British Aerospace, Mark Attrill, Enstrom. **11:** Andrew H. Cline (two), Enstrom. **12:** Graham Robson, Rockwell. **13:** McDonnell Douglas, Wes Wright, Ian Black. **14:** Boeing, Ian Black, Beech, Lockheed. **16:** Associated Press (two), via Robert F. Dorr. **17:** Bob Archer. **18-23:** Paul Jackson. **24:** Westland (two), Tom Ross. **25:** Paul Jackson. **26:** Westland (three). **27:** Westland. **28:** Peter R. Foster (two). **29:** Peter R. Foster (three). **30:** McDonnell Douglas. **31:** McDonnell Douglas (two), US Air Force. **32:** McDonnell Douglas (two), Deutsche Aerospace. **33:** McDonnell Douglas, US Air Force. **34:** McDonnell Douglas. **35:** Robert F. Dorr, McDonnell Douglas. **36:** McDonnell Douglas (two). **38-41:** McDonnell Douglas. **42:** Enterprise Aviation Photos via Jim Rotramel (JR). **43:** JR, Randy Jolly. **44:** General Dynamics (two). **45:** General Dynamics, US Navy (two), Joe Cupido. **46:** US Air Force (two), Joe Cupido. **47:** JR, Mike Grove via Robert L. Lawson, via Warren Thompson, David Donald. **48:** JR (three). **49:** General Dynamics via JR, Joe Cupido, JR. **50:** JR (two), Joe Cupido. **51:** JR (two), David Donald. **52:** Jeff Wilson, US Air Force, JR. **53:** James Benson, Hans Nijhuis. **54:** US Air Force (two). **55:** US Air Force, General Dynamics, Craig Kaston. **56:** JR (two), Craig Kaston. **57:** US Air Force, via JR. **58:** General Dynamics, Joe Cupido. **59:** Joe Cupido, General Dynamics, US Air Force. **60:** Royal Australian Air Force, US Air Force. **61:** US Air Force (two), David Donald (three), via Bob Archer, Joe Cupido, JR. **62:** JR. **67:** Grumman, Jeff Stout via Robert F. Dorr. **68:** Craig Kaston, James Benson. **69:** US Air Force, Richard Gennis. **70:** Grumman (two), Grumman via Robert L. Lawson, Peter R. Foster. **71:** US Air Force (two), Randy Jolly. **72:** via JR (two). **73:** US Air Force, via JR, via Warren Thompson. **74:** US Air Force, JR, D. Eklund. **75:** Photo Link, via Warren Thompson, General Dynamics, US Air Force. **76:** US Air Force, General Dynamics (two), JR. **77:** US Air Force, JR. **78:** US Air Force (two). **79:** via JR (two), US Air Force. **80:** via JR, US Air Force (two). **81:** via JR (two), US Air Force. **82:** US Air Force (two), JR. **83:** via JR (two), US Air Force. **84:** Randy Jolly. **85:** via JR, Craig Kaston. **86:** Craig Kaston, Hans Nijhuis, Photo Link, D. Eklund, US Air Force. **87:** Peter R. Foster, D. Eklund, Robert L. Lawson, General Dynamics, via JR, Joe Cupido. **88:** Jeff Rankin-Lowe, Mike Reyno, C.J. Lofting, Craig Kaston. **89:** via Michael Stroud, Richard Gennis, JR (two). **90:** Jeff Stout via Robert F. Dorr, JR (two), D. Eklund (two), US Air Force, via JR, David Donald. **91:** René Francillon, Stephen J. Brennan, US Air Force, Photo Link, Peter R. Foster, General Dynamics. **92:** W. Strandberg via JR, Bruce Robertson, Peter R. Foster, Joe Cupido. **93:** Randy Jolly (two), Robert F. Dorr, W. Strandberg via JR, Jeff Wilson, David Donald. **94:** US Air Force (four), via JR (four), General Dynamics. **95:** via JR, Joe Cupido, US Air Force (two), H. Zomers. **96:** General Dynamics, Bob Archer, Terry Waddington via Bob Archer, David Donald. **97:** Joe Cupido, Chris Ryan, D. Eklund, Associated Press, Joe Bruch via Bob Archer. **98:** Peter R. Foster, via JR (three), US Air Force, D. Eklund, Boeing. **99:** US Air Force, British Aerospace via Michael Stroud, Michael Grove via Robert L. Lawson, General Dynamics via JR. **100:** via Andrew H. Cline, Joe Cupido (two), Greg Meggs, Jelle Sjoerdsma, Peter Steinemann. **102:** Robert W. Holder, Dennis Thomsen. **103:** Jon Lake (three), Hendrik J. van Broekhuizen. **104:** Hendrik J. van Broekhuizen (two), Robert W. Holder, Dennis Thomsen. **105:** Jon Lake (two), Hendrik J. van Broekhuizen (two). **106:** Jon Lake (two), Hendrik J. van Broekhuizen, Dennis Thomsen. **107:** Jon Lake (two), Gerard Keysper, Robert W. Holder. **108:** Jon Lake (two), Dennis Thomsen, Gerard Keysper. **109:** Robert W. Holder, Hendrik J. van Broekhuizen, Dennis Thomsen. **110:** Jon Lake (two), Dennis Thomsen, Hendrik J. van Broekhuizen (three), Jon Lake. **112:** Herman Potgieter, Robbie Shaw. **113:** via Michael Stroud, Martin Baumann, Ben J. Ullings. **114:** Paul Jackson, via Michael Stroud. **115:** Dassault, via Michael Stroud (two). **116:** Frédéric Bezin, Mike Vines/Photo Link. **117:** Frédéric Bezin, Martin Baumann (three), Peter Wilson, Paul Jackson, H. Zomers, Jelle Sjoerdsma. **118:** Peter Steinemann (three), Jeff Puzzullo. **119:** Peter Steinemann (two), Dassault. **120:** Dassault (two). **121:** Dassault (four), Paul Jackson, via Michael Stroud. **122:** via Michael Stroud, Paul Jackson (two), Dassault. **123:** Hans Nijhuis, Dassault, Frédéric Bezin, via Michael Stroud, Peter R. Foster, Peter Steinemann. **124:** via Paul Jackson, Jean-Jacques Petit (two), Dassault, Chris Ryan, Paul Jackson. **125:** Martin Baumann, Paul Jackson, Jean-Jacques Petit (two), Dassault, Frédéric Bezin. **126:** Paul Jackson (three), Peter Steinemann (two), Dassault. **127:** Paul Jackson (three), Dassault, Paul Bennett, Salvador Mafé Huertas. **128:** via Paul Jackson (three), Dassault (two), Salvador Mafé Huertas. **129:** Dassault (two), Salvador Mafé Huertas. **130:** Dassault, via John W.R. Taylor (two). **131:** Dassault, via John W.R. Taylor (two). **132:** via Paul Jackson, Dassault, Jelle Sjoerdsma. **133:** via Paul Jackson, Jean-Jacques Petit, via Paul Jackson. **134:** Chris Brooks/Aerophoto, Martin Baumann (two), Hans Nijhuis, Paul Bennett. **135:** David Donald. **136:** Martin Baumann, Robbie Shaw, Dassault, Paul Jackson. **137:** Dassault (three), via Michael Stroud. **138-147:** Randy Jolly. **148:** Peter J. Bish, Lindsay Peacock (two), Georg Mader. **149:** Chris Lofting, Lindsay Peacock (two), Gabor Szekeres (six). **150:** Gabor Szekeres (two), Chris Lofting, Lindsay Peacock (three), Herman J. Sixma, Hans Nijhuis (two), Peter R. Foster. **151:** Jonny Bonny, Chris Lofting, Lindsay Peacock (three), Peter R. Foster (three). **152:** Lindsay Peacock, E.A. Sloot. **153:** Georg Mader, Gabor Szekeres (three), Jonny Bonny, Lindsay Peacock (two), Peter R. Foster, Hans Nijhuis. **154:** Gabor Szekeres (two), Hans Nijhuis, Jonny Bonny, Georg Mader, Herman J. Sixma (two), Peter R. Foster, Peter J. Bish, Chris Lofting. **155:** Gabor Szekeres (four), Jonny Bonny, Georg Mader, Herman J. Sixma (two), Peter R. Foster, Peter J. Bish, Chris Lofting. **156:** Lindsay Peacock, Peter R. Foster (three), Hans Nijhuis, Jonny Bonny, Herman J. Sixma, Gabor Szekeres. **157:** Gabor Szekeres (two), Jonny Bonny, Herman J. Sixma, Lindsay Peacock (two), Peter J. Bish, Chris Lofting.